"Ladies and gentlemen...
This town just got a
**WHOLE LOT MORE
INTERESTING!**"
Impossible Jones

SCOUT
COMICS

FB/TW/IG:
@scoutcomics

LEARN MORE AT:
www.scoutcomics.com

Brendan Deneen, *CEO*
James Haick III, *President*
Don Handfield, *CCO*
Lesa Miller, *COO*
Richard Rivera, *Exec. VP*
David Byrne, *Co-Publisher*
Charlie Stickney, *Co-Publisher*
Andrea Lorenzo Molinari, *Editorial Director*
Marcus Guillory, *Head of Design*
Trent Miller, *General Counsel*
Nicole D'Andria, *Director of Digital Content*

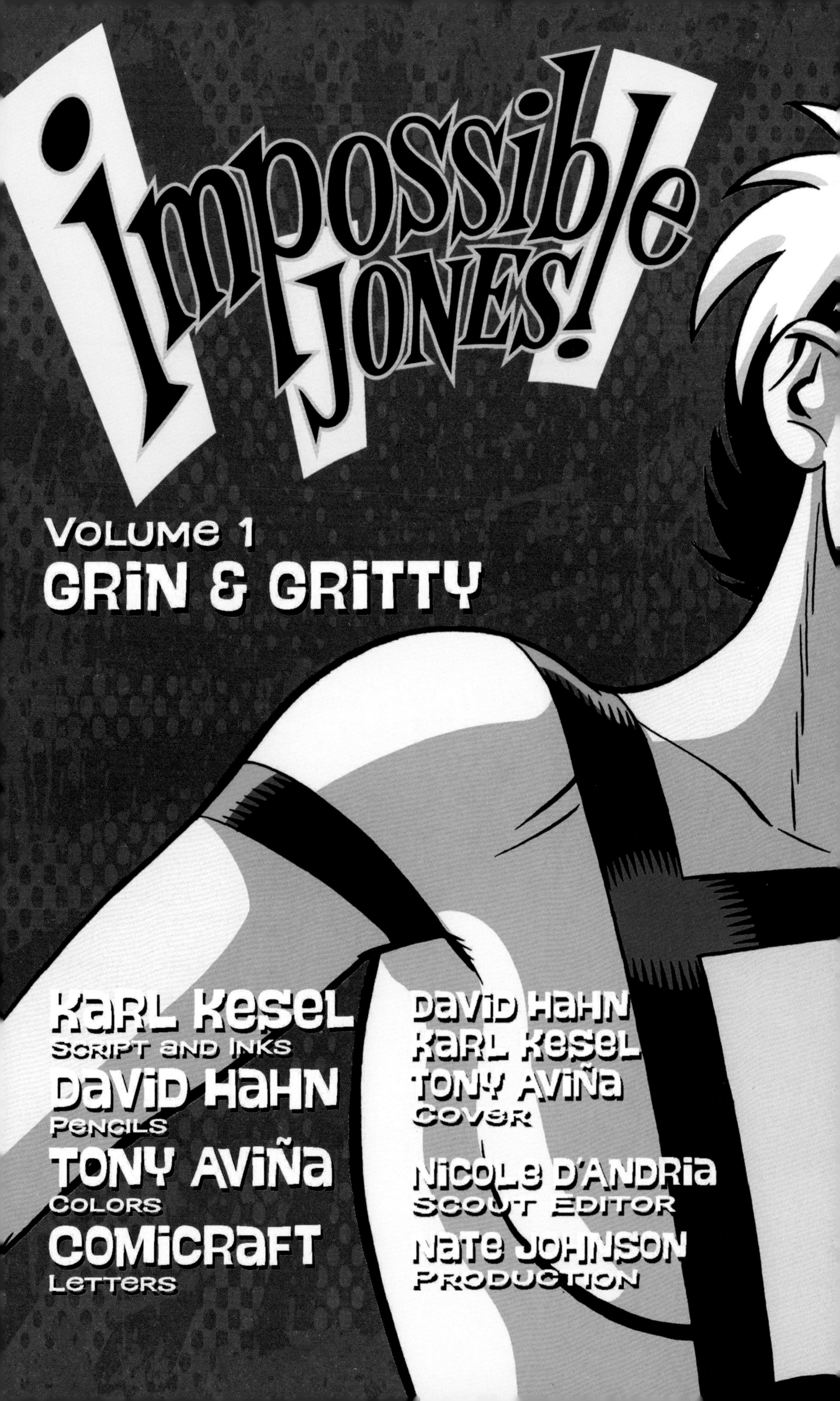

Impossible Jones!

Volume 1
Grin & Gritty

Karl Kesel
Script and Inks

David Hahn
Pencils

Tony Aviña
Colors

Comicraft
Letters

David Hahn
Karl Kesel
Tony Aviña
Cover

Nicole D'Andria
Scout Editor

Nate Johnson
Production

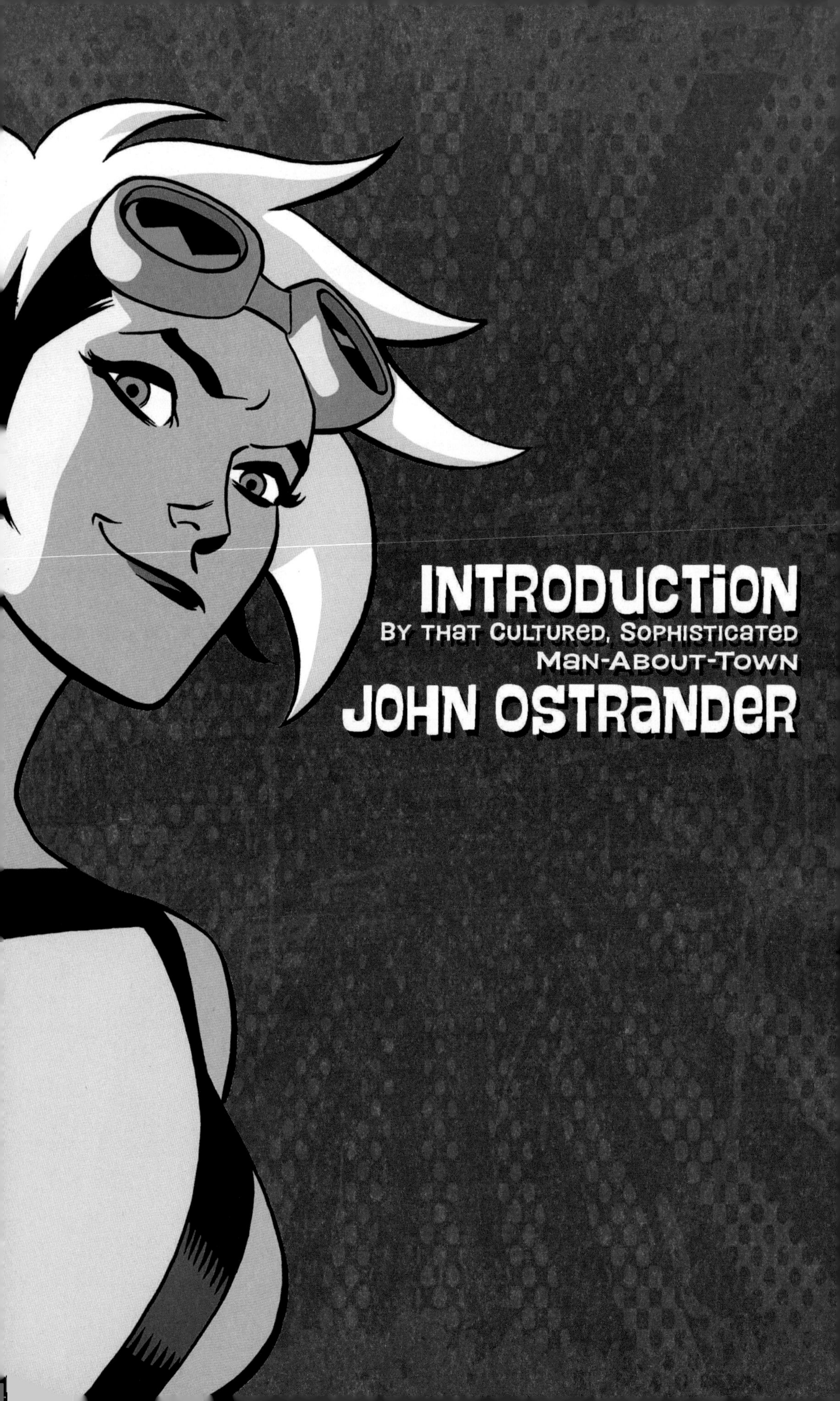

INTRODUCTION

By that Cultured, Sophisticated
Man-About-Town

JOHN OSTRANDER

Do You Remember When Comics Were Fun?

Karl Kesel, David Hahn, and Company do. I think the principal hallmark of **Impossible Jones** is fun. The basic concept is fun – a young thief acquires superpowers and gets mistaken as a superhero. Brightly, she decides to use the cover of being a superhero to continue being a thief. That's a great idea right there and rife with possibilities and Karl and David, et al, exploit it.

The setting is also fun – New Hope City, which sounds a little like New YORK City but isn't. (The gang does that a lot in this book; places and people that are reminiscent of other places and characters but are not quite). The place is teeming with masked heroes and villains; characters like **Holly Daze**, **Captain Lightning**, **Polecat** (one of my faves), **Even Steven** (very Ditko-esque and another of my faves), **Saint of Knives**, **Homewrecker**, **Mr. (Gila) Monster** and lots and lots more. The gang has a riot of imagination and reminds me of the days when Karl and I worked on **Suicide Squad** for DC. I'd get what I called "Kesel Epistles" – long notes (which I had invited) brimming with characters and ideas.

And then there's **Impossible Jones** herself, aka Isabelle "Belle" Castillo, an accomplished thief who finds herself betrayed on her latest job. Belle's caught in an explosion that should have killed her but, impossibly, leaves her with total molecular control over her whole body, including her clothes. Sounds relatively simple but is very adaptable, as is Belle. There are LOTS of ways she can use her body; she can take any shape, much like Plastic Man or Elongated Man (who were always a lot of fun) or even Mr. Fantastic of the Fantastic Four (who is not as much fun; I swear, that man, hasn't a drop of whimsy in his whole rubbery body). Her shadow has acquired a rather ferocious and nasty shape; I suspect that will be explained at a later date and, no doubt, will create further problems for our (anti)heroine.

The story is fun, the art is fun, the colors and the lettering are fun and let's be honest – in these troubled times, we could all use a bit more fun, right? So stop reading me and go read Impossible Jones.

Go have some **FUN!**

John Ostrander
October 2021

John Ostrander created the modern version of DC Comics' **SUICIDE SQUAD**, where he patiently listened to an endless stream of ideas from the inker, Karl Kesel. John's attitude of "We're all in this together, and if you think of something that makes this book better, I want to hear it" is a philosophy Kesel has followed ever since.

Part 1

"My So-Called Secret Origin."

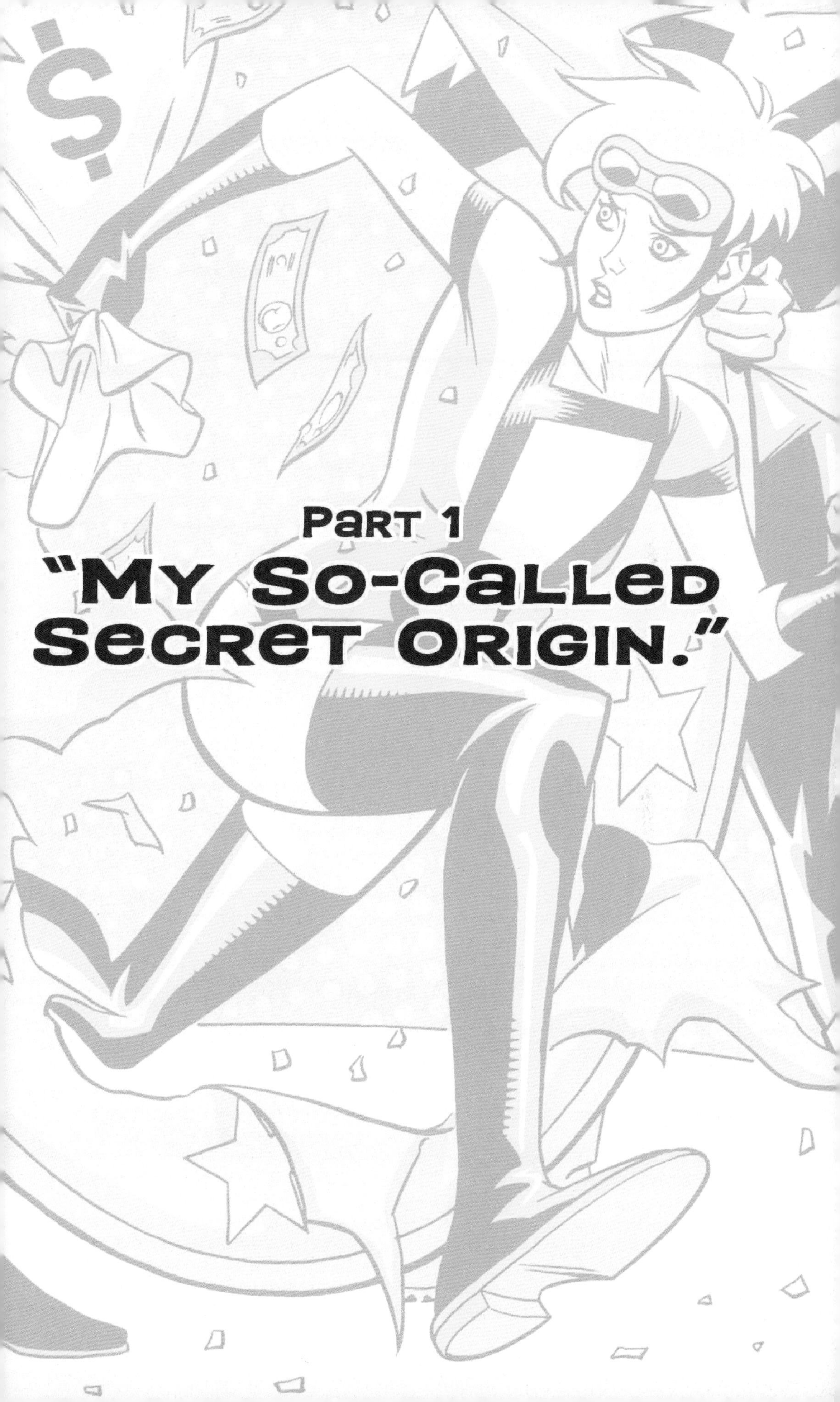

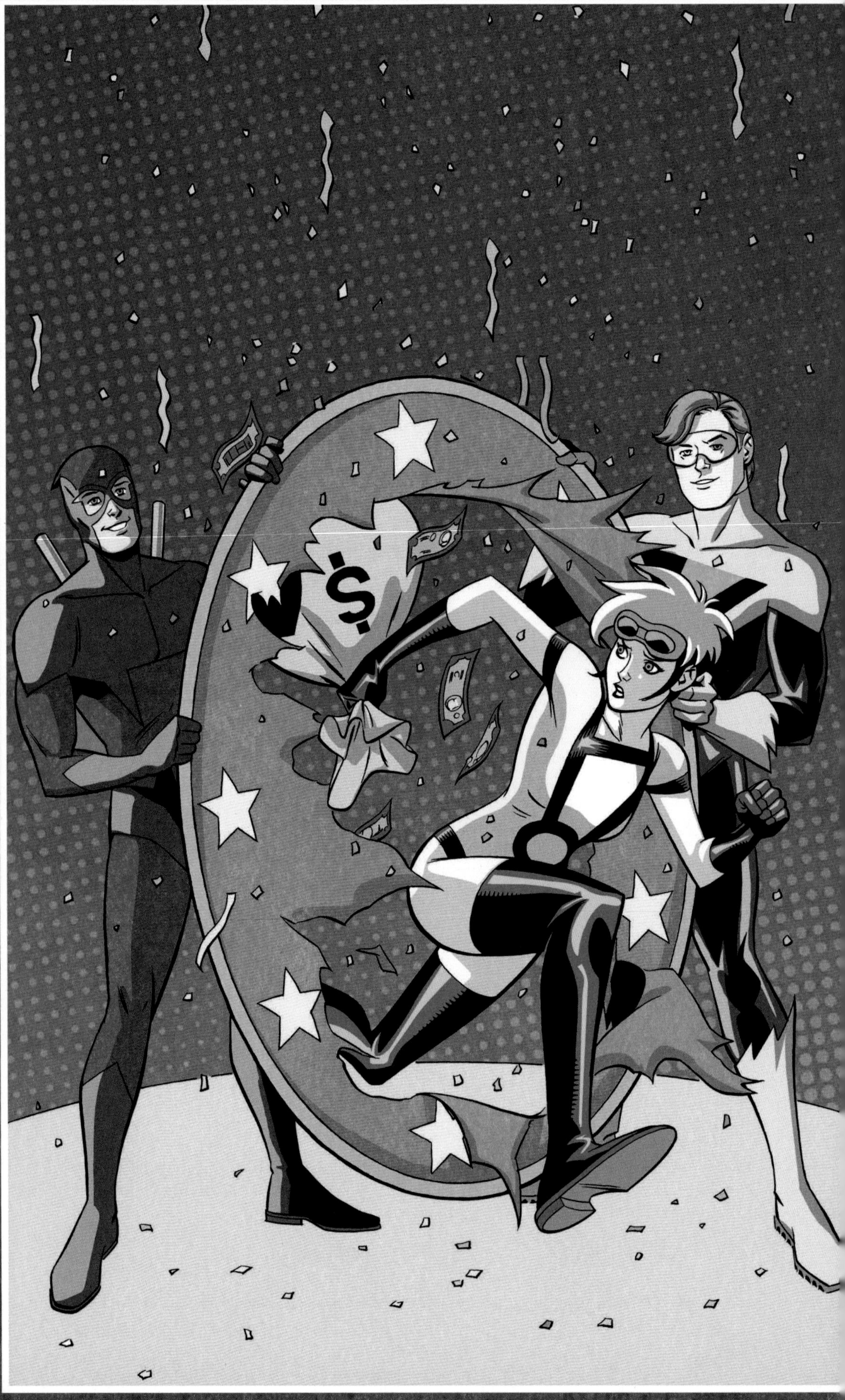

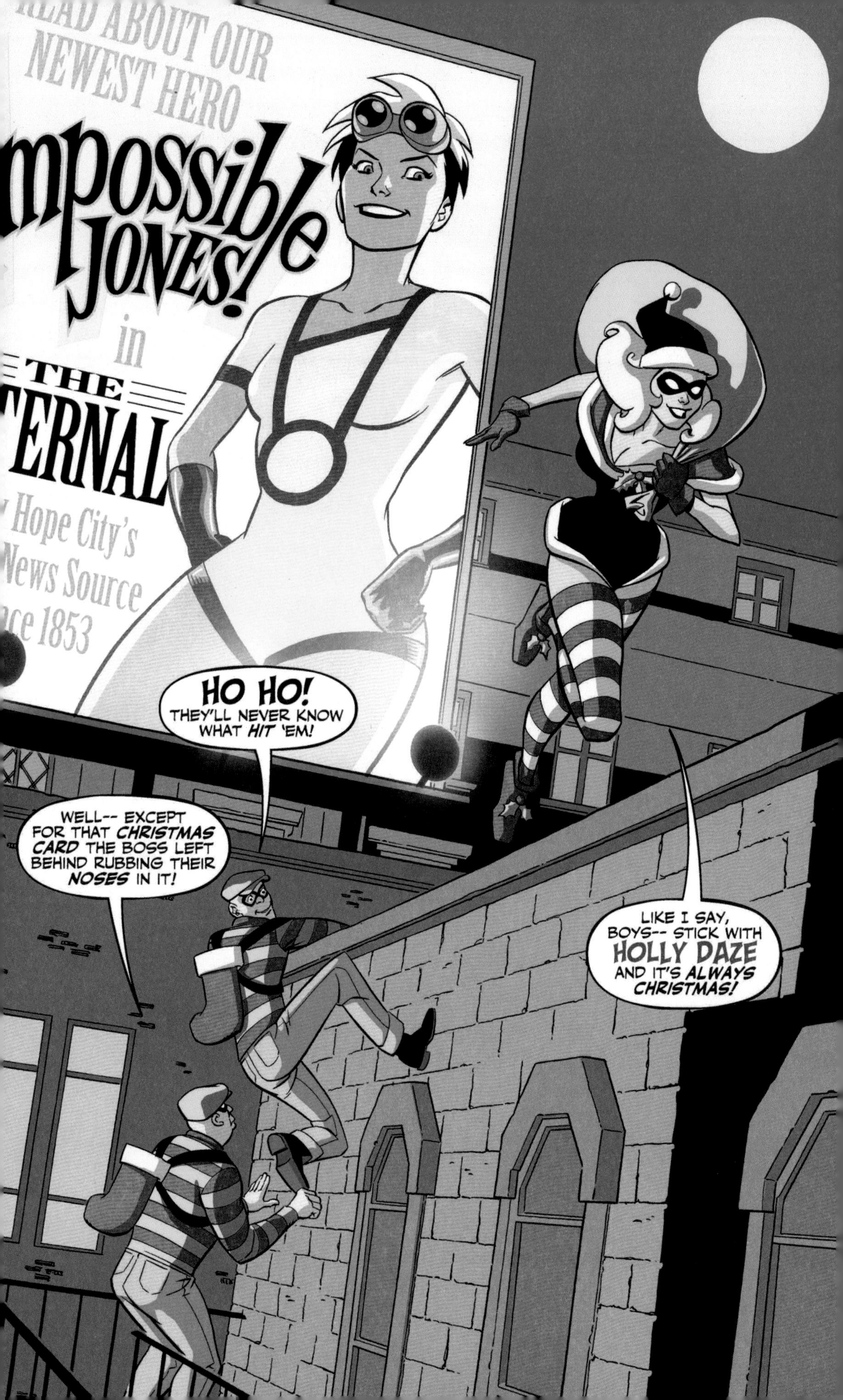

READ ABOUT OUR NEWEST HERO
Impossible JONES!
in
THE
TERNAL
Hope City's
News Source
ce 1853
HO HO! THEY'LL NEVER KNOW WHAT HIT 'EM!
WELL-- EXCEPT FOR THAT CHRISTMAS CARD THE BOSS LEFT BEHIND RUBBING THEIR NOSES IN IT!
LIKE I SAY, BOYS-- STICK WITH HOLLY DAZE AND IT'S ALWAYS CHRISTMAS!

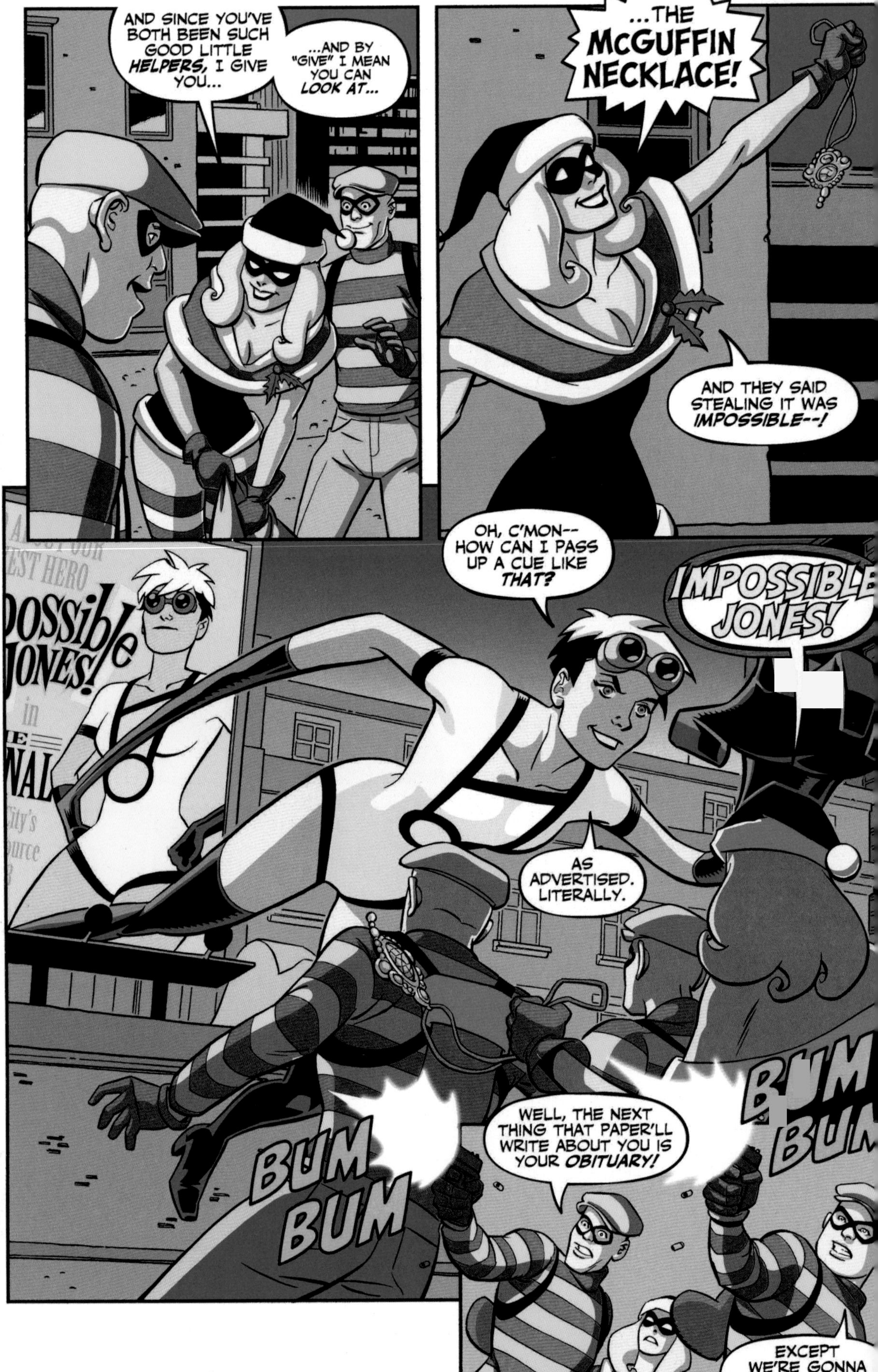
AND SINCE YOU'VE BOTH BEEN SUCH GOOD LITTLE HELPERS, I GIVE YOU...
...AND BY "GIVE" I MEAN YOU CAN LOOK AT...
...THE McGUFFIN NECKLACE!
AND THEY SAID STEALING IT WAS IMPOSSIBLE--!
OH, C'MON--HOW CAN I PASS UP A CUE LIKE THAT?
IMPOSSIBLE JONES!
AS ADVERTISED. LITERALLY.
BUM BUM
BUM BUM
WELL, THE NEXT THING THAT PAPER'LL WRITE ABOUT YOU IS YOUR OBITUARY!
EXCEPT WE'RE GONNA WRITE IT FIRST-IN LEAD!

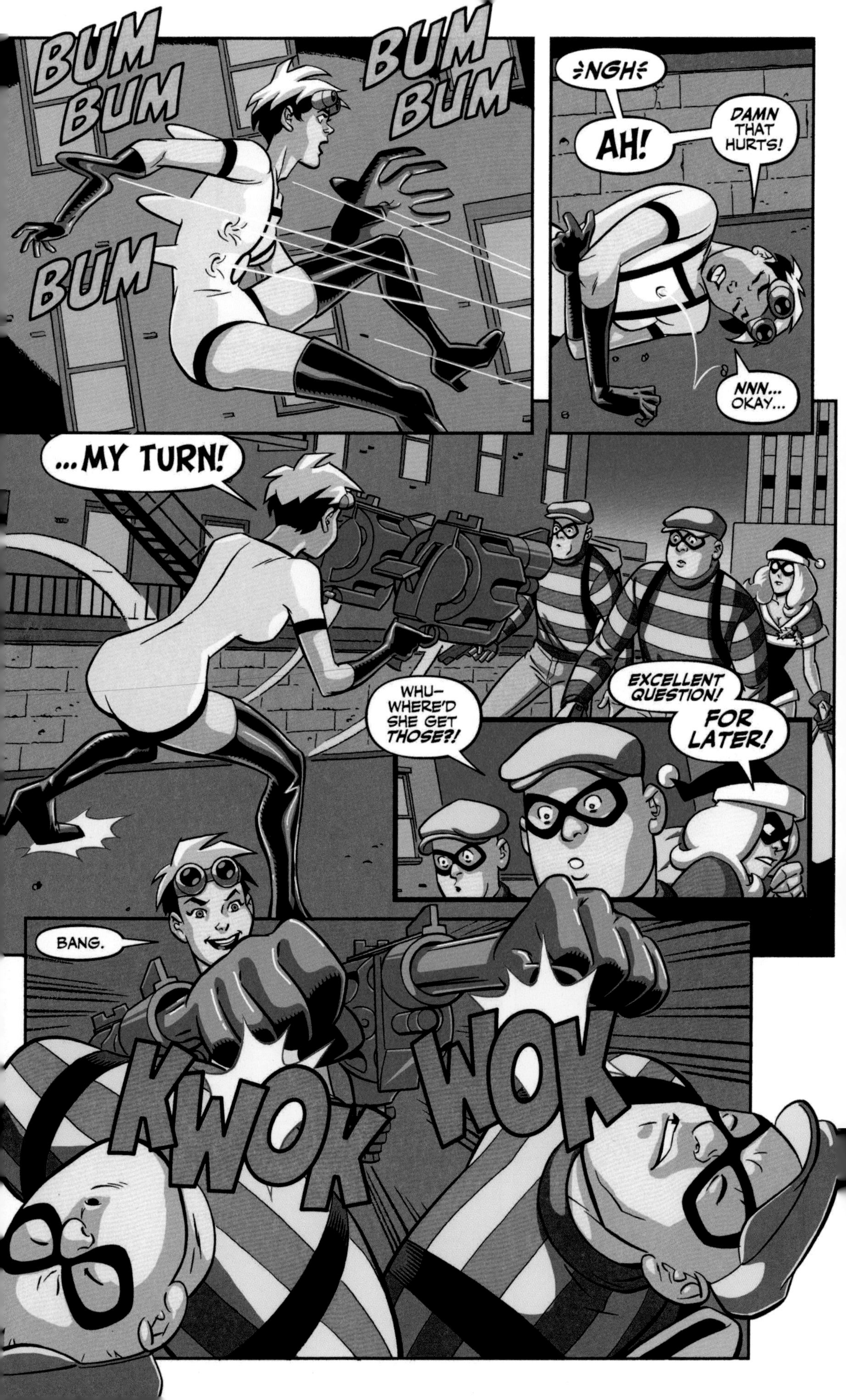

BUM BUM
BUM BUM
BUM
NGH
AH!
DAMN THAT HURTS!
NNN... OKAY...
...MY TURN!
WHU-WHERE'D SHE GET THOSE?!
EXCELLENT QUESTION!
FOR LATER!
BANG.
KWOK
WOK

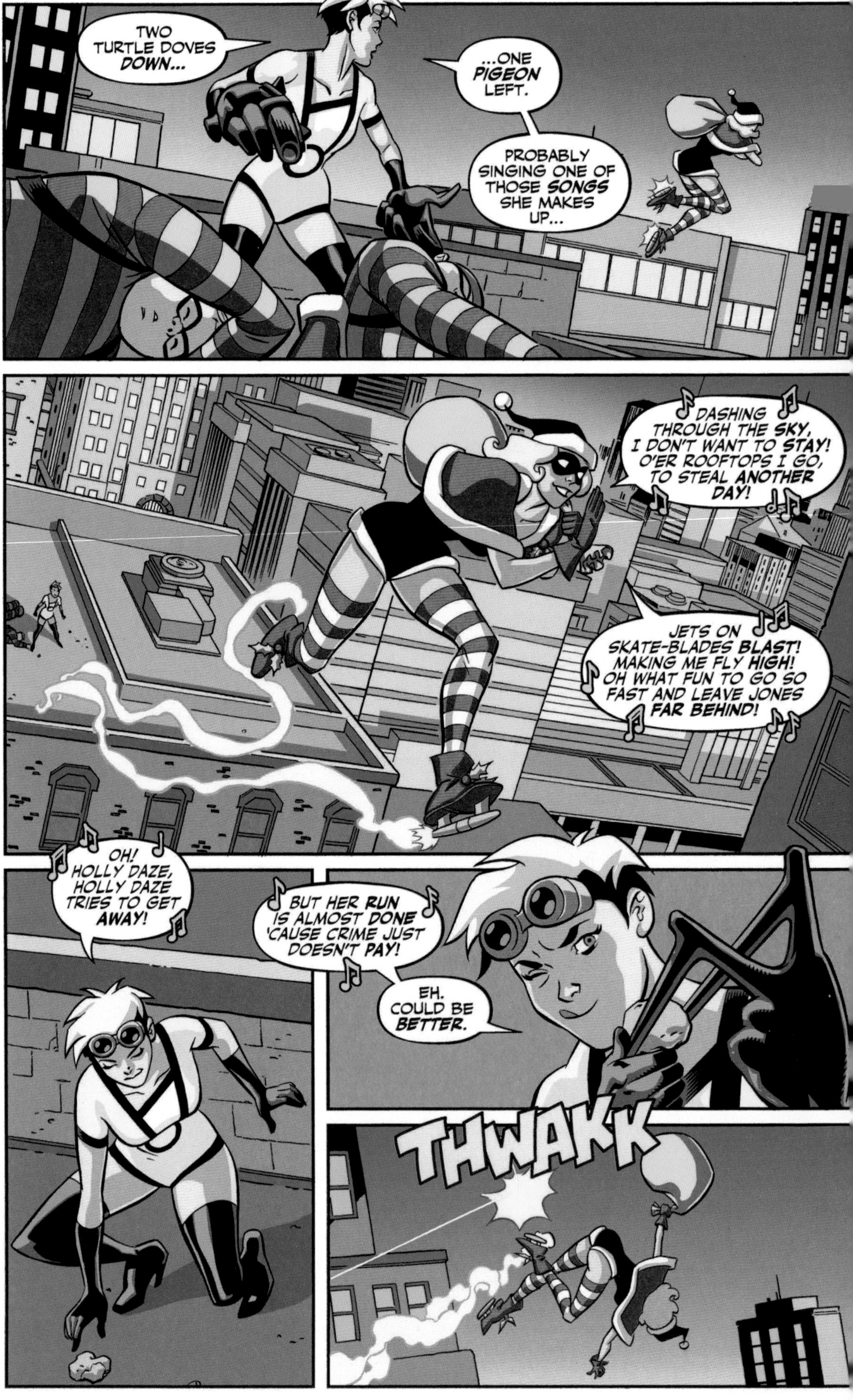
TWO TURTLE DOVES DOWN...
...ONE PIGEON LEFT.
PROBABLY SINGING ONE OF THOSE SONGS SHE MAKES UP...
DASHING THROUGH THE SKY, I DON'T WANT TO STAY! O'ER ROOFTOPS I GO, TO STEAL ANOTHER DAY!
JETS ON SKATE-BLADES BLAST! MAKING ME FLY HIGH! OH WHAT FUN TO GO SO FAST AND LEAVE JONES FAR BEHIND!
OH! HOLLY DAZE, HOLLY DAZE TRIES TO GET AWAY!
BUT HER RUN IS ALMOST DONE 'CAUSE CRIME JUST DOESN'T PAY!
EH. COULD BE BETTER.
THWAKK

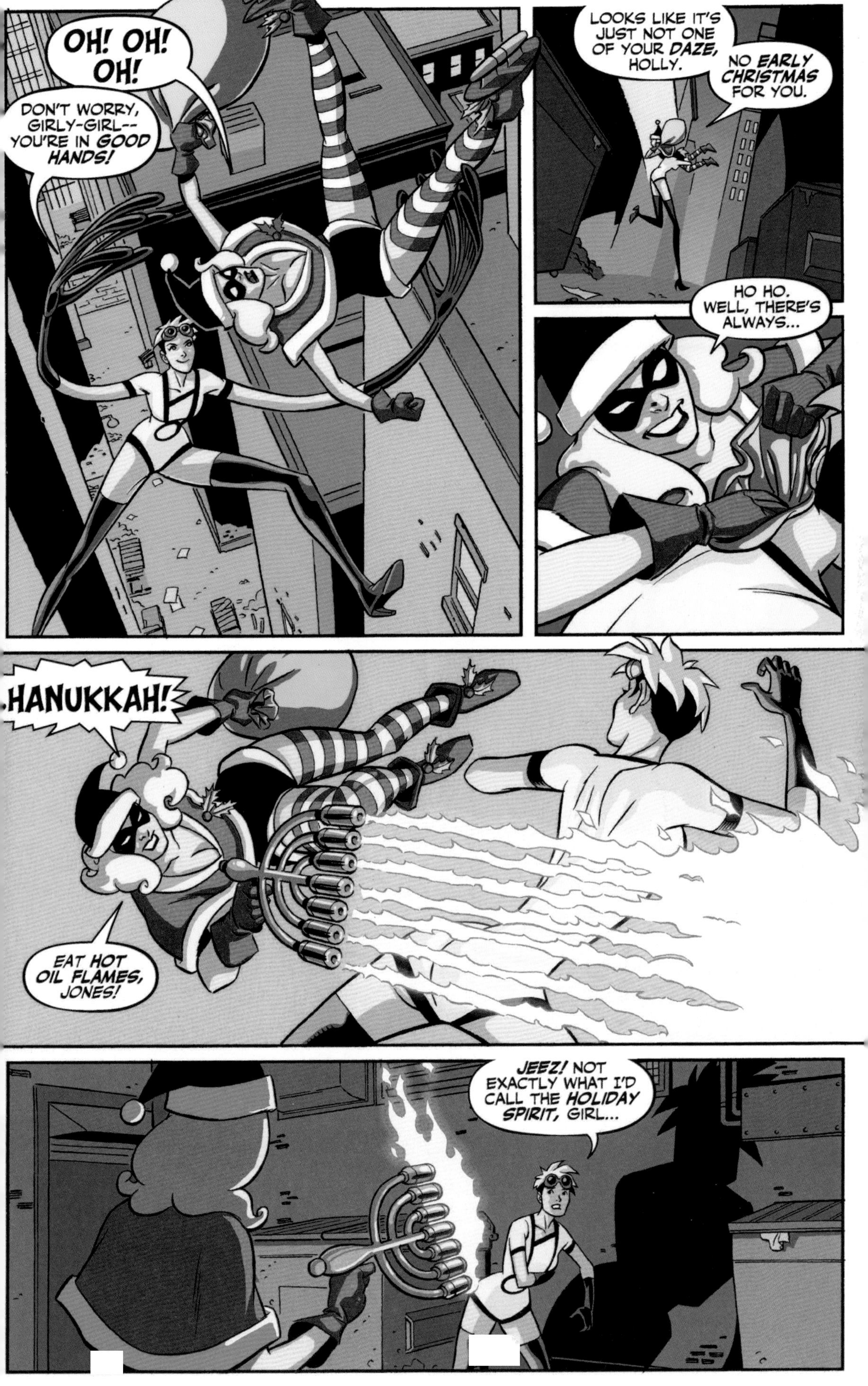
OH! OH! OH!
DON'T WORRY, GIRLY-GIRL-- YOU'RE IN GOOD HANDS!
LOOKS LIKE IT'S JUST NOT ONE OF YOUR DAZE, HOLLY.
NO EARLY CHRISTMAS FOR YOU.
HO HO. WELL, THERE'S ALWAYS...
HANUKKAH!
EAT HOT OIL FLAMES, JONES!
JEEZ! NOT EXACTLY WHAT I'D CALL THE HOLIDAY SPIRIT, GIRL...

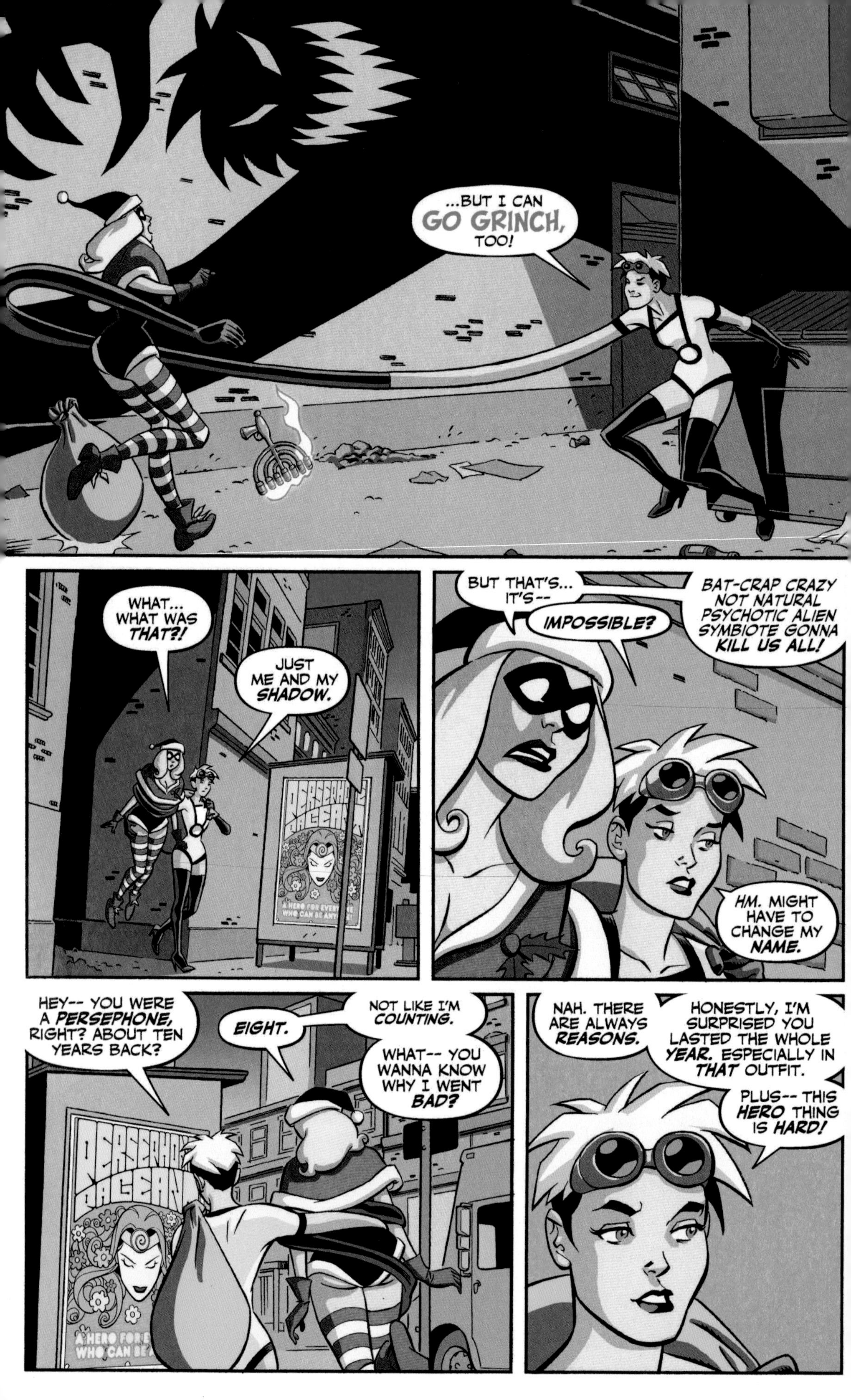

...BUT I CAN GO GRINCH, TOO!
WHAT... WHAT WAS *THAT?!*
JUST ME AND MY *SHADOW.*
BUT THAT'S... IT'S--
IMPOSSIBLE?
BAT-CRAP CRAZY NOT NATURAL PSYCHOTIC ALIEN SYMBIOTE GONNA *KILL US ALL!*
HM. MIGHT HAVE TO CHANGE MY *NAME.*
HEY-- YOU WERE A *PERSEPHONE,* RIGHT? ABOUT TEN YEARS BACK?
EIGHT.
NOT LIKE I'M *COUNTING.*
WHAT-- YOU WANNA KNOW WHY I WENT *BAD?*
NAH. THERE ARE ALWAYS *REASONS.*
HONESTLY, I'M SURPRISED YOU LASTED THE WHOLE *YEAR.* ESPECIALLY IN *THAT* OUTFIT.
PLUS-- THIS *HERO* THING IS *HARD!*

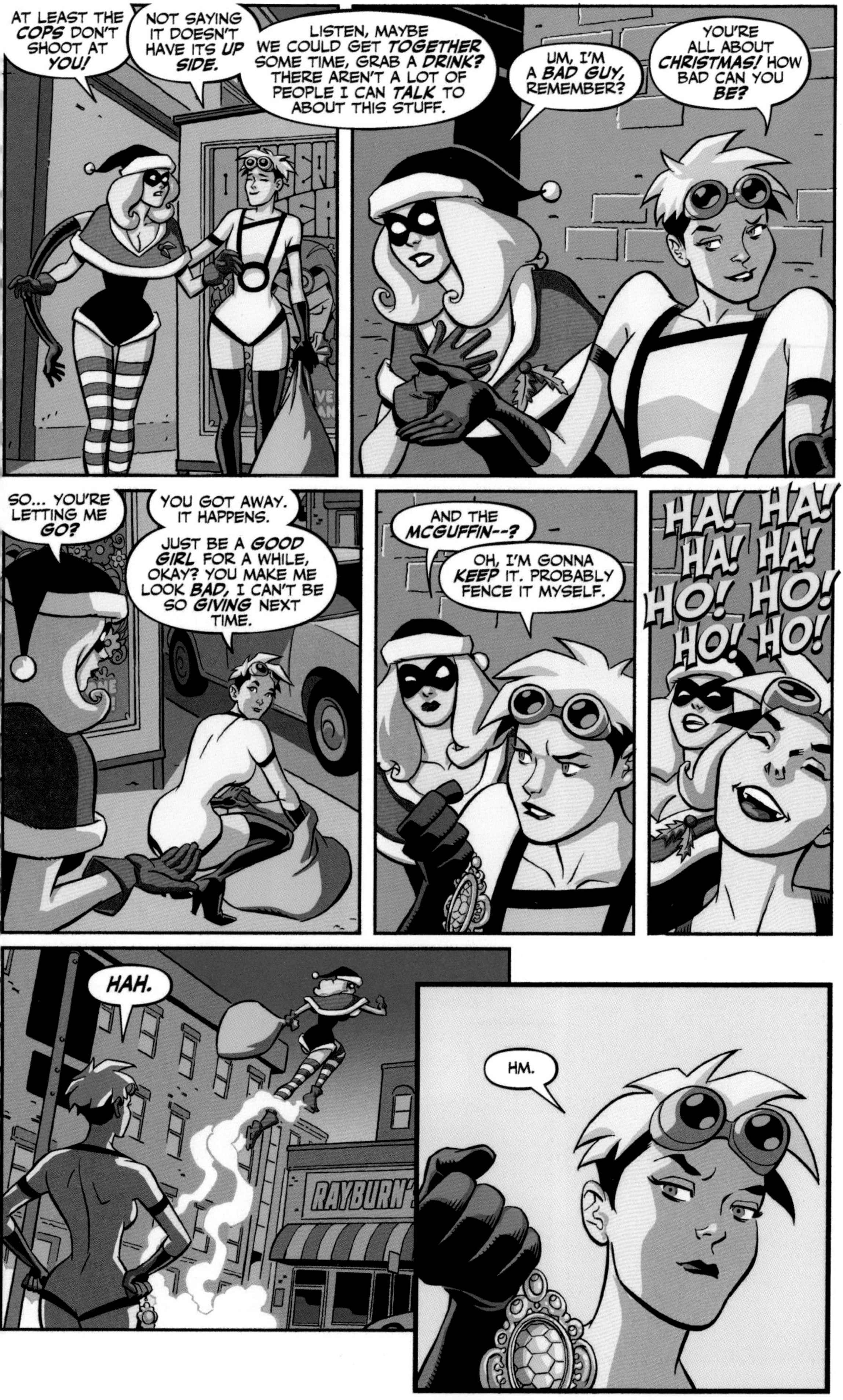
AT LEAST THE COPS DON'T SHOOT AT YOU!
NOT SAYING IT DOESN'T HAVE ITS UP SIDE.
LISTEN, MAYBE WE COULD GET TOGETHER SOME TIME, GRAB A DRINK? THERE AREN'T A LOT OF PEOPLE I CAN TALK TO ABOUT THIS STUFF.
UM, I'M A BAD GUY, REMEMBER?
YOU'RE ALL ABOUT CHRISTMAS! HOW BAD CAN YOU BE?
SO... YOU'RE LETTING ME GO?
YOU GOT AWAY. IT HAPPENS.
JUST BE A GOOD GIRL FOR A WHILE, OKAY? YOU MAKE ME LOOK BAD, I CAN'T BE SO GIVING NEXT TIME.
AND THE MCGUFFIN--?
OH, I'M GONNA KEEP IT. PROBABLY FENCE IT MYSELF.
HA! HA! HA! HA! HO! HO! HO! HO!
HAH.
RAYBURN'
HM.

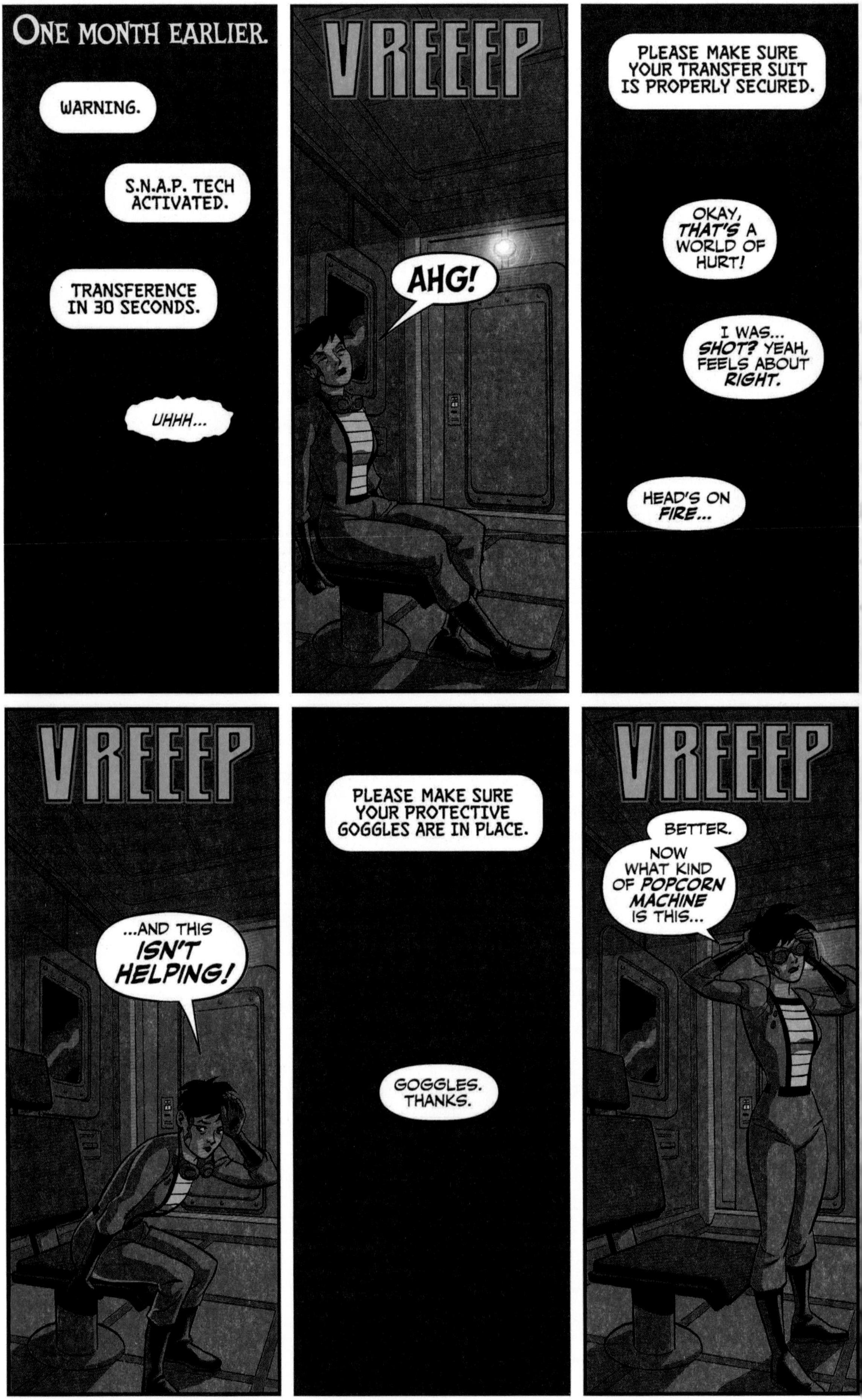
ONE MONTH EARLIER.
WARNING.
S.N.A.P. TECH ACTIVATED.
TRANSFERENCE IN 30 SECONDS.
UHHH...
VREEEP
AHG!
PLEASE MAKE SURE YOUR TRANSFER SUIT IS PROPERLY SECURED.
OKAY, THAT'S A WORLD OF HURT!
I WAS... SHOT? YEAH, FEELS ABOUT RIGHT.
HEAD'S ON FIRE...
VREEEP
...AND THIS ISN'T HELPING!
PLEASE MAKE SURE YOUR PROTECTIVE GOGGLES ARE IN PLACE.
GOGGLES. THANKS.
VREEEP
BETTER.
NOW WHAT KIND OF POPCORN MACHINE IS THIS...

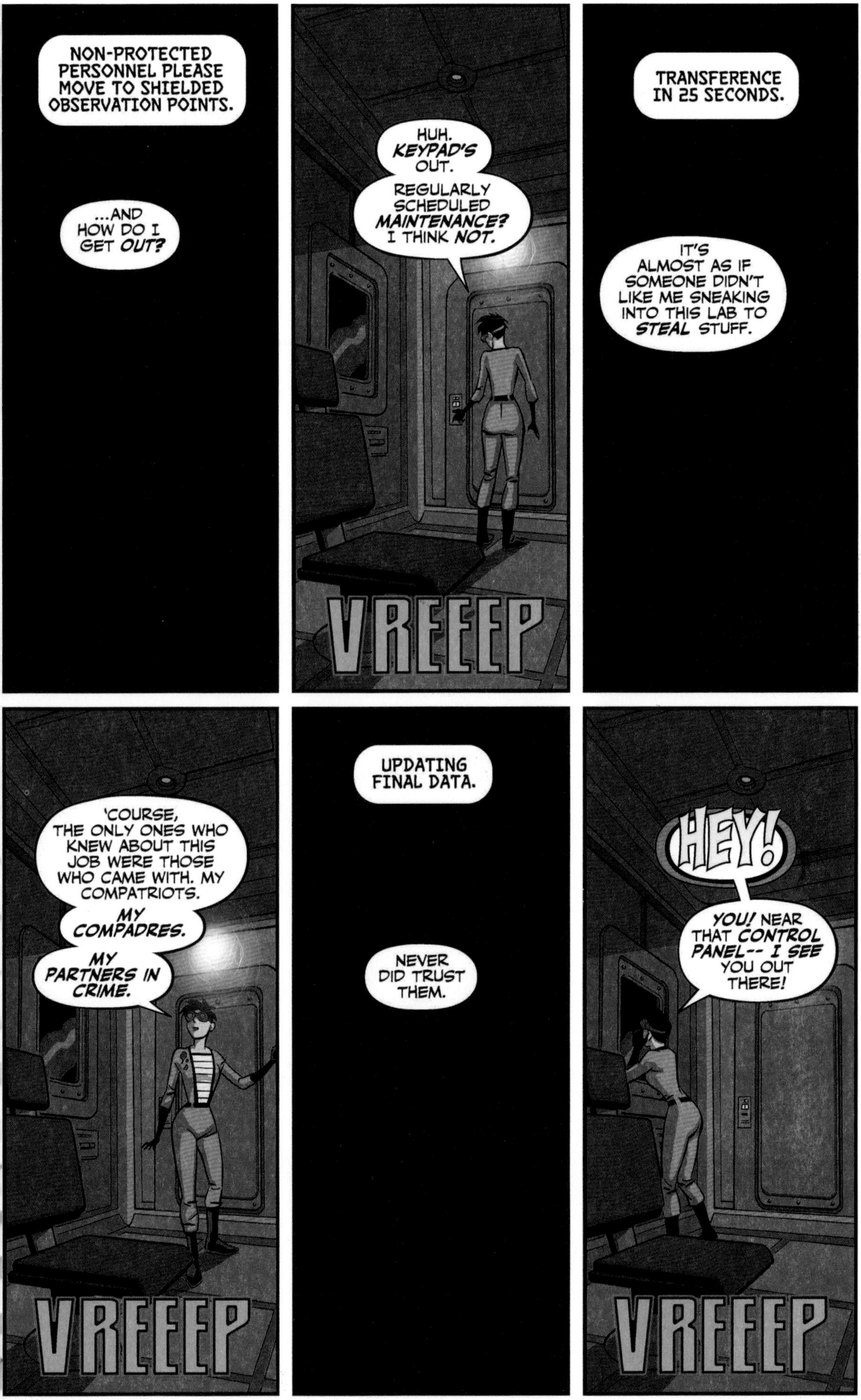

NON-PROTECTED PERSONNEL PLEASE MOVE TO SHIELDED OBSERVATION POINTS.
...AND HOW DO I GET OUT?
HUH. KEYPAD'S OUT.
REGULARLY SCHEDULED MAINTENANCE? I THINK NOT.
VREEEP
TRANSFERENCE IN 25 SECONDS.
IT'S ALMOST AS IF SOMEONE DIDN'T LIKE ME SNEAKING INTO THIS LAB TO STEAL STUFF.
'COURSE, THE ONLY ONES WHO KNEW ABOUT THIS JOB WERE THOSE WHO CAME WITH. MY COMPATRIOTS.
MY COMPADRES.
MY PARTNERS IN CRIME.
VREEEP
UPDATING FINAL DATA.
NEVER DID TRUST THEM.
HEY!
YOU! NEAR THAT CONTROL PANEL-- I SEE YOU OUT THERE!
VREEEP

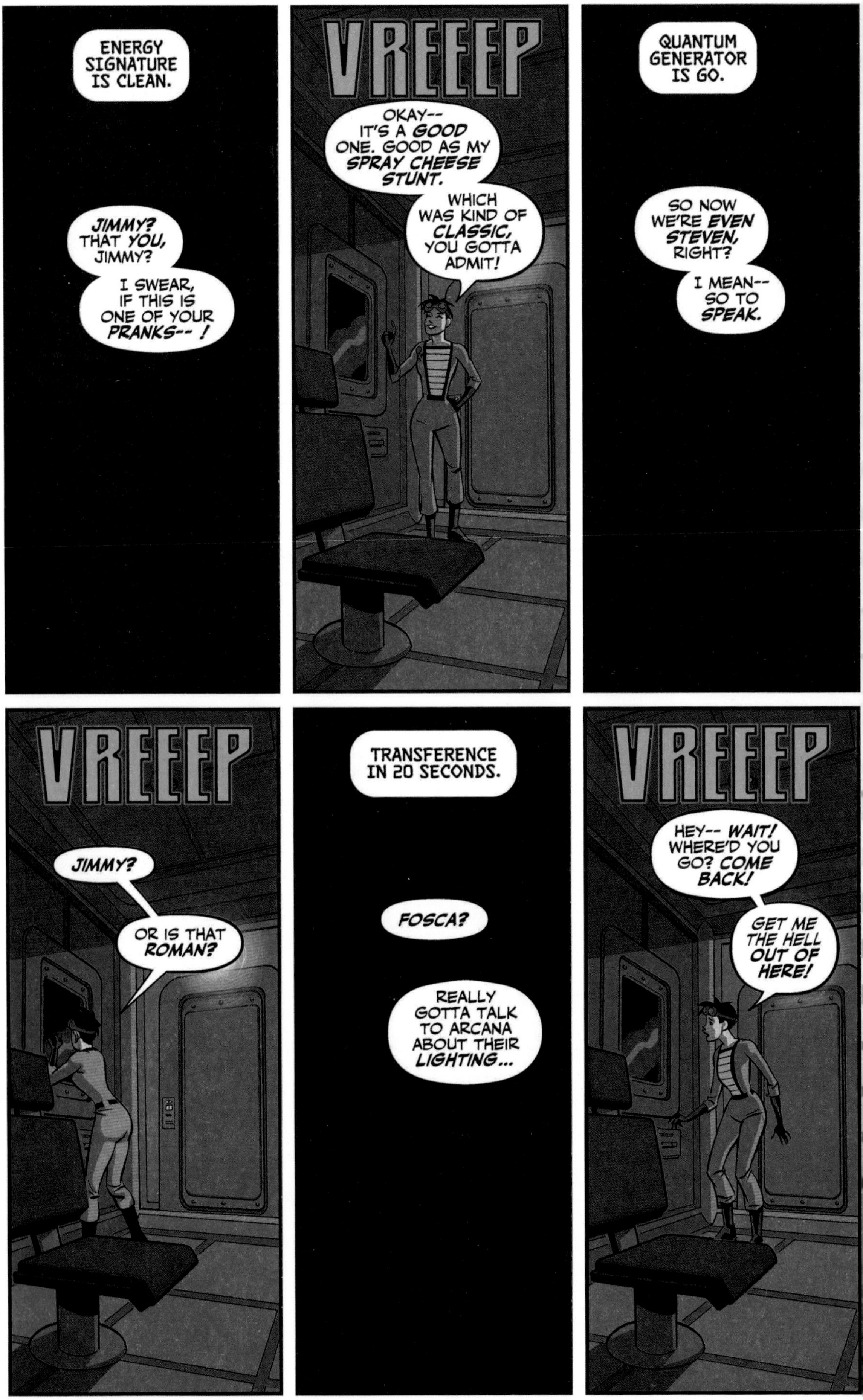
ENERGY SIGNATURE IS CLEAN.
JIMMY? THAT YOU, JIMMY?
I SWEAR, IF THIS IS ONE OF YOUR PRANKS-- !
VREEEP
OKAY-- IT'S A GOOD ONE. GOOD AS MY SPRAY CHEESE STUNT.
WHICH WAS KIND OF CLASSIC, YOU GOTTA ADMIT!
QUANTUM GENERATOR IS GO.
SO NOW WE'RE EVEN STEVEN, RIGHT?
I MEAN-- SO TO SPEAK.
VREEEP
JIMMY?
OR IS THAT ROMAN?
TRANSFERENCE IN 20 SECONDS.
FOSCA?
REALLY GOTTA TALK TO ARCANA ABOUT THEIR LIGHTING...
VREEEP
HEY-- WAIT! WHERE'D YOU GO? COME BACK!
GET ME THE HELL OUT OF HERE!

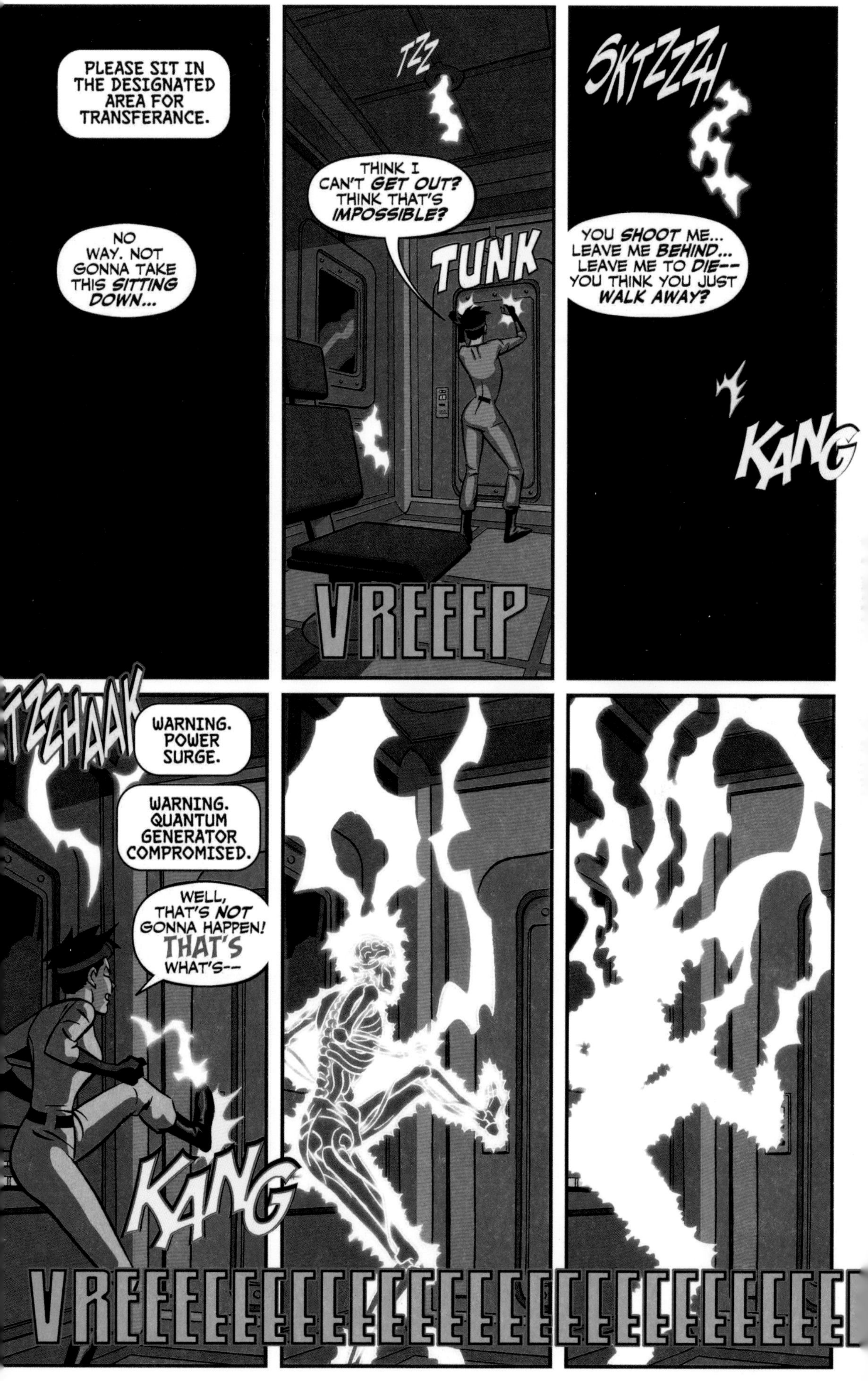
PLEASE SIT IN THE DESIGNATED AREA FOR TRANSFERANCE.
NO WAY. NOT GONNA TAKE THIS SITTING DOWN...
TZZ
THINK I CAN'T GET OUT? THINK THAT'S IMPOSSIBLE?
TUNK
VREEEP
SKTZZZH
YOU SHOOT ME... LEAVE ME BEHIND... LEAVE ME TO DIE-- YOU THINK YOU JUST WALK AWAY?
KANG
TZZHAAK
WARNING. POWER SURGE.
WARNING. QUANTUM GENERATOR COMPROMISED.
WELL, THAT'S NOT GONNA HAPPEN! THAT'S WHAT'S--
KANG
VREEEEEEEEEEEEEEEEEEEEEEEEE

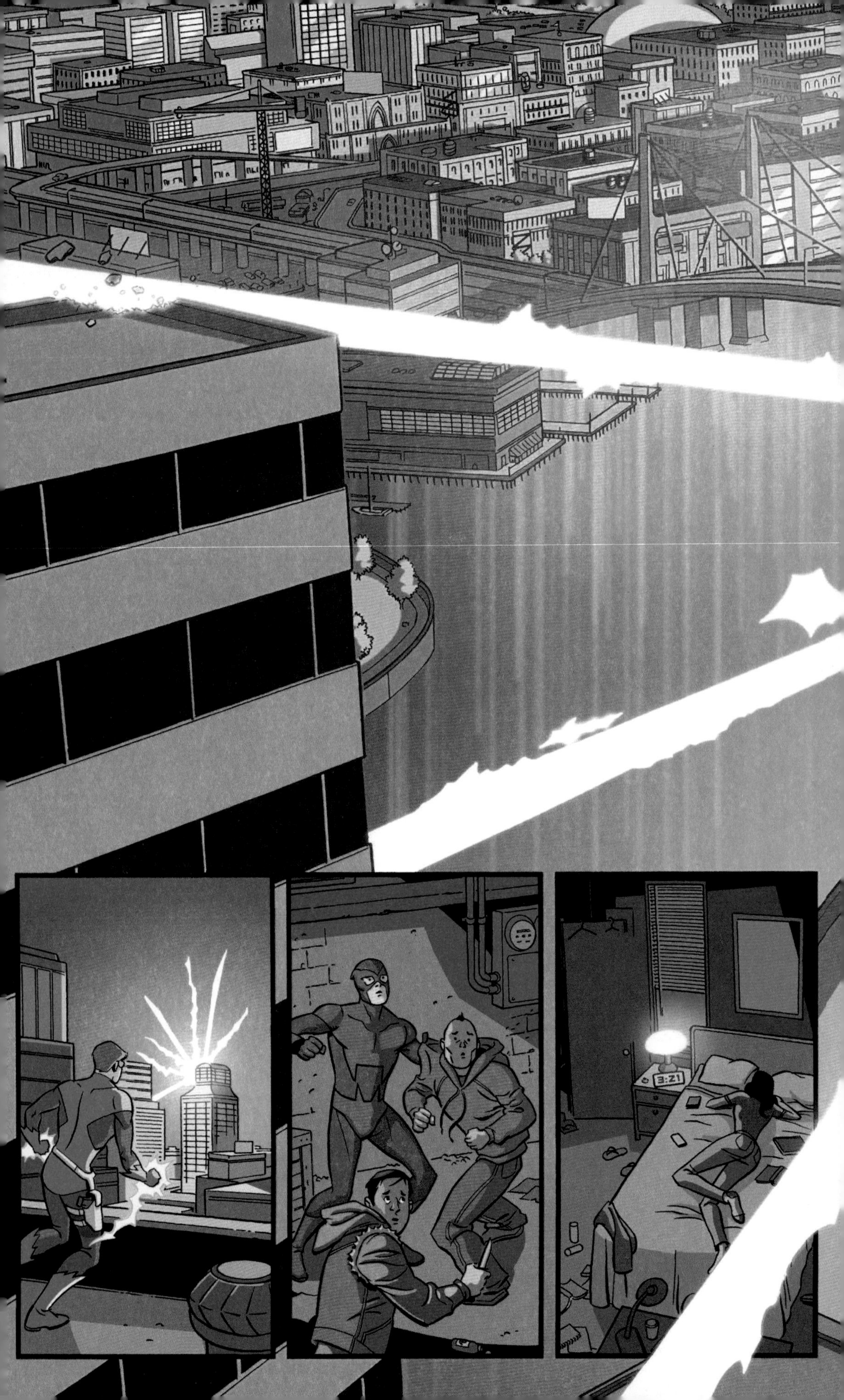
3:21

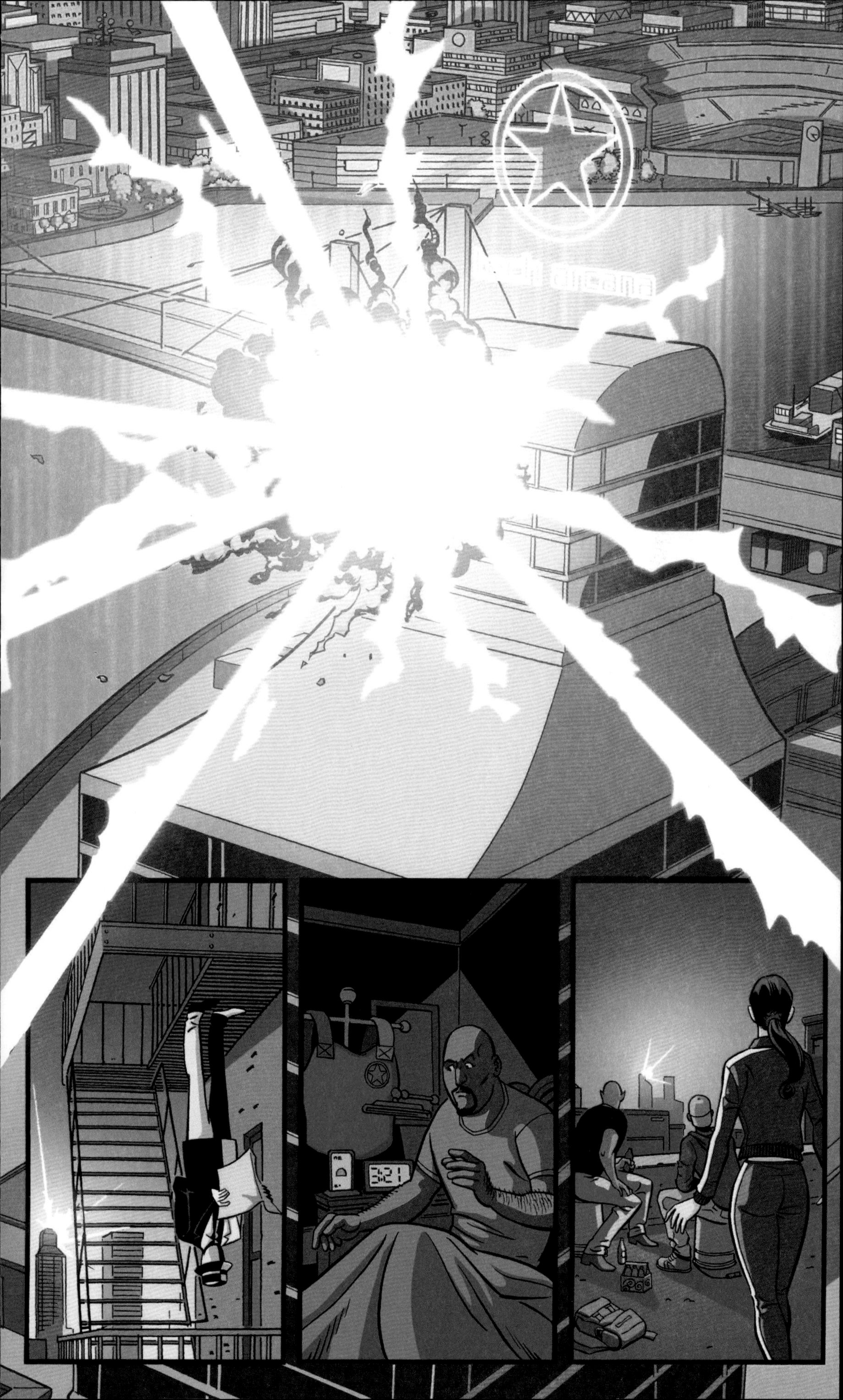

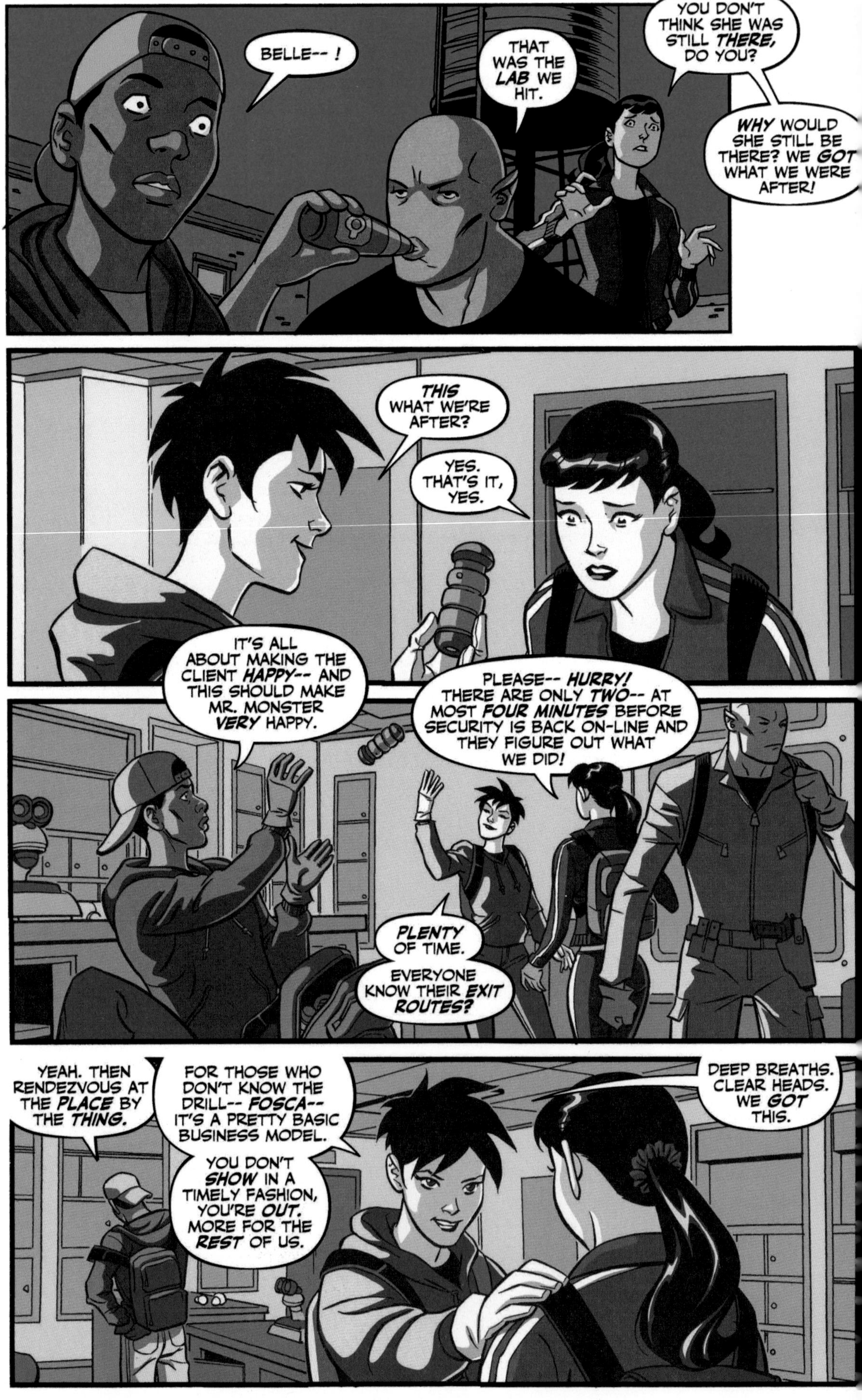

BELLE-- !
THAT WAS THE LAB WE HIT.
YOU DON'T THINK SHE WAS STILL THERE, DO YOU?
WHY WOULD SHE STILL BE THERE? WE GOT WHAT WE WERE AFTER!
THIS WHAT WE'RE AFTER?
YES. THAT'S IT, YES.
IT'S ALL ABOUT MAKING THE CLIENT HAPPY-- AND THIS SHOULD MAKE MR. MONSTER VERY HAPPY.
PLEASE-- HURRY! THERE ARE ONLY TWO-- AT MOST FOUR MINUTES BEFORE SECURITY IS BACK ON-LINE AND THEY FIGURE OUT WHAT WE DID!
PLENTY OF TIME.
EVERYONE KNOW THEIR EXIT ROUTES?
YEAH. THEN RENDEZVOUS AT THE PLACE BY THE THING.
FOR THOSE WHO DON'T KNOW THE DRILL-- FOSCA-- IT'S A PRETTY BASIC BUSINESS MODEL.
YOU DON'T SHOW IN A TIMELY FASHION, YOU'RE OUT. MORE FOR THE REST OF US.
DEEP BREATHS. CLEAR HEADS. WE GOT THIS.

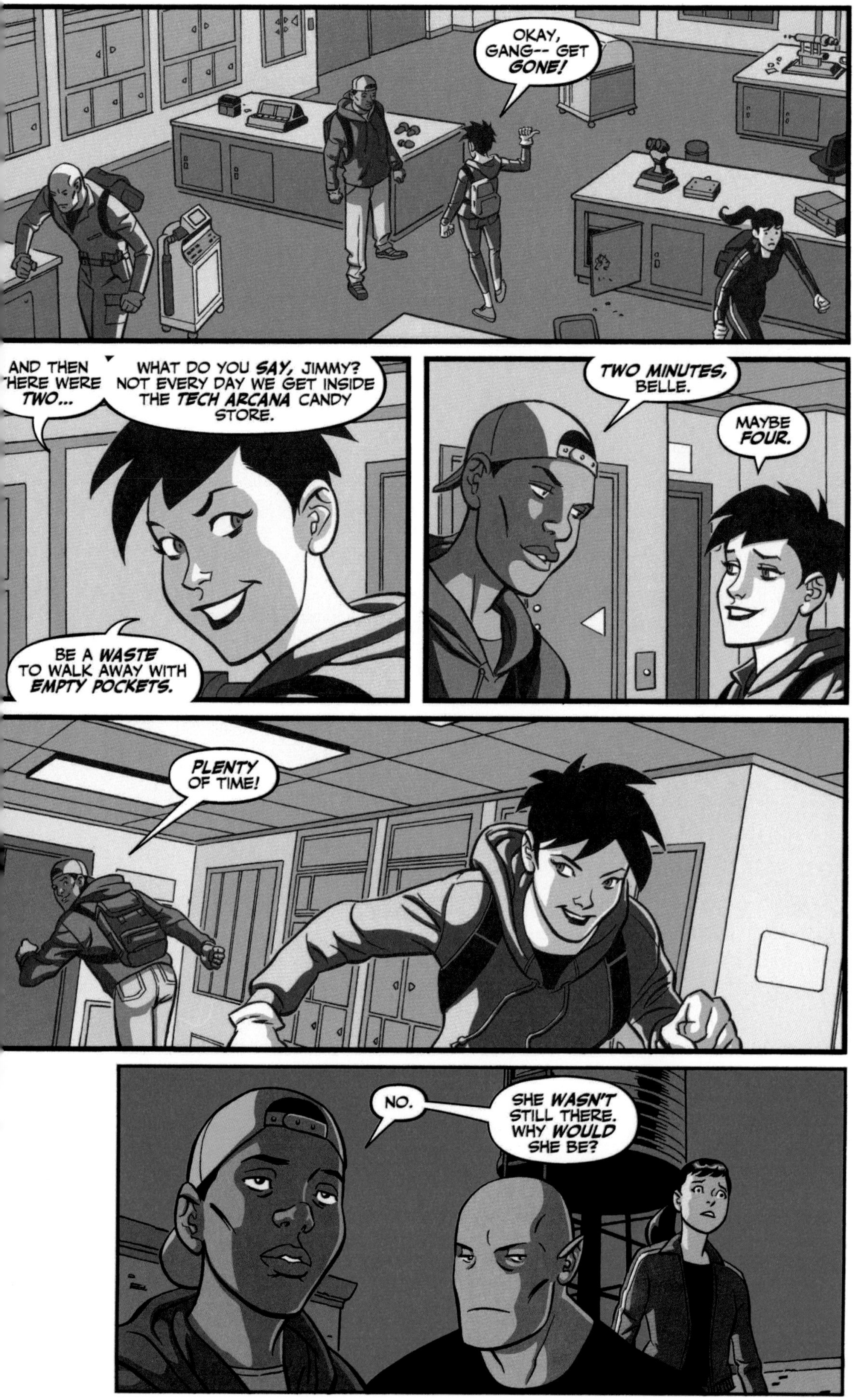

OKAY, GANG-- GET GONE!
AND THEN THERE WERE TWO...
WHAT DO YOU SAY, JIMMY? NOT EVERY DAY WE GET INSIDE THE TECH ARCANA CANDY STORE.
BE A WASTE TO WALK AWAY WITH EMPTY POCKETS.
TWO MINUTES, BELLE.
MAYBE FOUR.
PLENTY OF TIME!
NO.
SHE WASN'T STILL THERE. WHY WOULD SHE BE?

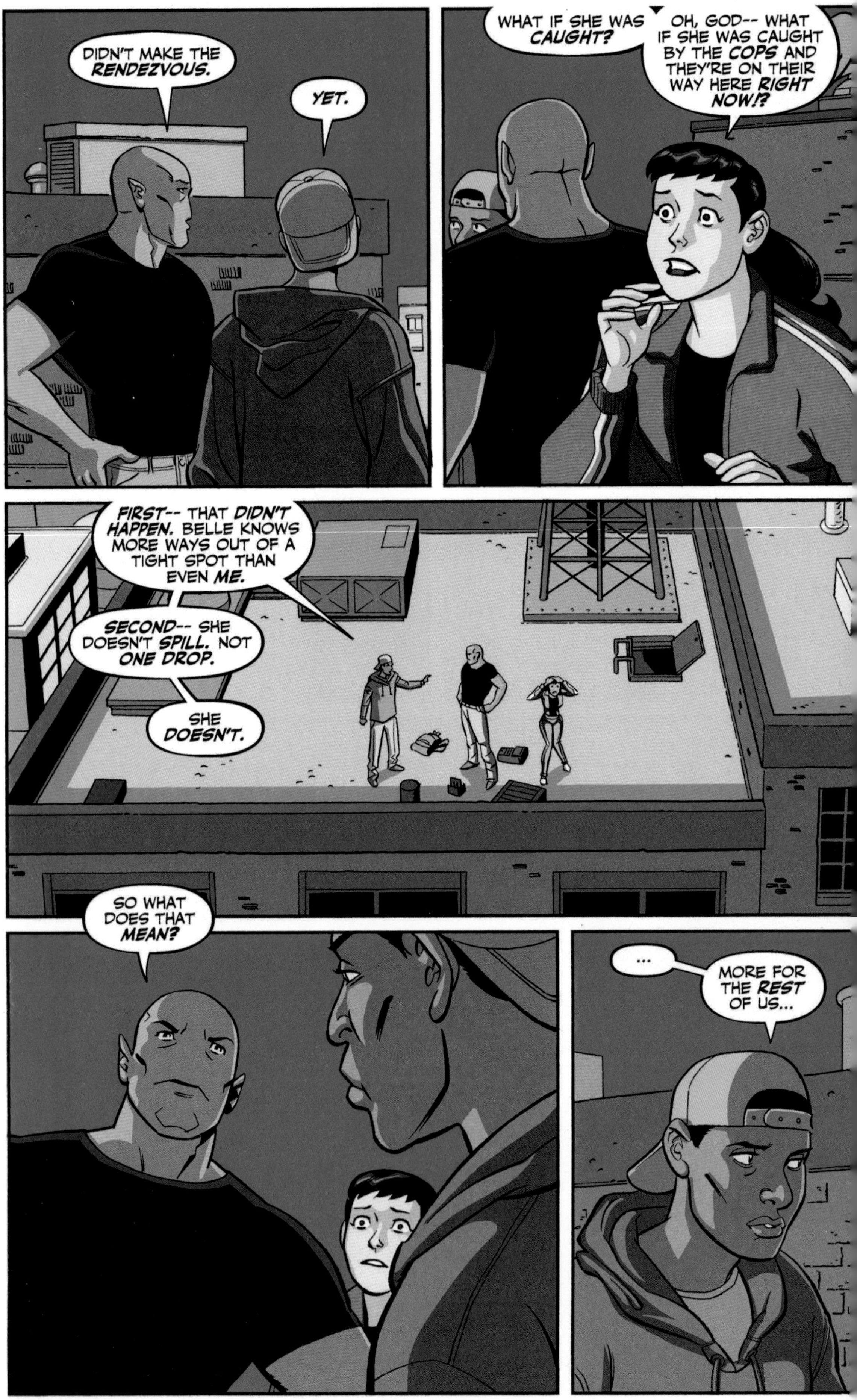
DIDN'T MAKE THE RENDEZVOUS.
YET.
WHAT IF SHE WAS CAUGHT?
OH, GOD-- WHAT IF SHE WAS CAUGHT BY THE COPS AND THEY'RE ON THEIR WAY HERE RIGHT NOW!?
FIRST-- THAT DIDN'T HAPPEN. BELLE KNOWS MORE WAYS OUT OF A TIGHT SPOT THAN EVEN ME.
SECOND-- SHE DOESN'T SPILL. NOT ONE DROP.
SHE DOESN'T.
SO WHAT DOES THAT MEAN?
...
MORE FOR THE REST OF US...

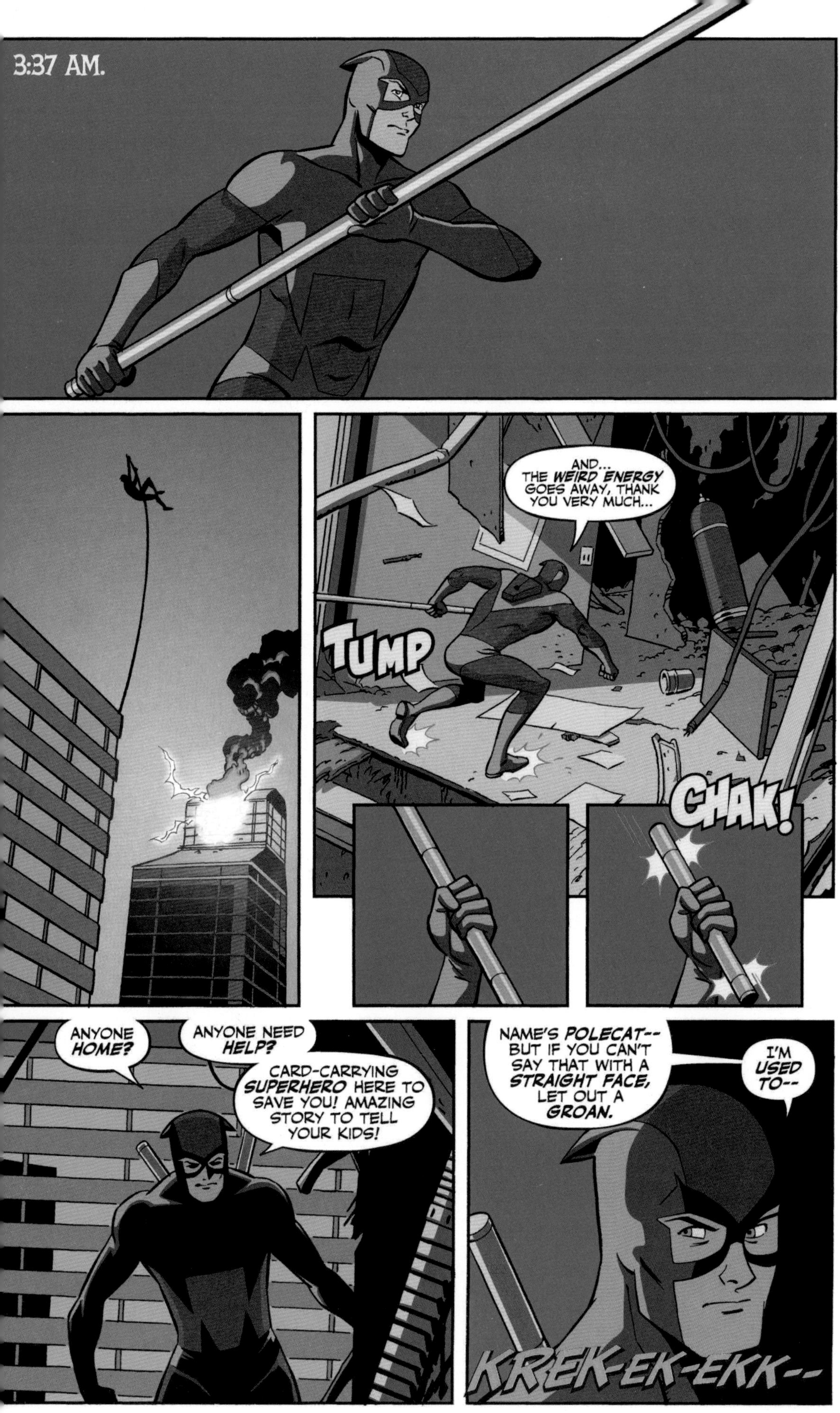

3:37 AM.
AND... THE WEIRD ENERGY GOES AWAY, THANK YOU VERY MUCH...
TUMP
CHAK!
ANYONE HOME?
ANYONE NEED HELP?
CARD-CARRYING SUPERHERO HERE TO SAVE YOU! AMAZING STORY TO TELL YOUR KIDS!
NAME'S POLECAT-- BUT IF YOU CAN'T SAY THAT WITH A STRAIGHT FACE, LET OUT A GROAN.
I'M USED TO--
KREK-EK-EKK--

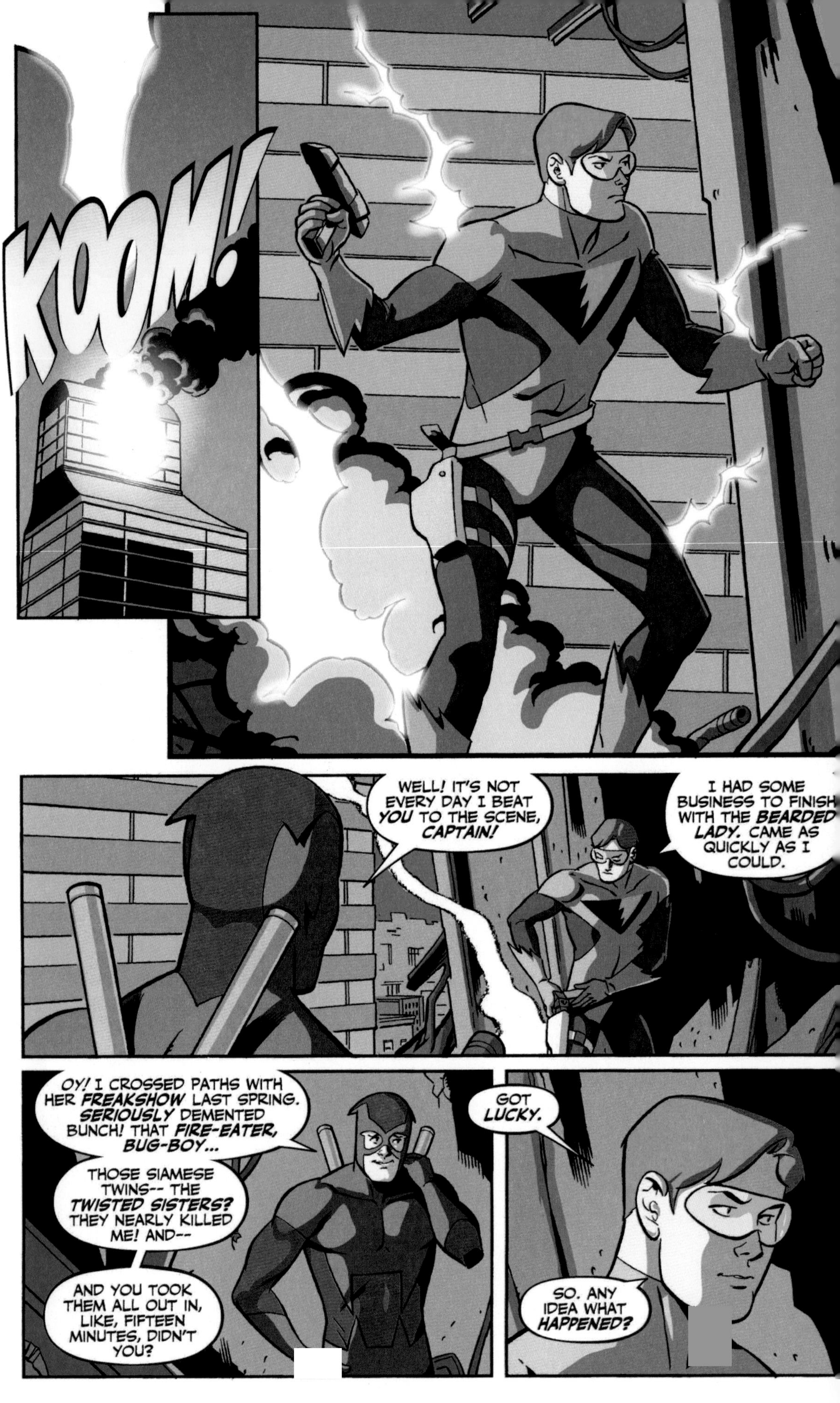
KOOM!
WELL! IT'S NOT EVERY DAY I BEAT YOU TO THE SCENE, CAPTAIN!
I HAD SOME BUSINESS TO FINISH WITH THE BEARDED LADY. CAME AS QUICKLY AS I COULD.
OY! I CROSSED PATHS WITH HER FREAKSHOW LAST SPRING. SERIOUSLY DEMENTED BUNCH! THAT FIRE-EATER, BUG-BOY...
THOSE SIAMESE TWINS-- THE TWISTED SISTERS? THEY NEARLY KILLED ME! AND--
AND YOU TOOK THEM ALL OUT IN, LIKE, FIFTEEN MINUTES, DIDN'T YOU?
GOT LUCKY.
SO. ANY IDEA WHAT HAPPENED?

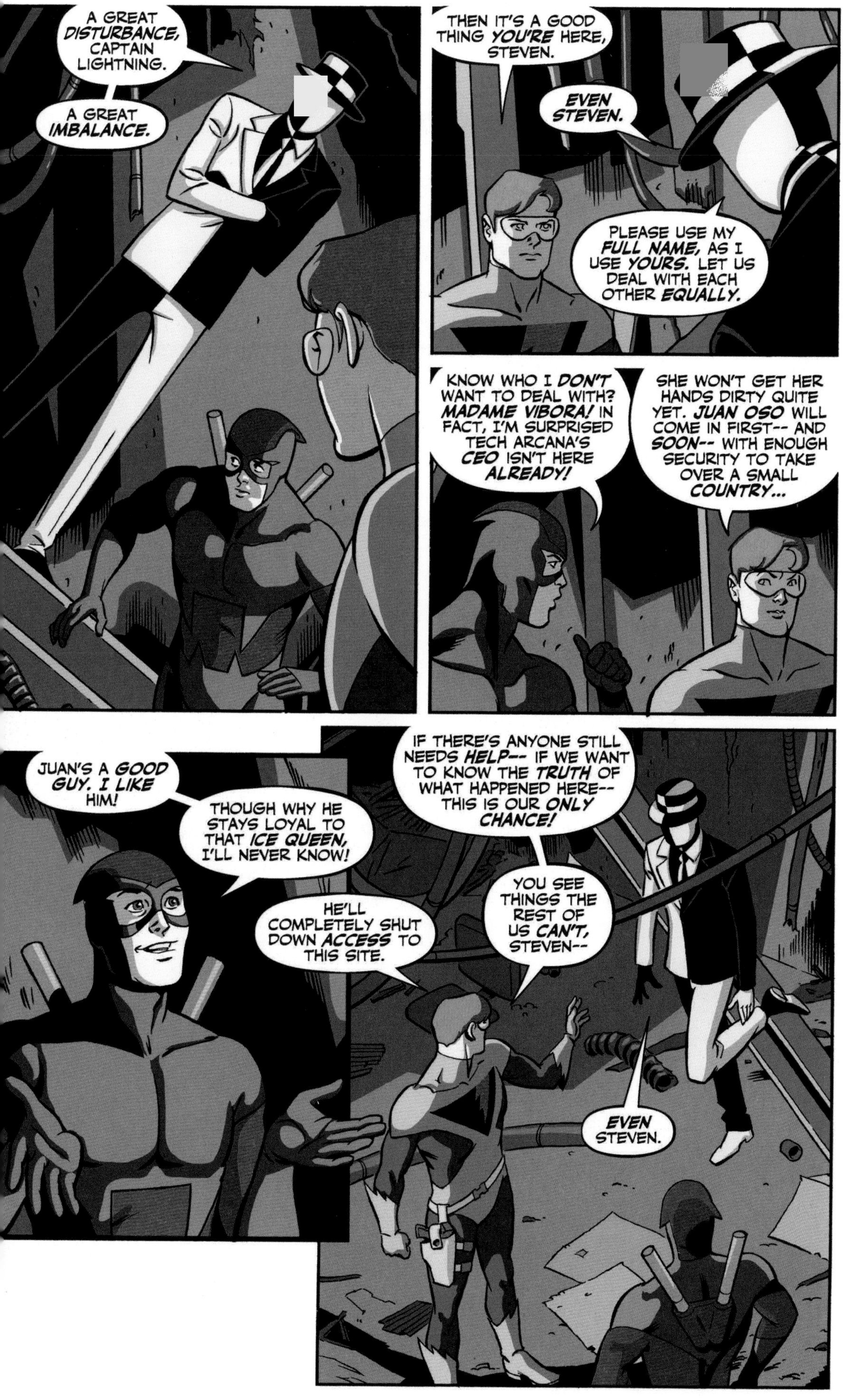
A GREAT DISTURBANCE, CAPTAIN LIGHTNING.
A GREAT IMBALANCE.
THEN IT'S A GOOD THING YOU'RE HERE, STEVEN.
EVEN STEVEN.
PLEASE USE MY FULL NAME, AS I USE YOURS. LET US DEAL WITH EACH OTHER EQUALLY.
KNOW WHO I DON'T WANT TO DEAL WITH? MADAME VIBORA! IN FACT, I'M SURPRISED TECH ARCANA'S CEO ISN'T HERE ALREADY!
SHE WON'T GET HER HANDS DIRTY QUITE YET. JUAN OSO WILL COME IN FIRST-- AND SOON-- WITH ENOUGH SECURITY TO TAKE OVER A SMALL COUNTRY...
JUAN'S A GOOD GUY. I LIKE HIM!
THOUGH WHY HE STAYS LOYAL TO THAT ICE QUEEN, I'LL NEVER KNOW!
HE'LL COMPLETELY SHUT DOWN ACCESS TO THIS SITE.
IF THERE'S ANYONE STILL NEEDS HELP-- IF WE WANT TO KNOW THE TRUTH OF WHAT HAPPENED HERE-- THIS IS OUR ONLY CHANCE!
YOU SEE THINGS THE REST OF US CAN'T, STEVEN--
EVEN STEVEN.

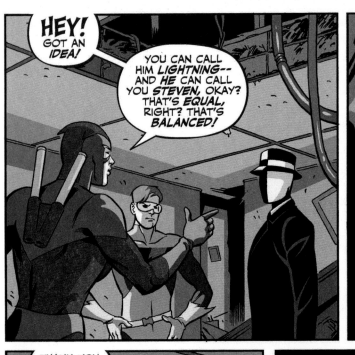

HEY! GOT AN IDEA!

YOU CAN CALL HIM *LIGHTNING*-- AND *HE* CAN CALL YOU *STEVEN*, OKAY? THAT'S *EQUAL*, RIGHT? THAT'S *BALANCED!*

...

YES. THAT WORKS.

THANK YOU. *NOW...*

WHAT CAN YOU SENSE ABOUT THE *EXPLOSION*, STEVEN?

WHAT SET IT *OFF?* IS THERE ANYONE WE CAN STILL *SAVE?* WERE ANY LIVES *LOST?*

LOST. YES. BUT MATTER AND ENERGY CANNOT BE *DESTROYED.* IT CAN ONLY BE TRANSFORMED... *RESHAPED.*

WHAT WAS *LOST* MAY STILL BE *FOUND.*

THE BALANCE IS *SHIFTING.*

WHAT... DOES THAT *MEAN?*

IT MEANS WE'RE *OUT OF TIME*-- !

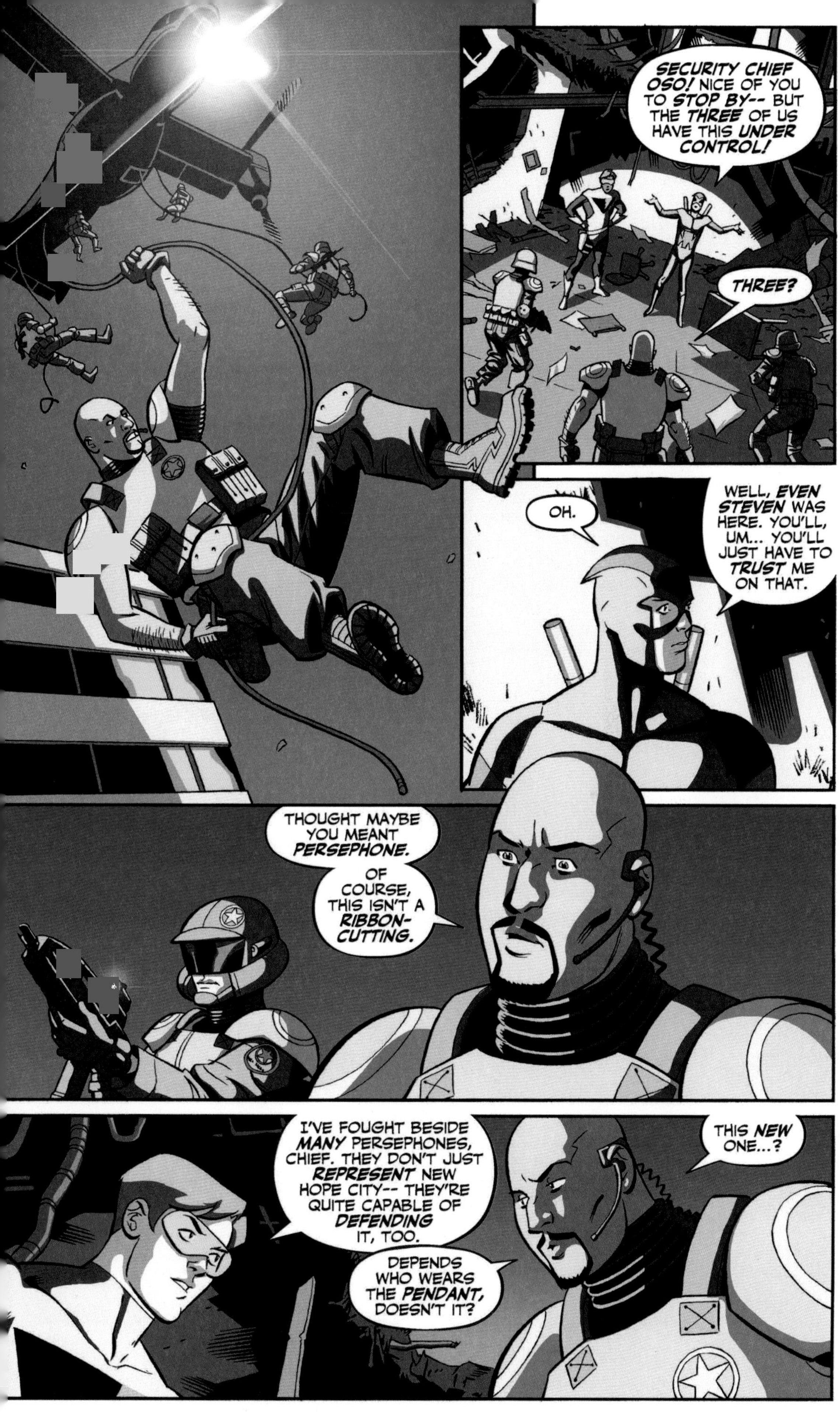
SECURITY CHIEF OSO! NICE OF YOU TO STOP BY-- BUT THE THREE OF US HAVE THIS UNDER CONTROL!
THREE?
OH.
WELL, EVEN STEVEN WAS HERE. YOU'LL, UM... YOU'LL JUST HAVE TO TRUST ME ON THAT.
THOUGHT MAYBE YOU MEANT PERSEPHONE.
OF COURSE, THIS ISN'T A RIBBON-CUTTING.
I'VE FOUGHT BESIDE MANY PERSEPHONES, CHIEF. THEY DON'T JUST REPRESENT NEW HOPE CITY-- THEY'RE QUITE CAPABLE OF DEFENDING IT, TOO.
THIS NEW ONE...?
DEPENDS WHO WEARS THE PENDANT, DOESN'T IT?

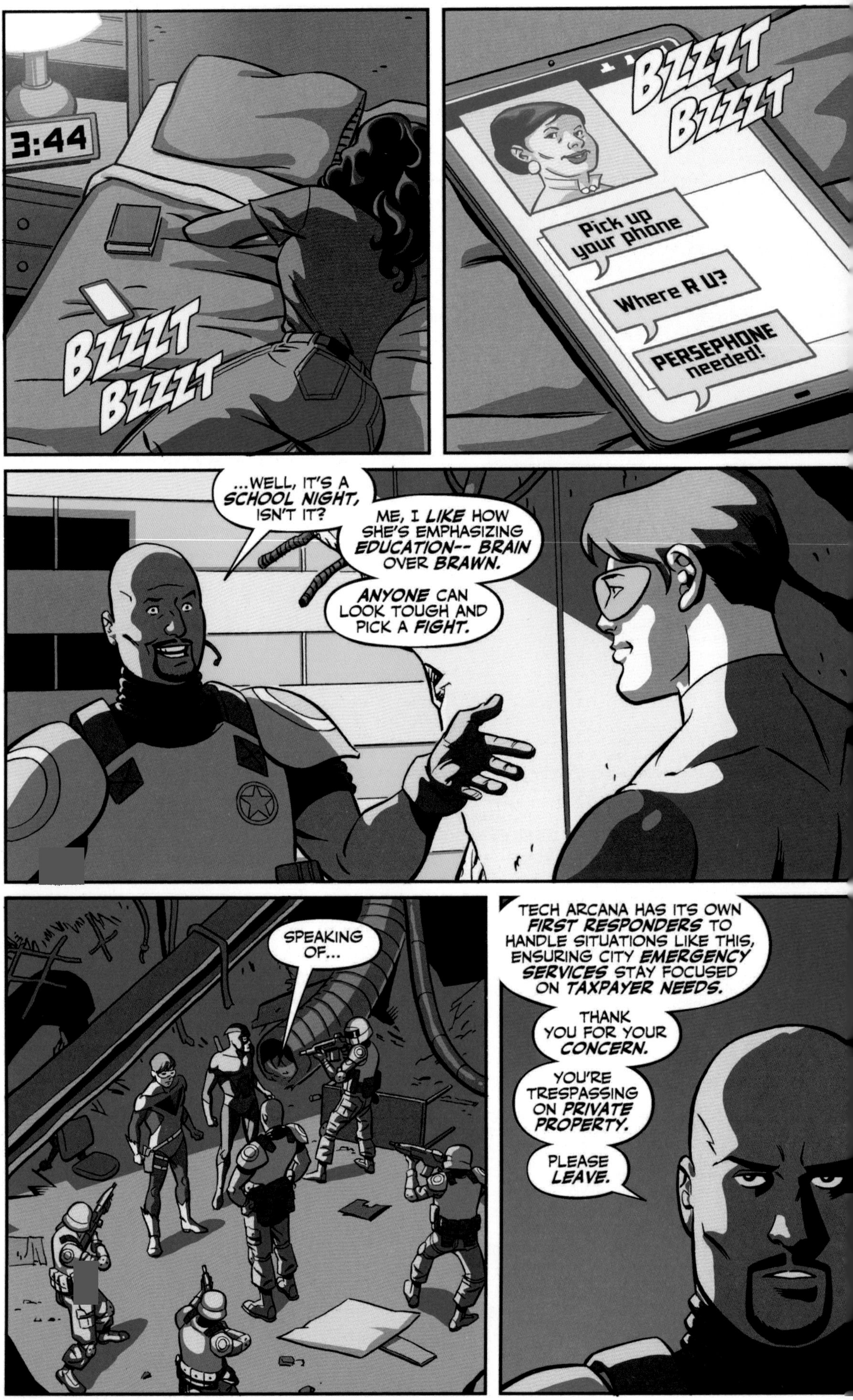
3:44
BZZZT BZZZT
BZZZT BZZZT
Pick up your phone
Where R U?
PERSEPHONE needed!
...WELL, IT'S A SCHOOL NIGHT, ISN'T IT?
ME, I LIKE HOW SHE'S EMPHASIZING EDUCATION-- BRAIN OVER BRAWN.
ANYONE CAN LOOK TOUGH AND PICK A FIGHT.
SPEAKING OF...
TECH ARCANA HAS ITS OWN FIRST RESPONDERS TO HANDLE SITUATIONS LIKE THIS, ENSURING CITY EMERGENCY SERVICES STAY FOCUSED ON TAXPAYER NEEDS.
THANK YOU FOR YOUR CONCERN.
YOU'RE TRESPASSING ON PRIVATE PROPERTY.
PLEASE LEAVE.

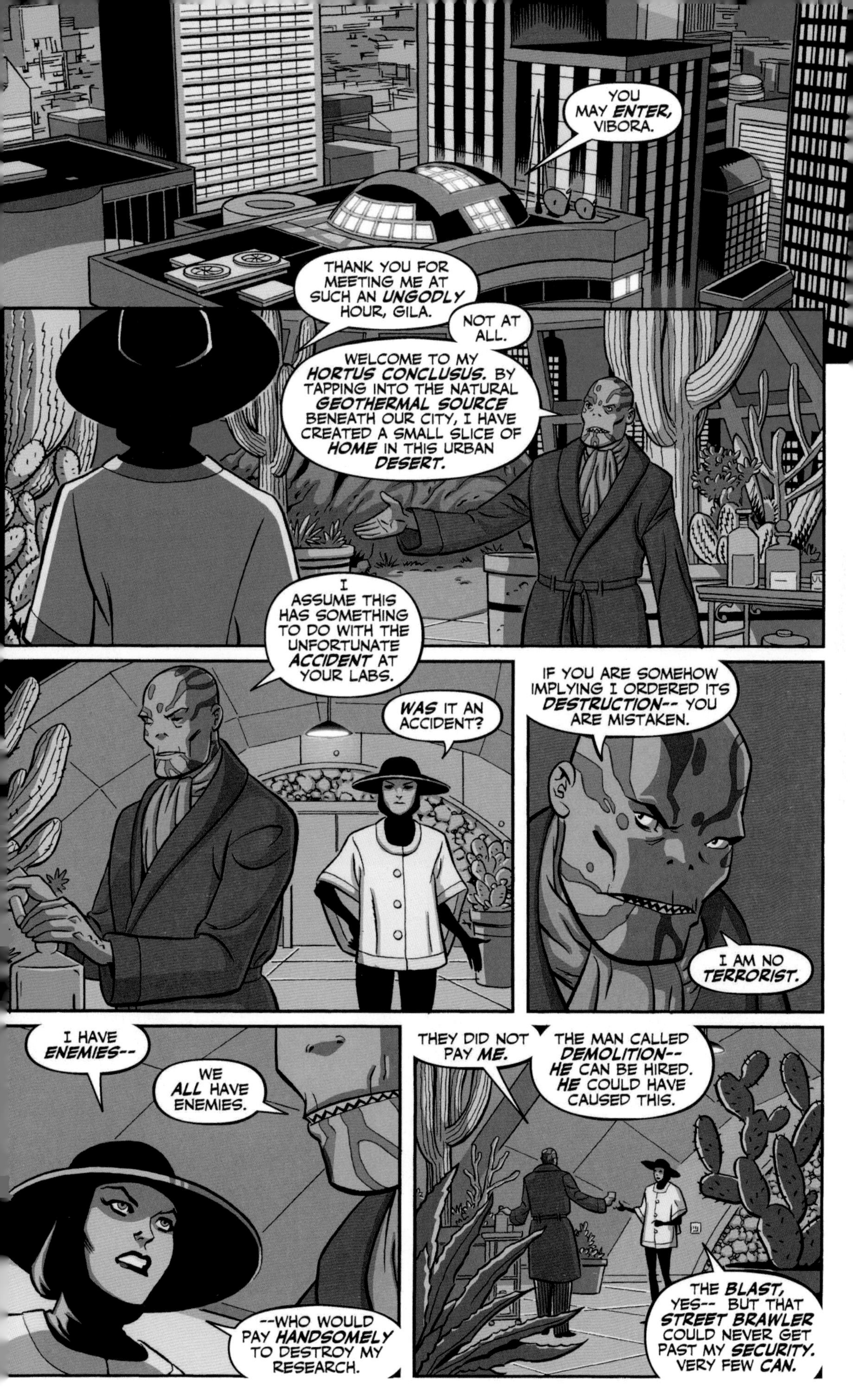
YOU MAY ENTER, VIBORA.
THANK YOU FOR MEETING ME AT SUCH AN UNGODLY HOUR, GILA.
NOT AT ALL.
WELCOME TO MY HORTUS CONCLUSUS. BY TAPPING INTO THE NATURAL GEOTHERMAL SOURCE BENEATH OUR CITY, I HAVE CREATED A SMALL SLICE OF HOME IN THIS URBAN DESERT.
I ASSUME THIS HAS SOMETHING TO DO WITH THE UNFORTUNATE ACCIDENT AT YOUR LABS.
WAS IT AN ACCIDENT?
IF YOU ARE SOMEHOW IMPLYING I ORDERED ITS DESTRUCTION-- YOU ARE MISTAKEN.
I AM NO TERRORIST.
I HAVE ENEMIES--
WE ALL HAVE ENEMIES.
--WHO WOULD PAY HANDSOMELY TO DESTROY MY RESEARCH.
THEY DID NOT PAY ME.
THE MAN CALLED DEMOLITION-- HE CAN BE HIRED. HE COULD HAVE CAUSED THIS.
THE BLAST, YES-- BUT THAT STREET BRAWLER COULD NEVER GET PAST MY SECURITY. VERY FEW CAN.

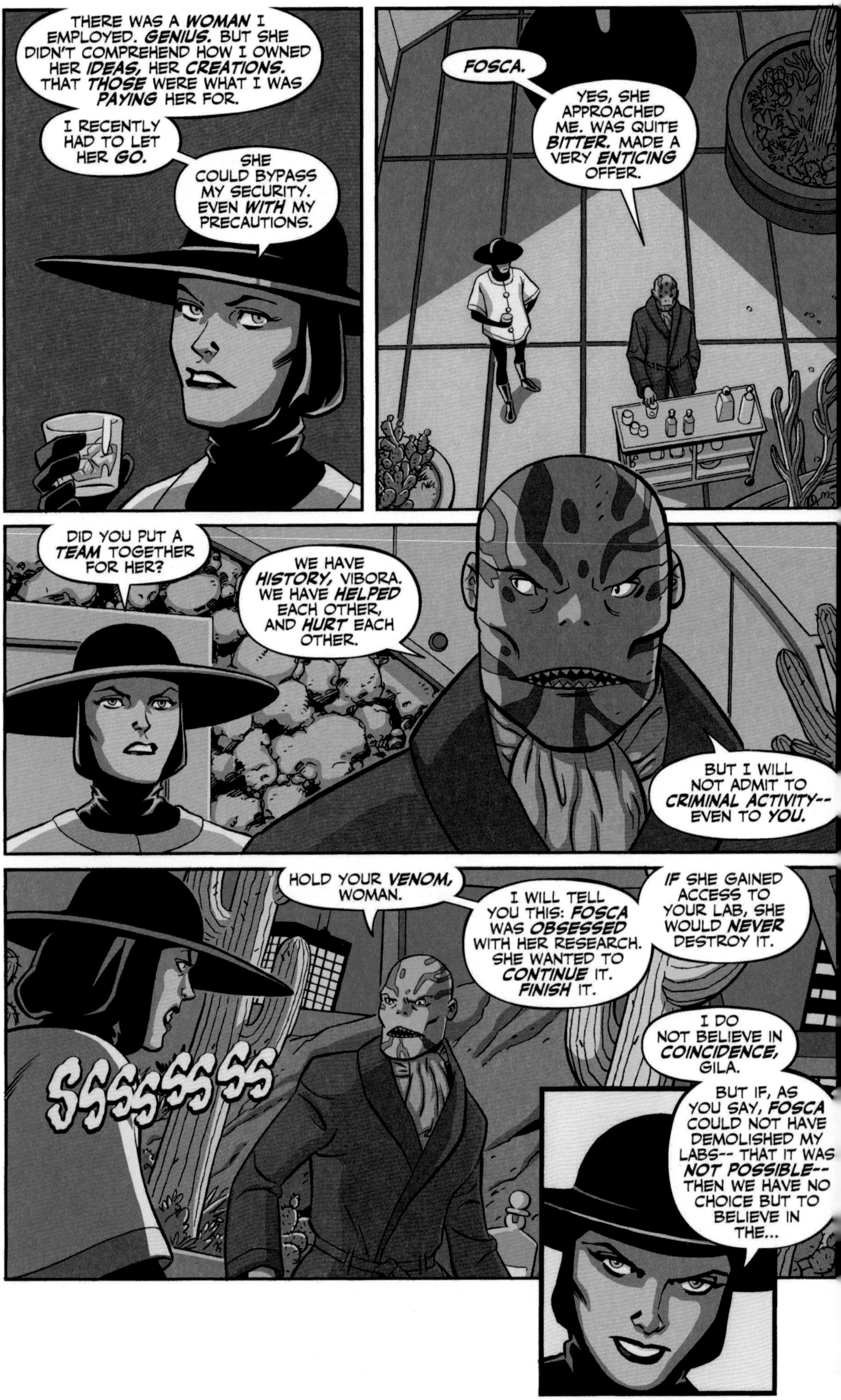

THERE WAS A WOMAN I EMPLOYED. GENIUS. BUT SHE DIDN'T COMPREHEND HOW I OWNED HER IDEAS, HER CREATIONS. THAT THOSE WERE WHAT I WAS PAYING HER FOR.
I RECENTLY HAD TO LET HER GO.
SHE COULD BYPASS MY SECURITY. EVEN WITH MY PRECAUTIONS.
FOSCA.
YES, SHE APPROACHED ME. WAS QUITE BITTER. MADE A VERY ENTICING OFFER.
DID YOU PUT A TEAM TOGETHER FOR HER?
WE HAVE HISTORY, VIBORA. WE HAVE HELPED EACH OTHER, AND HURT EACH OTHER.
BUT I WILL NOT ADMIT TO CRIMINAL ACTIVITY-- EVEN TO YOU.
SSSSSSSSS
HOLD YOUR VENOM, WOMAN.
I WILL TELL YOU THIS: FOSCA WAS OBSESSED WITH HER RESEARCH. SHE WANTED TO CONTINUE IT. FINISH IT.
IF SHE GAINED ACCESS TO YOUR LAB, SHE WOULD NEVER DESTROY IT.
I DO NOT BELIEVE IN COINCIDENCE, GILA.
BUT IF, AS YOU SAY, FOSCA COULD NOT HAVE DEMOLISHED MY LABS-- THAT IT WAS NOT POSSIBLE-- THEN WE HAVE NO CHOICE BUT TO BELIEVE IN THE...

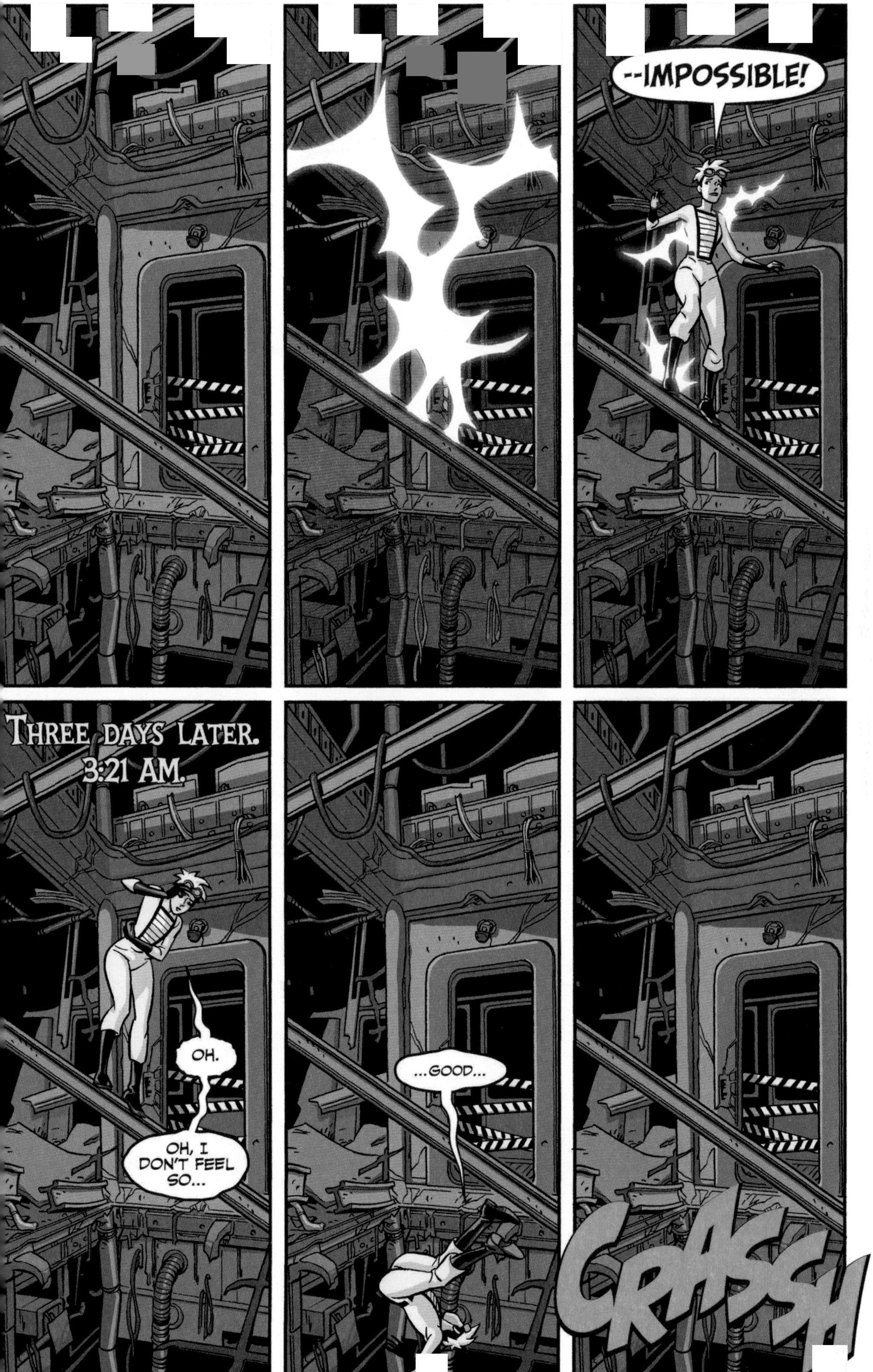
--IMPOSSIBLE!
THREE DAYS LATER.
3:21 AM.
OH.
OH, I DON'T FEEL SO...
...GOOD...
CRASH

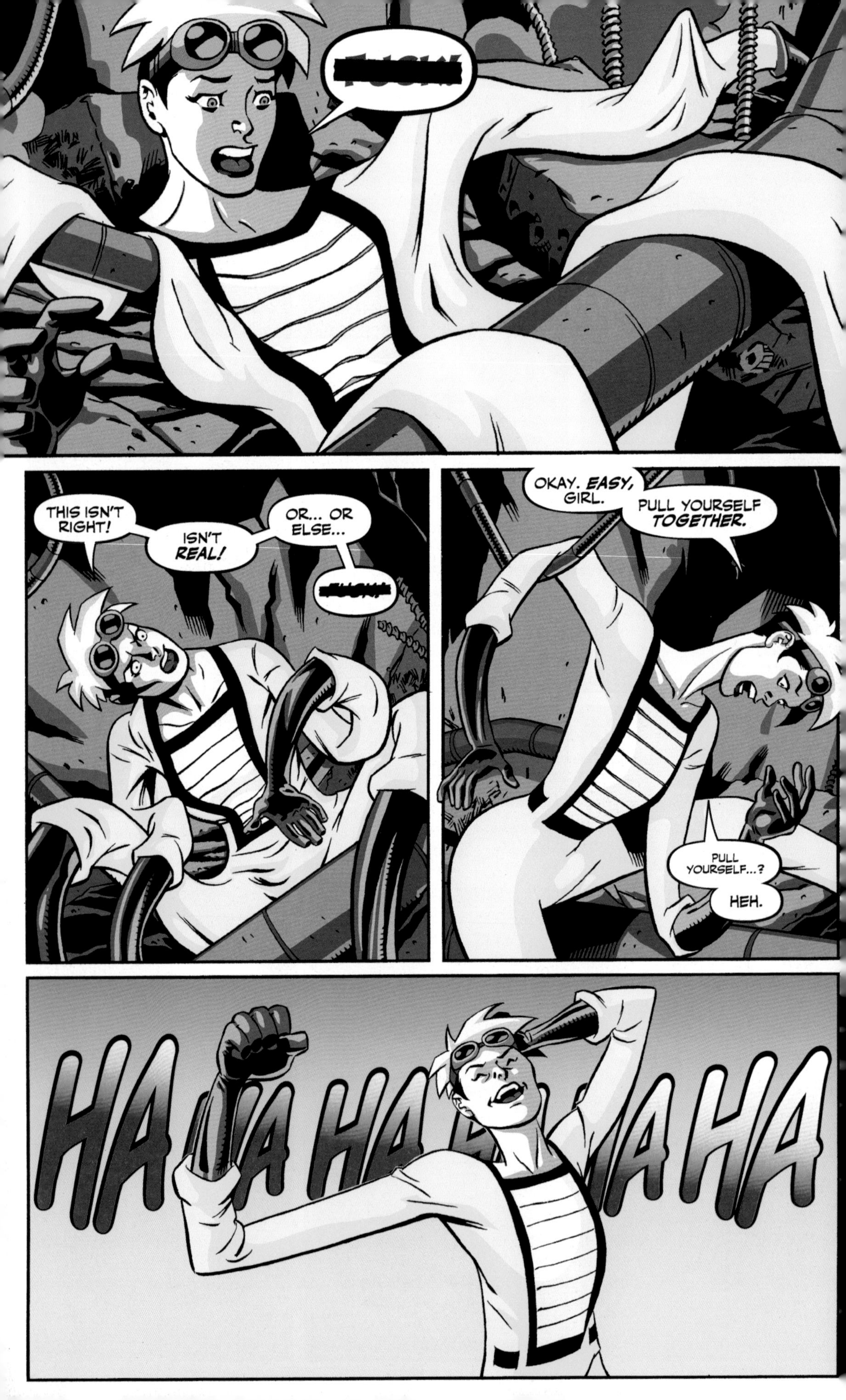
[redacted]
THIS ISN'T RIGHT!
ISN'T REAL!
OR... OR ELSE...
[redacted]
OKAY. EASY, GIRL.
PULL YOURSELF TOGETHER.
PULL YOURSELF...?
HEH.
HA HA HA HA HA HA

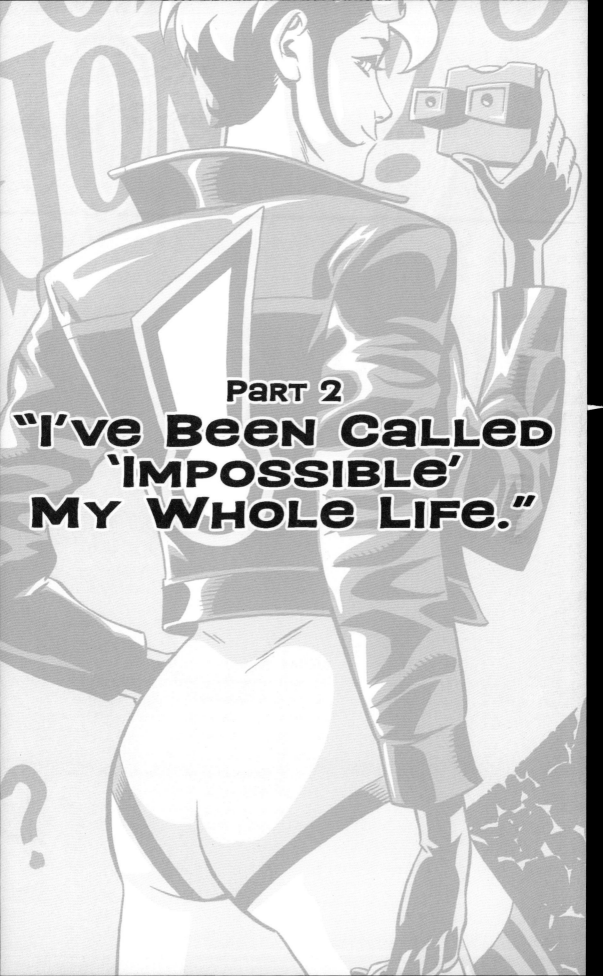

PART 2
"I've Been Called 'Impossible' My Whole Life."

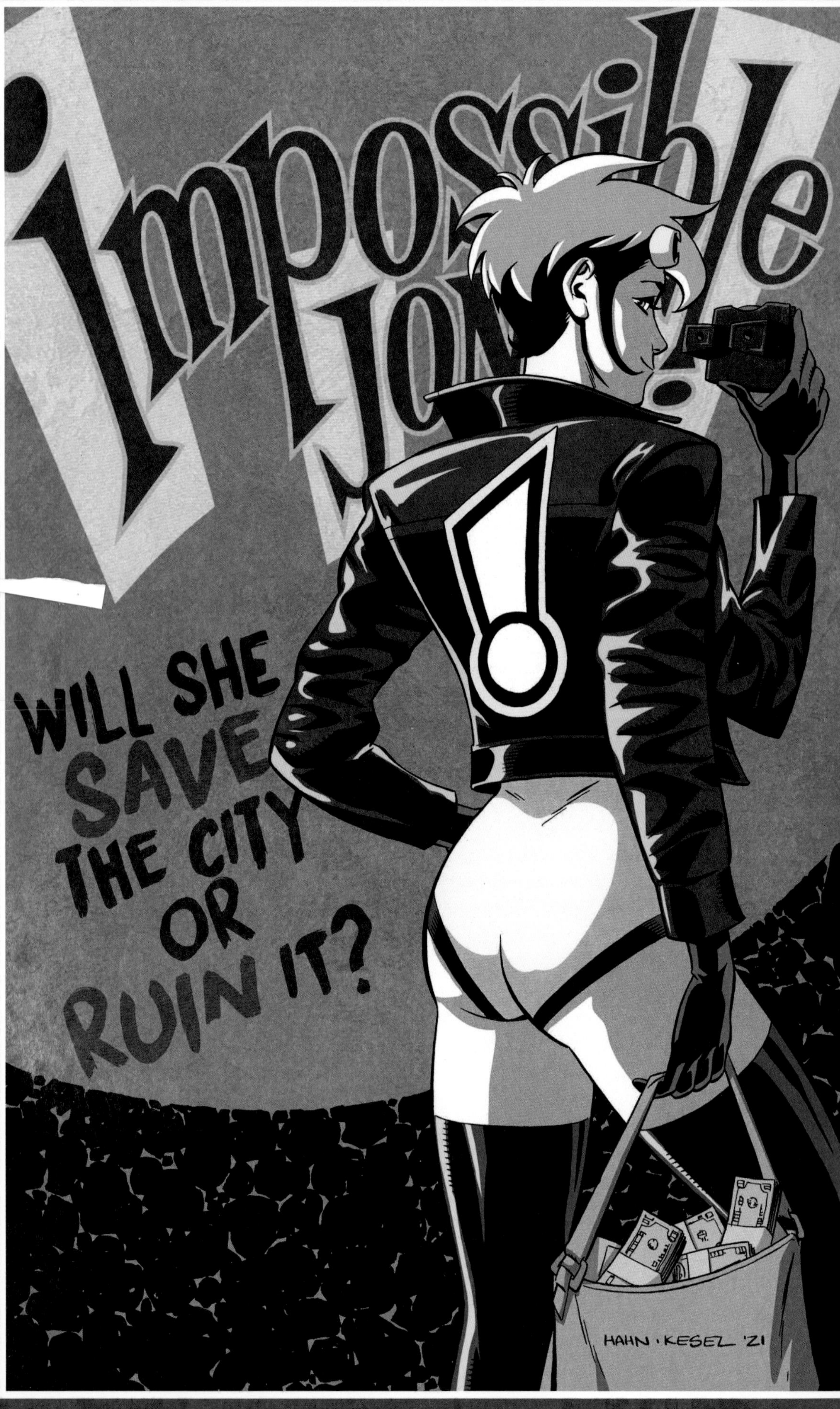
Impossible
WILL SHE SAVE THE CITY OR RUIN IT?
HAHN · KESEL '21

OKAY, PEOPLE--FAN OUT, STAY SHARP.

EYES OPEN FOR RANDALL.

SOUNDS LIKE SECURITY!

HIS LAST REPORT CUT OFF *TOO QUICKLY,* AND HE HASN'T RESPONDED *SINCE.*

LET'S HOPE HE'S JUST OFF READING THOSE DAMN *TREKKER* COMICS OF HIS!

THEY *ARE* PRETTY GOOD, CHIEF.

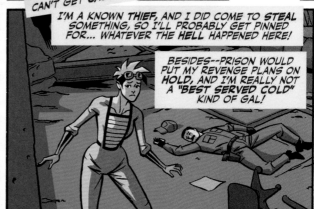

CAN'T GET *CAUGHT.*

I'M A KNOWN *THIEF,* AND I DID COME TO *STEAL* SOMETHING, SO I'LL PROBABLY GET PINNED FOR... WHATEVER THE *HELL* HAPPENED HERE!

BESIDES--PRISON WOULD PUT MY REVENGE PLANS ON *HOLD,* AND I'M REALLY NOT A *"BEST SERVED COLD"* KIND OF GAL!

ALSO NOT THE *"LEAP OF FAITH"* KIND.

HAS TO BE ANOTHER WAY OUT.

HAVE TO FIND IT *NOW!*

ANYTHING YOUR WAY, APPLEBY?

NO, SIR. NOT A--

HOLD IT.

MOVEMENT. ...

SON OF A BITCH--!

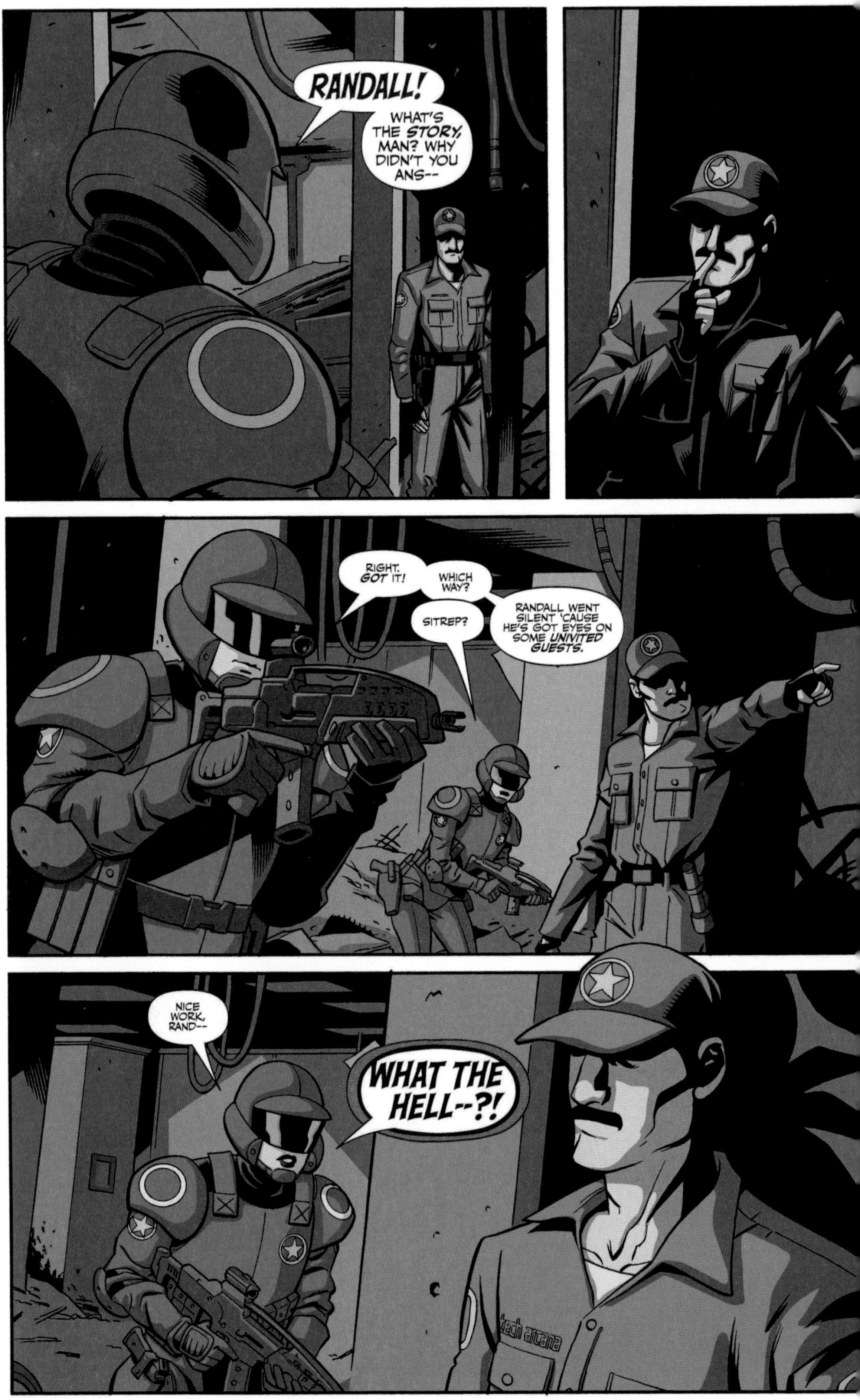
RANDALL!
WHAT'S THE STORY, MAN? WHY DIDN'T YOU ANS--
RIGHT. GOT IT!
WHICH WAY?
SITREP?
RANDALL WENT SILENT 'CAUSE HE'S GOT EYES ON SOME UNIVITED GUESTS.
NICE WORK, RAND--
WHAT THE HELL--?!
tech arcana

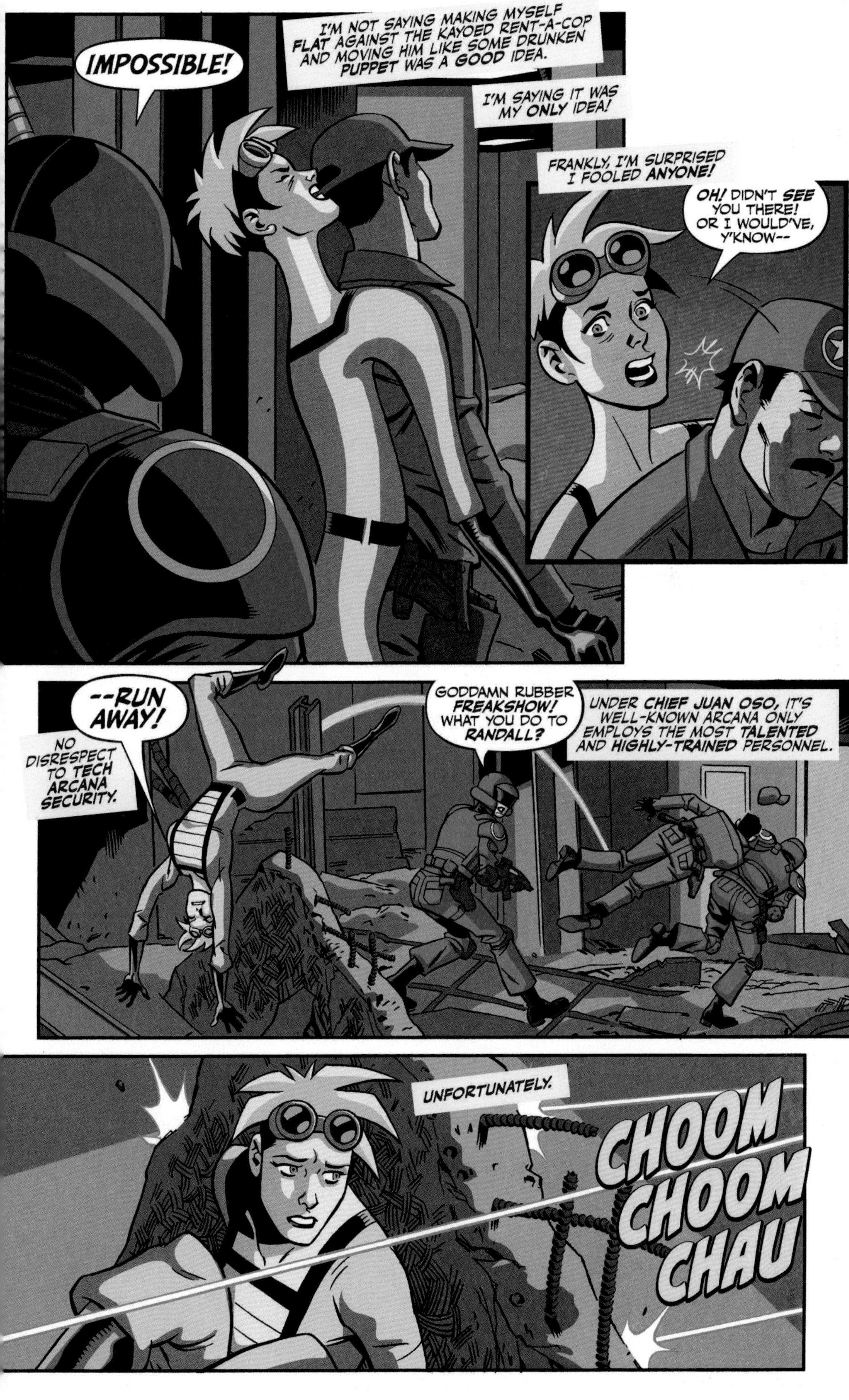
IMPOSSIBLE!
I'M NOT SAYING MAKING MYSELF FLAT AGAINST THE KAYOED RENT-A-COP AND MOVING HIM LIKE SOME DRUNKEN PUPPET WAS A GOOD IDEA.
I'M SAYING IT WAS MY ONLY IDEA!
FRANKLY, I'M SURPRISED I FOOLED ANYONE!
OH! DIDN'T SEE YOU THERE! OR I WOULD'VE, Y'KNOW--
--RUN AWAY!
NO DISRESPECT TO TECH ARCANA SECURITY.
GODDAMN RUBBER FREAKSHOW! WHAT YOU DO TO RANDALL?
UNDER CHIEF JUAN OSO, IT'S WELL-KNOWN ARCANA ONLY EMPLOYS THE MOST TALENTED AND HIGHLY-TRAINED PERSONNEL.
UNFORTUNATELY.
CHOOM
CHOOM
CHAU

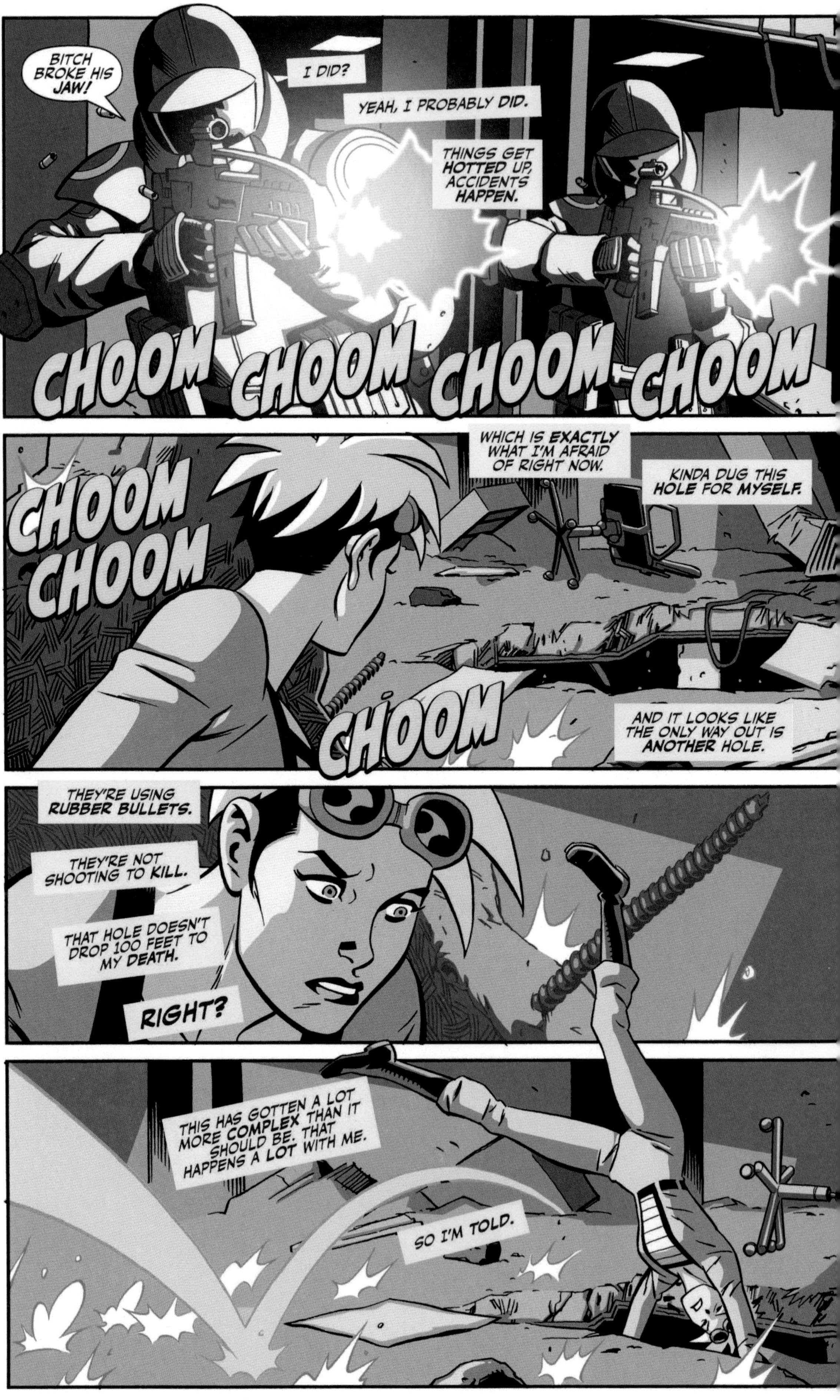

BITCH BROKE HIS JAW!
I DID?
YEAH, I PROBABLY DID.
THINGS GET HOTTED UP, ACCIDENTS HAPPEN.
CHOOM CHOOM CHOOM CHOOM
WHICH IS EXACTLY WHAT I'M AFRAID OF RIGHT NOW.
KINDA DUG THIS HOLE FOR MYSELF.
CHOOM
CHOOM
CHOOM
AND IT LOOKS LIKE THE ONLY WAY OUT IS ANOTHER HOLE.
THEY'RE USING RUBBER BULLETS.
THEY'RE NOT SHOOTING TO KILL.
THAT HOLE DOESN'T DROP 100 FEET TO MY DEATH.
RIGHT?
THIS HAS GOTTEN A LOT MORE COMPLEX THAN IT SHOULD BE. THAT HAPPENS A LOT WITH ME.
SO I'M TOLD.

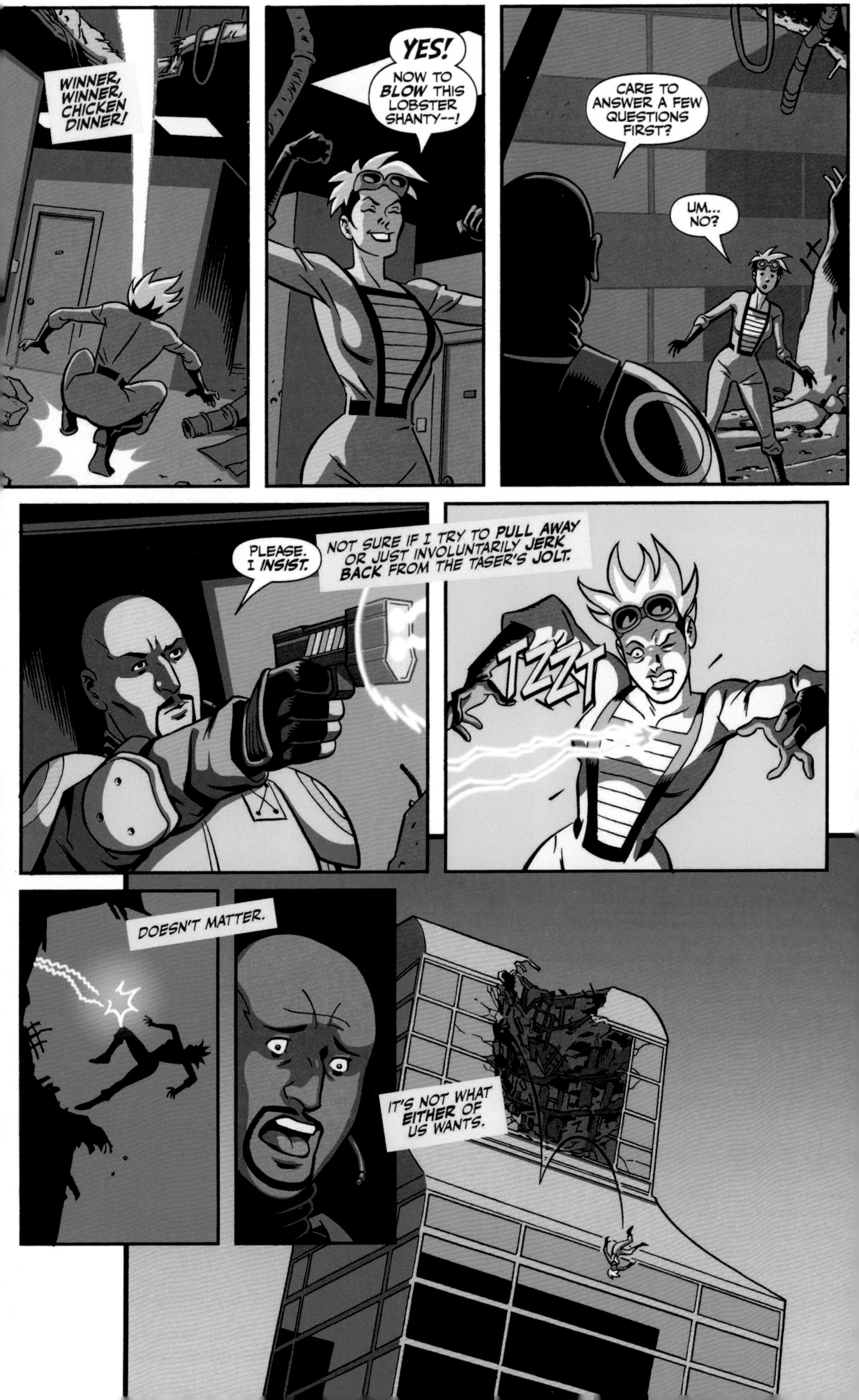
WINNER, WINNER, CHICKEN DINNER!
YES!
NOW TO BLOW THIS LOBSTER SHANTY--!
CARE TO ANSWER A FEW QUESTIONS FIRST?
UM... NO?
PLEASE. I INSIST.
NOT SURE IF I TRY TO PULL AWAY OR JUST INVOLUNTARILY JERK BACK FROM THE TASER'S JOLT.
TZZT
DOESN'T MATTER.
IT'S NOT WHAT EITHER OF US WANTS.

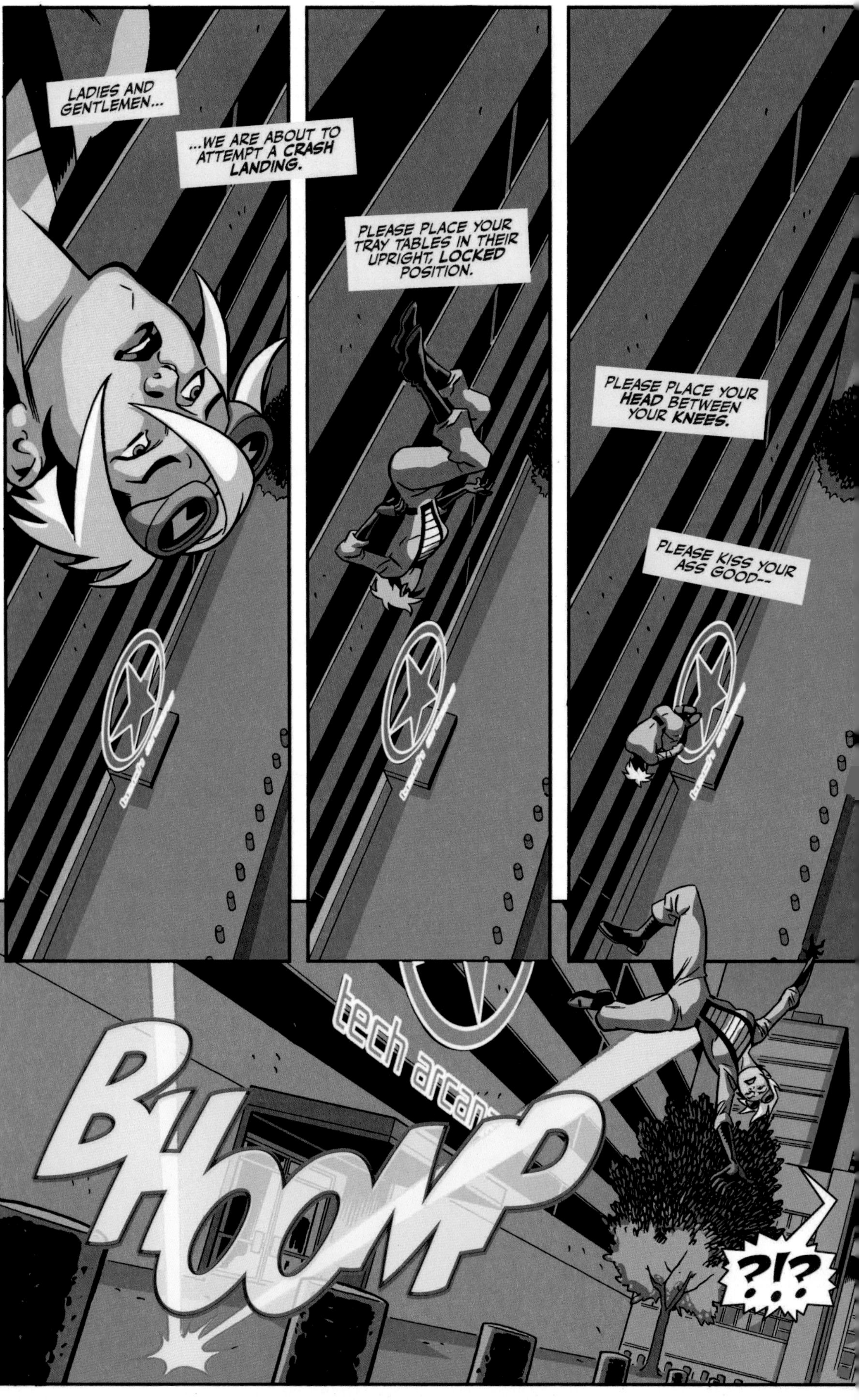
LADIES AND GENTLEMEN...
...WE ARE ABOUT TO ATTEMPT A CRASH LANDING.
PLEASE PLACE YOUR TRAY TABLES IN THEIR UPRIGHT, LOCKED POSITION.
PLEASE PLACE YOUR HEAD BETWEEN YOUR KNEES.
PLEASE KISS YOUR ASS GOOD--
tech arcana
BHOOMP
?!?

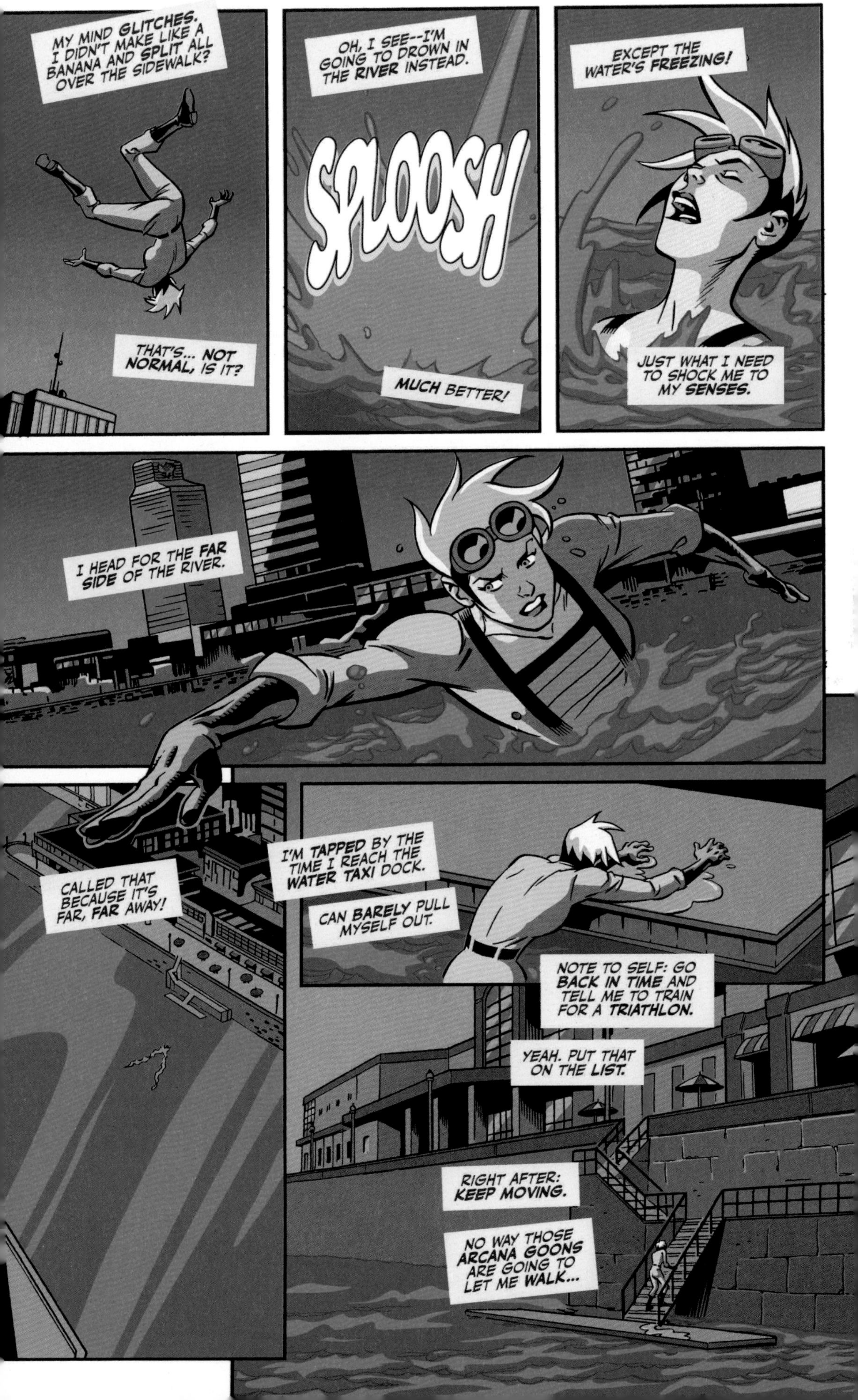

MY MIND GLITCHES. I DIDN'T MAKE LIKE A BANANA AND SPLIT ALL OVER THE SIDEWALK?
THAT'S... NOT NORMAL, IS IT?
OH, I SEE--I'M GOING TO DROWN IN THE RIVER INSTEAD.
SPLOOSH
MUCH BETTER!
EXCEPT THE WATER'S FREEZING!
JUST WHAT I NEED TO SHOCK ME TO MY SENSES.
I HEAD FOR THE FAR SIDE OF THE RIVER.
CALLED THAT BECAUSE IT'S FAR, FAR AWAY!
I'M TAPPED BY THE TIME I REACH THE WATER TAXI DOCK.
CAN BARELY PULL MYSELF OUT.
NOTE TO SELF: GO BACK IN TIME AND TELL ME TO TRAIN FOR A TRIATHLON.
YEAH. PUT THAT ON THE LIST.
RIGHT AFTER: KEEP MOVING.
NO WAY THOSE ARCANA GOONS ARE GOING TO LET ME WALK...

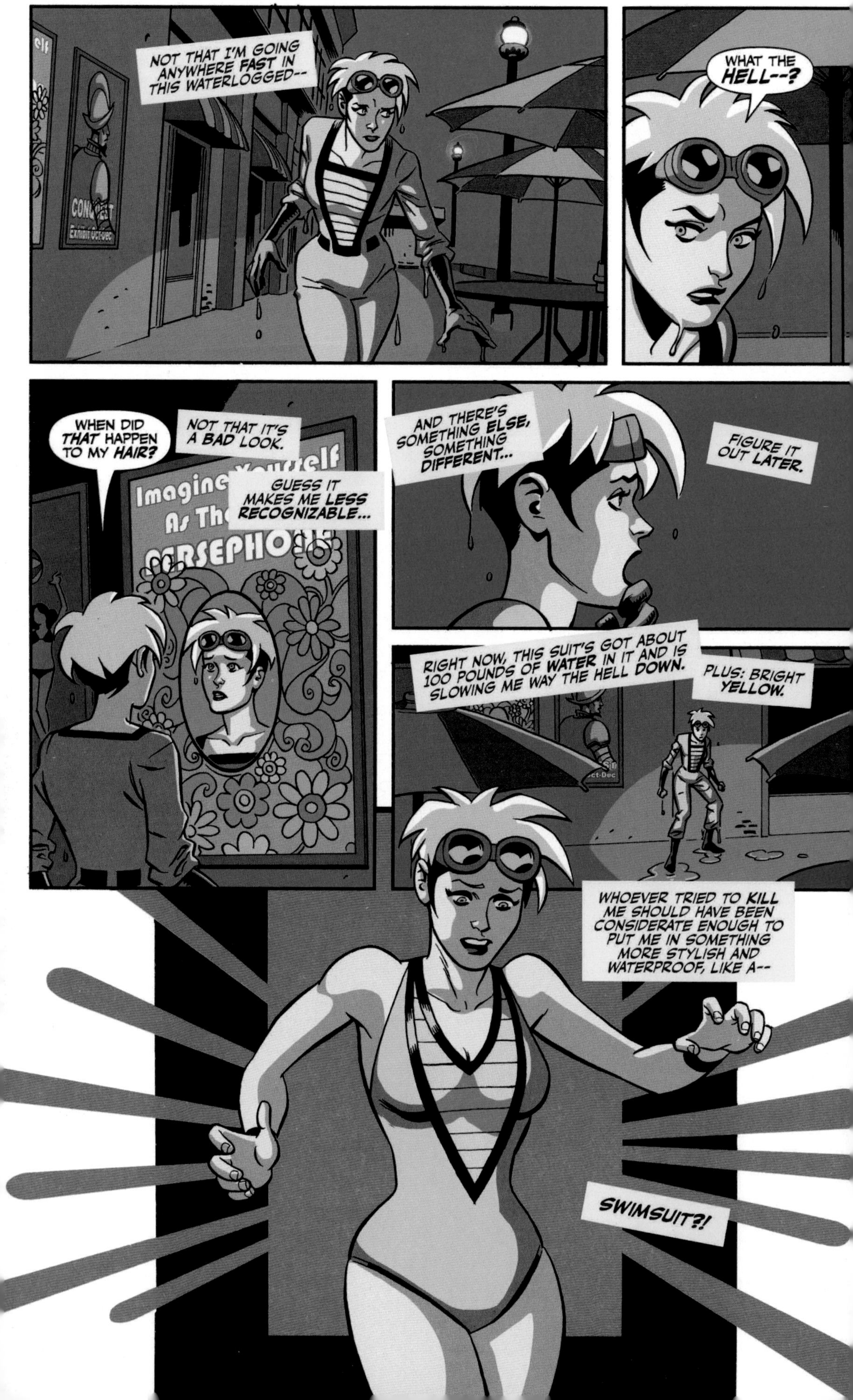
NOT THAT I'M GOING ANYWHERE FAST IN THIS WATERLOGGED--
CONQUEST Exhibit Oct-Dec
WHAT THE HELL--?
WHEN DID THAT HAPPEN TO MY HAIR?
NOT THAT IT'S A BAD LOOK.
GUESS IT MAKES ME LESS RECOGNIZABLE...
AND THERE'S SOMETHING ELSE, SOMETHING DIFFERENT...
FIGURE IT OUT LATER.
RIGHT NOW, THIS SUIT'S GOT ABOUT 100 POUNDS OF WATER IN IT AND IS SLOWING ME WAY THE HELL DOWN.
PLUS: BRIGHT YELLOW.
WHOEVER TRIED TO KILL ME SHOULD HAVE BEEN CONSIDERATE ENOUGH TO PUT ME IN SOMETHING MORE STYLISH AND WATERPROOF, LIKE A--
SWIMSUIT?!

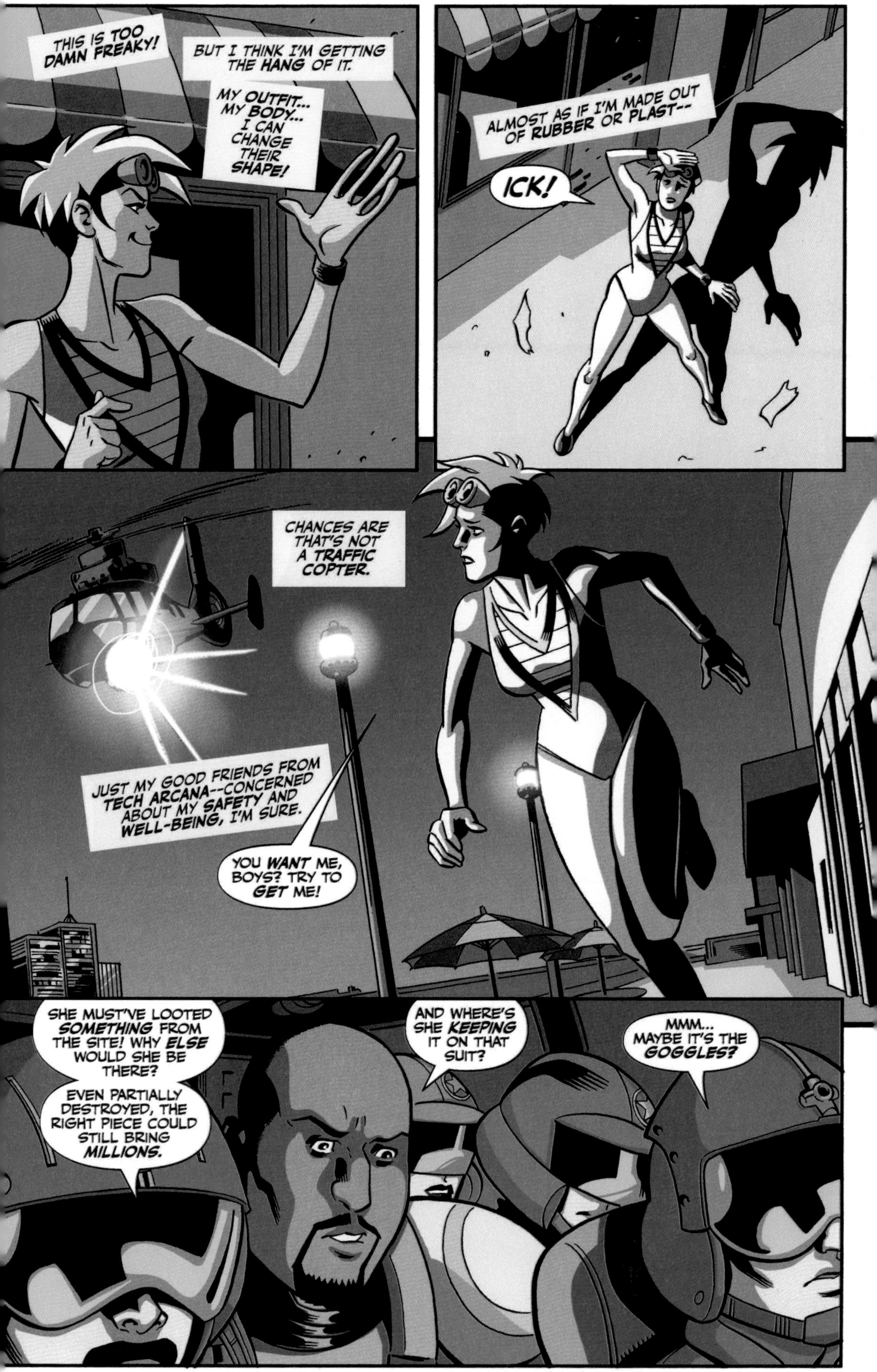
THIS IS TOO DAMN FREAKY!
BUT I THINK I'M GETTING THE HANG OF IT.
MY OUTFIT... MY BODY... I CAN CHANGE THEIR SHAPE!
ALMOST AS IF I'M MADE OUT OF RUBBER OR PLAST--
ICK!
CHANCES ARE THAT'S NOT A TRAFFIC COPTER.
JUST MY GOOD FRIENDS FROM TECH ARCANA--CONCERNED ABOUT MY SAFETY AND WELL-BEING, I'M SURE.
YOU WANT ME, BOYS? TRY TO GET ME!
SHE MUST'VE LOOTED SOMETHING FROM THE SITE! WHY ELSE WOULD SHE BE THERE?
EVEN PARTIALLY DESTROYED, THE RIGHT PIECE COULD STILL BRING MILLIONS.
AND WHERE'S SHE KEEPING IT ON THAT SUIT?
MMM... MAYBE IT'S THE GOGGLES?

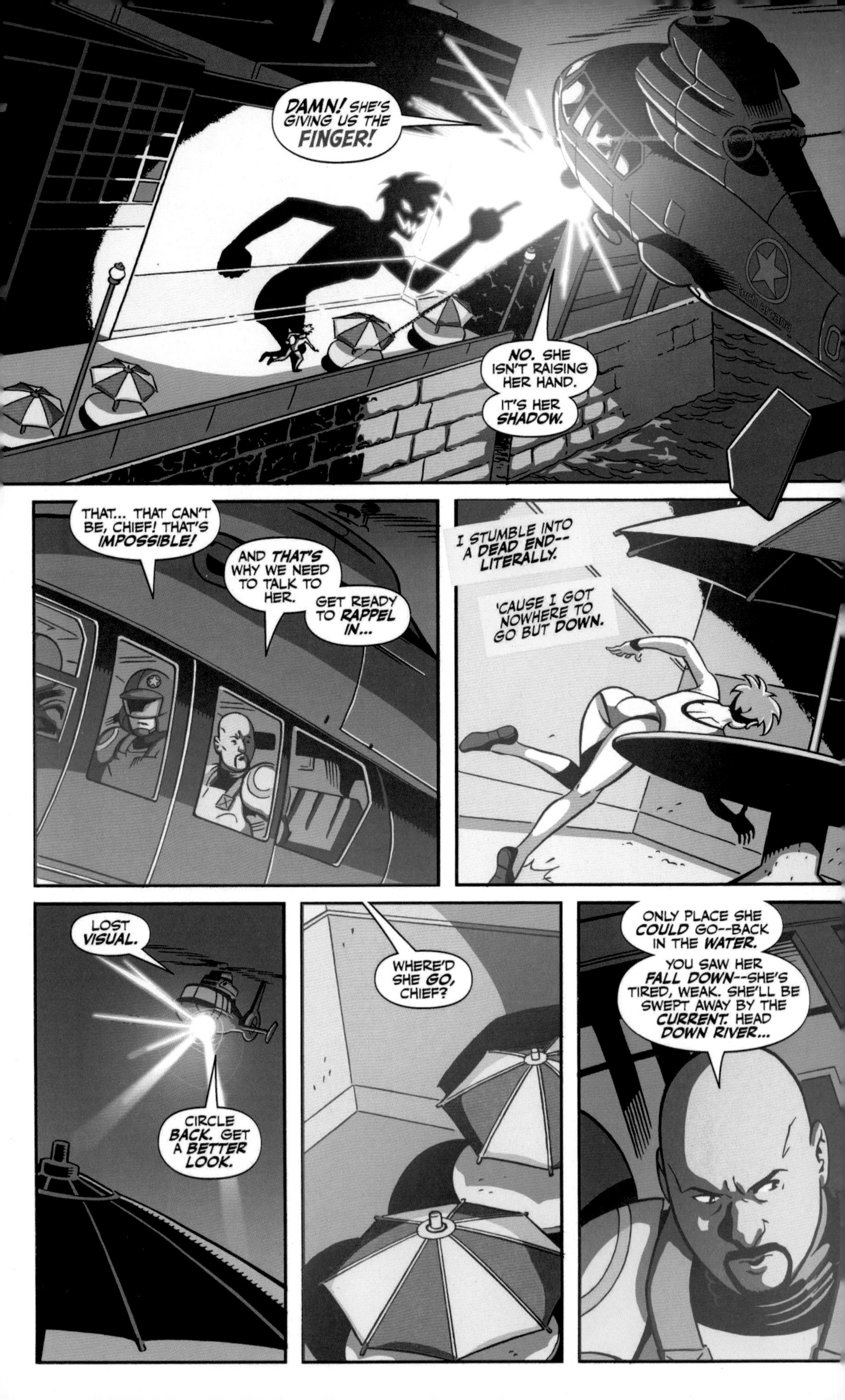
DAMN! SHE'S GIVING US THE FINGER!
NO. SHE ISN'T RAISING HER HAND.
IT'S HER SHADOW.
THAT... THAT CAN'T BE, CHIEF! THAT'S IMPOSSIBLE!
AND THAT'S WHY WE NEED TO TALK TO HER.
GET READY TO RAPPEL IN...
I STUMBLE INTO A DEAD END-- LITERALLY.
'CAUSE I GOT NOWHERE TO GO BUT DOWN.
LOST VISUAL.
CIRCLE BACK. GET A BETTER LOOK.
WHERE'D SHE GO, CHIEF?
ONLY PLACE SHE COULD GO--BACK IN THE WATER.
YOU SAW HER FALL DOWN--SHE'S TIRED, WEAK. SHE'LL BE SWEPT AWAY BY THE CURRENT. HEAD DOWN RIVER...

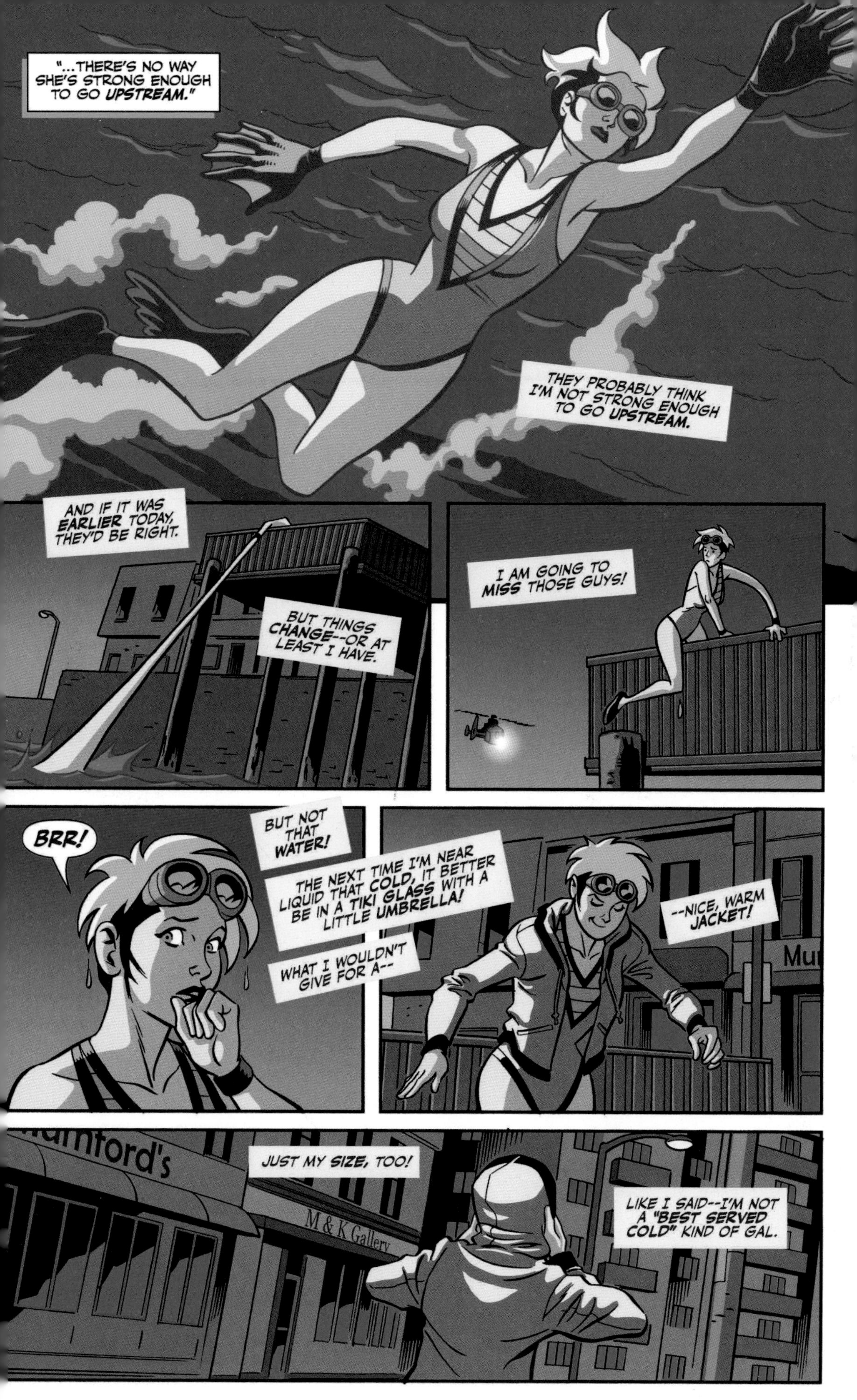
"...THERE'S NO WAY SHE'S STRONG ENOUGH TO GO UPSTREAM."
THEY PROBABLY THINK I'M NOT STRONG ENOUGH TO GO UPSTREAM.
AND IF IT WAS EARLIER TODAY, THEY'D BE RIGHT.
BUT THINGS CHANGE--OR AT LEAST I HAVE.
I AM GOING TO MISS THOSE GUYS!
BRR!
BUT NOT THAT WATER!
THE NEXT TIME I'M NEAR LIQUID THAT COLD, IT BETTER BE IN A TIKI GLASS WITH A LITTLE UMBRELLA!
WHAT I WOULDN'T GIVE FOR A--
--NICE, WARM JACKET!
Mamford's
M & K Gallery
JUST MY SIZE, TOO!
LIKE I SAID--I'M NOT A "BEST SERVED COLD" KIND OF GAL.

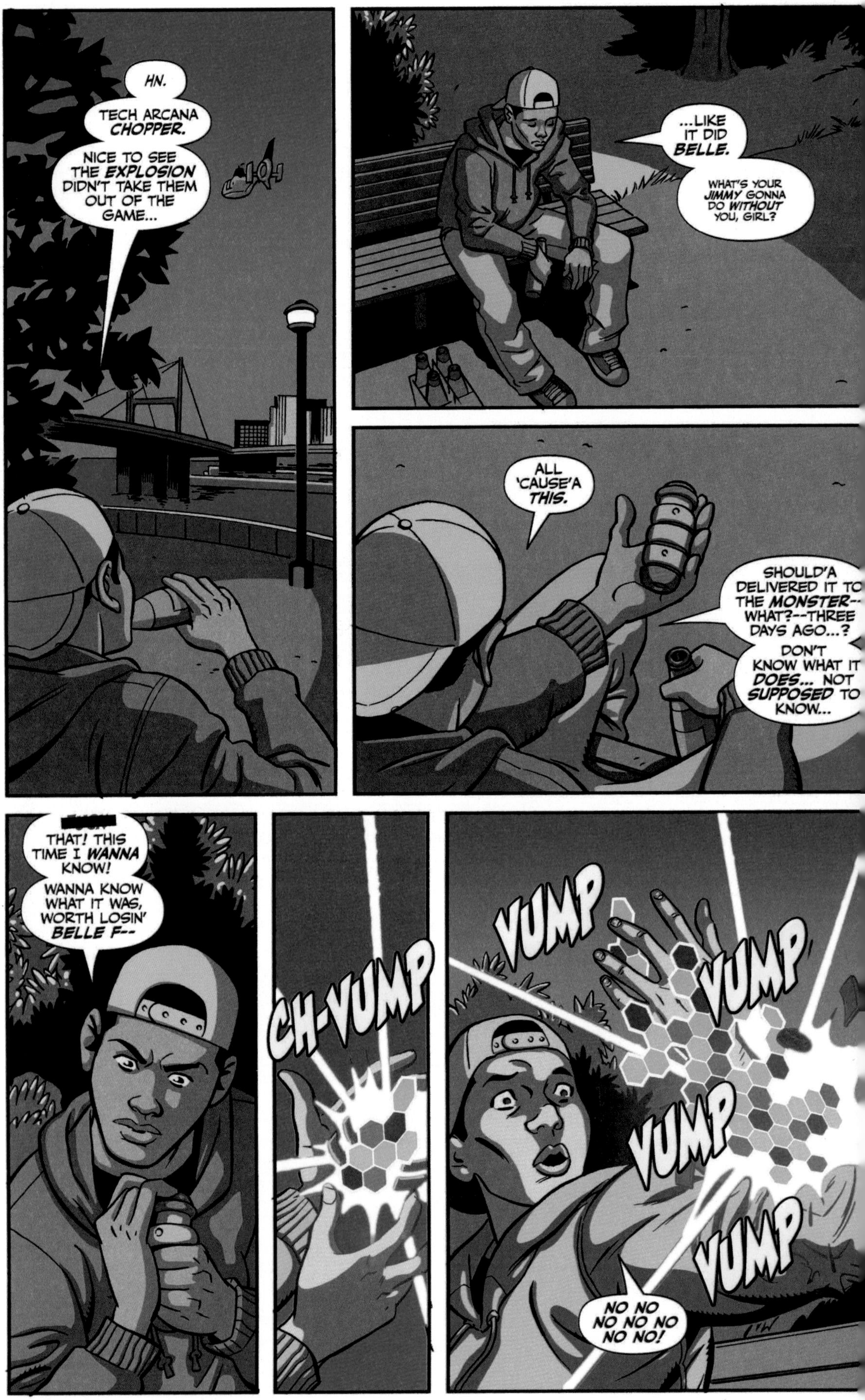
HN.
TECH ARCANA CHOPPER.
NICE TO SEE THE EXPLOSION DIDN'T TAKE THEM OUT OF THE GAME...
...LIKE IT DID BELLE.
WHAT'S YOUR JIMMY GONNA DO WITHOUT YOU, GIRL?
ALL 'CAUSE'A THIS.
SHOULD'A DELIVERED IT TO THE MONSTER--WHAT?--THREE DAYS AGO...?
DON'T KNOW WHAT IT DOES... NOT SUPPOSED TO KNOW...
[redacted] THAT! THIS TIME I WANNA KNOW!
WANNA KNOW WHAT IT WAS, WORTH LOSIN' BELLE F--
CH-VUMP
VUMP
VUMP
VUMP
VUMP
NO NO NO NO NO NO NO!

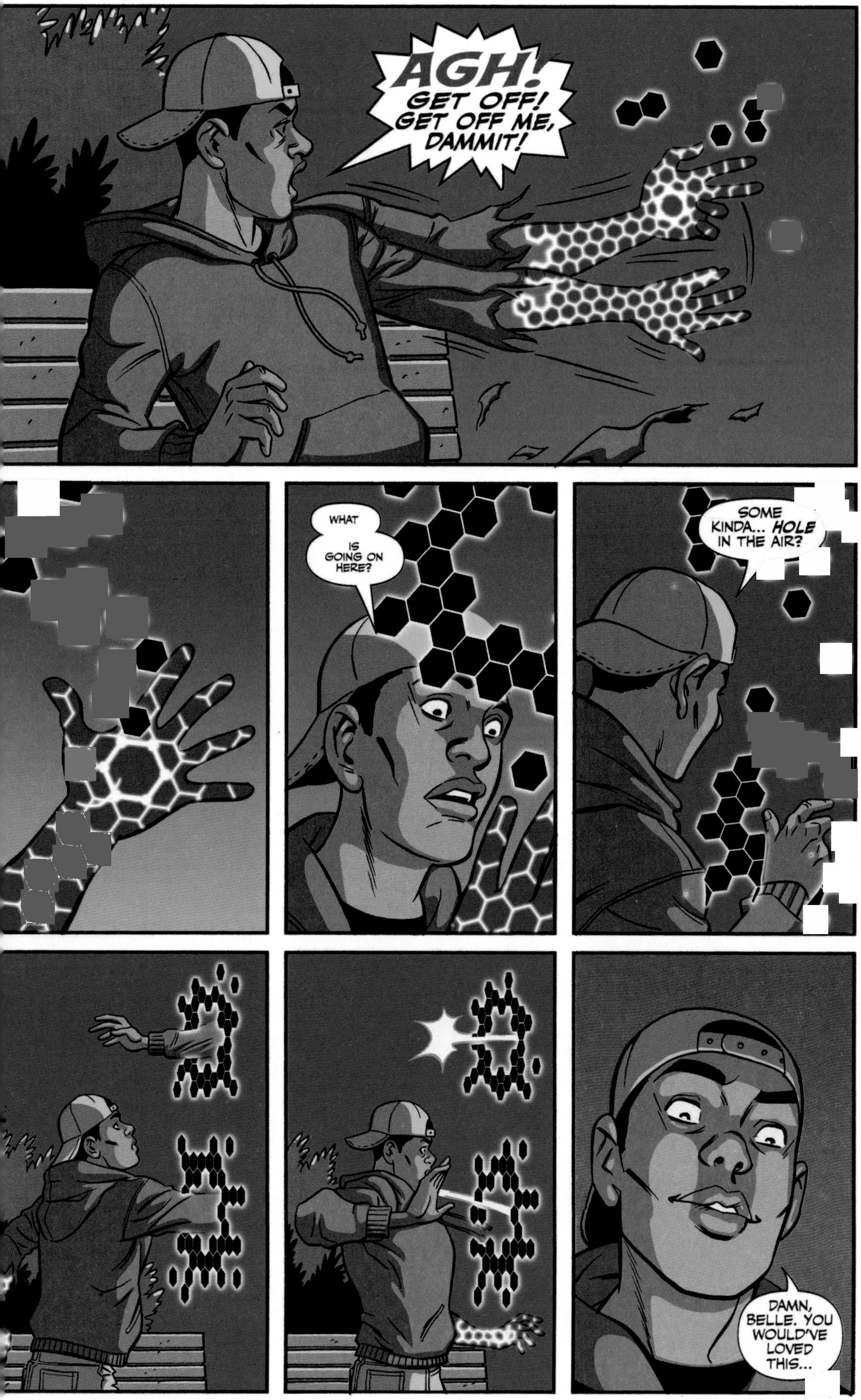
AGH! GET OFF! GET OFF ME, DAMMIT!
WHAT IS GOING ON HERE?
SOME KINDA... HOLE IN THE AIR?
DAMN, BELLE. YOU WOULD'VE LOVED THIS...

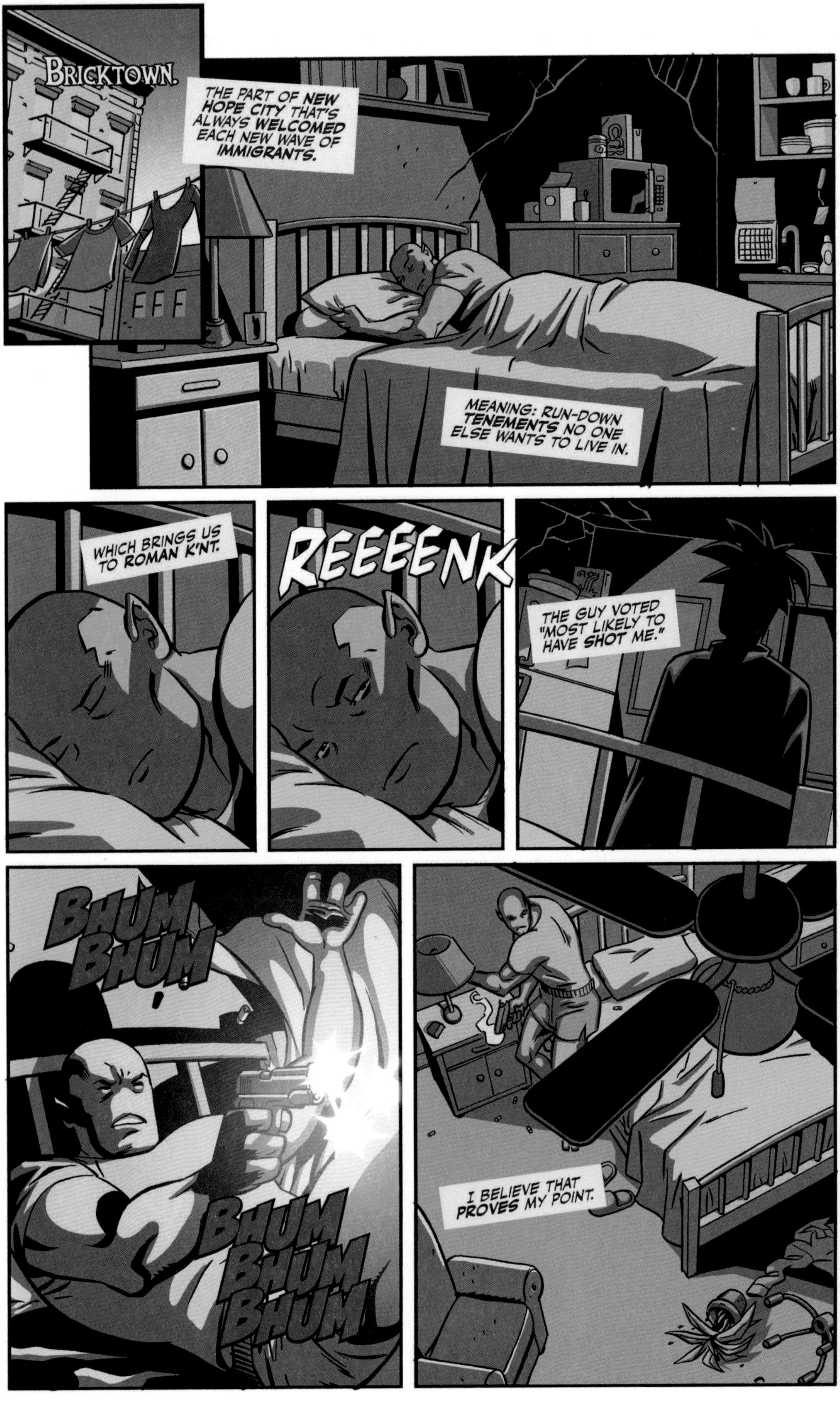
BRICKTOWN.
THE PART OF NEW HOPE CITY THAT'S ALWAYS WELCOMED EACH NEW WAVE OF IMMIGRANTS.
MEANING: RUN-DOWN TENEMENTS NO ONE ELSE WANTS TO LIVE IN.
WHICH BRINGS US TO ROMAN K'NT.
REEEENK
THE GUY VOTED "MOST LIKELY TO HAVE SHOT ME."
BHUM BHUM
BHUM BHUM BHUM
I BELIEVE THAT PROVES MY POINT.

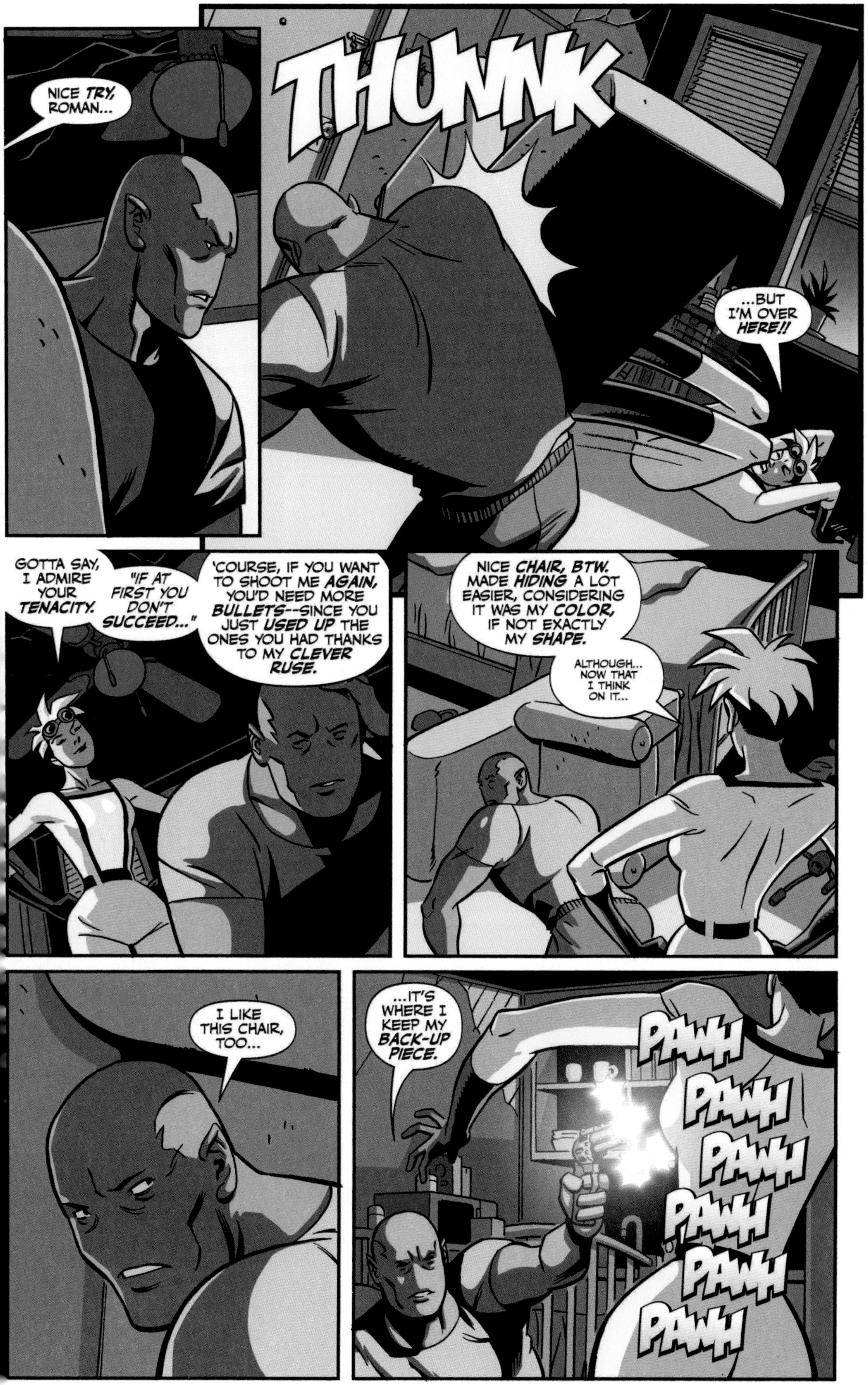

NICE TRY, ROMAN...
THUNNK
...BUT I'M OVER HERE!!
GOTTA SAY, I ADMIRE YOUR TENACITY.
"IF AT FIRST YOU DON'T SUCCEED..."
'COURSE, IF YOU WANT TO SHOOT ME AGAIN, YOU'D NEED MORE BULLETS--SINCE YOU JUST USED UP THE ONES YOU HAD THANKS TO MY CLEVER RUSE.
NICE CHAIR, BTW. MADE HIDING A LOT EASIER, CONSIDERING IT WAS MY COLOR, IF NOT EXACTLY MY SHAPE.
ALTHOUGH... NOW THAT I THINK ON IT...
I LIKE THIS CHAIR, TOO...
...IT'S WHERE I KEEP MY BACK-UP PIECE.
PAWH
PAWH
PAWH
PAWH
PAWH
PAWH

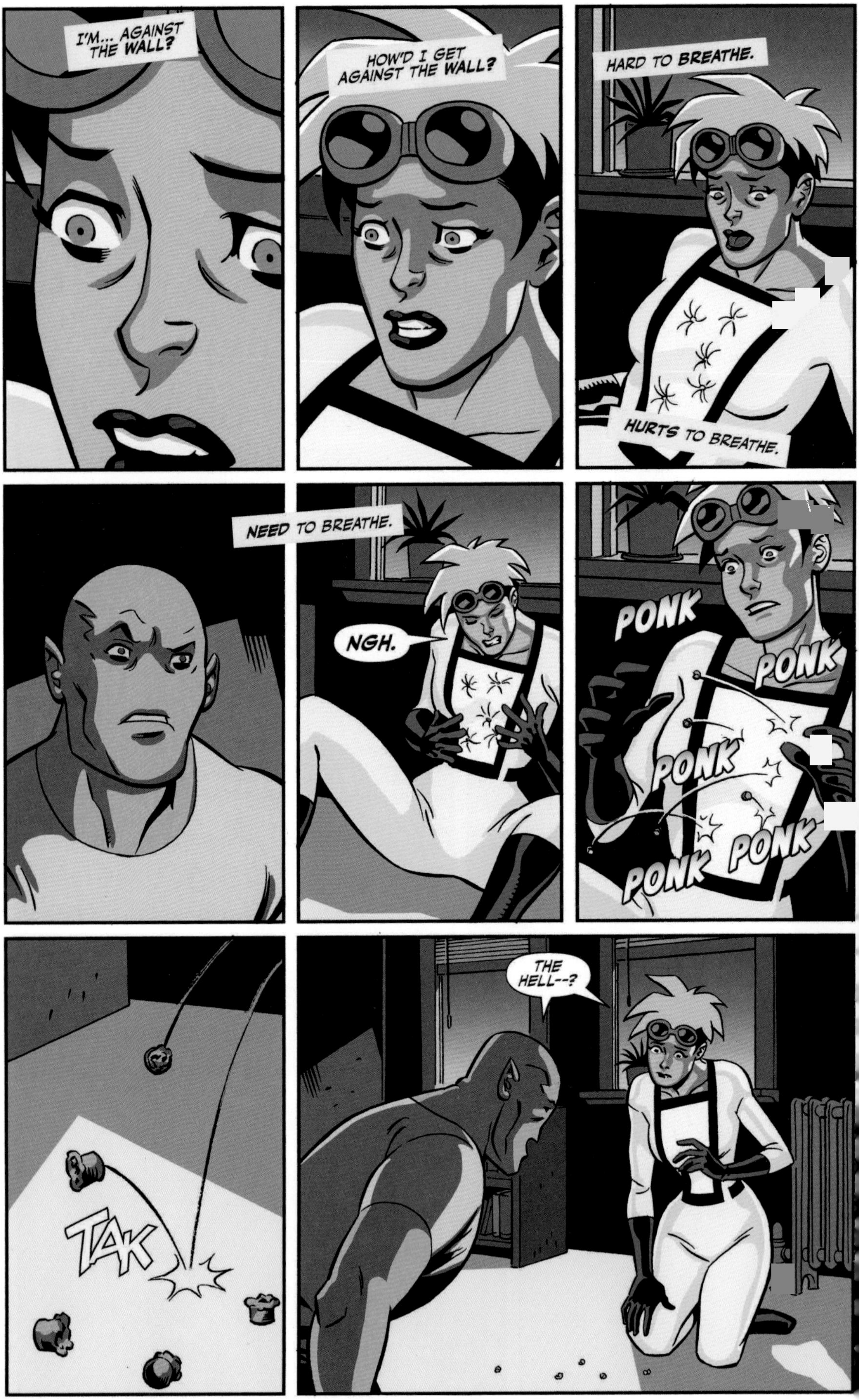
I'M... AGAINST THE WALL?
HOW'D I GET AGAINST THE WALL?
HARD TO BREATHE.
HURTS TO BREATHE.
NEED TO BREATHE.
NGH.
PONK
PONK
PONK
PONK
PONK
TAK
THE HELL--?

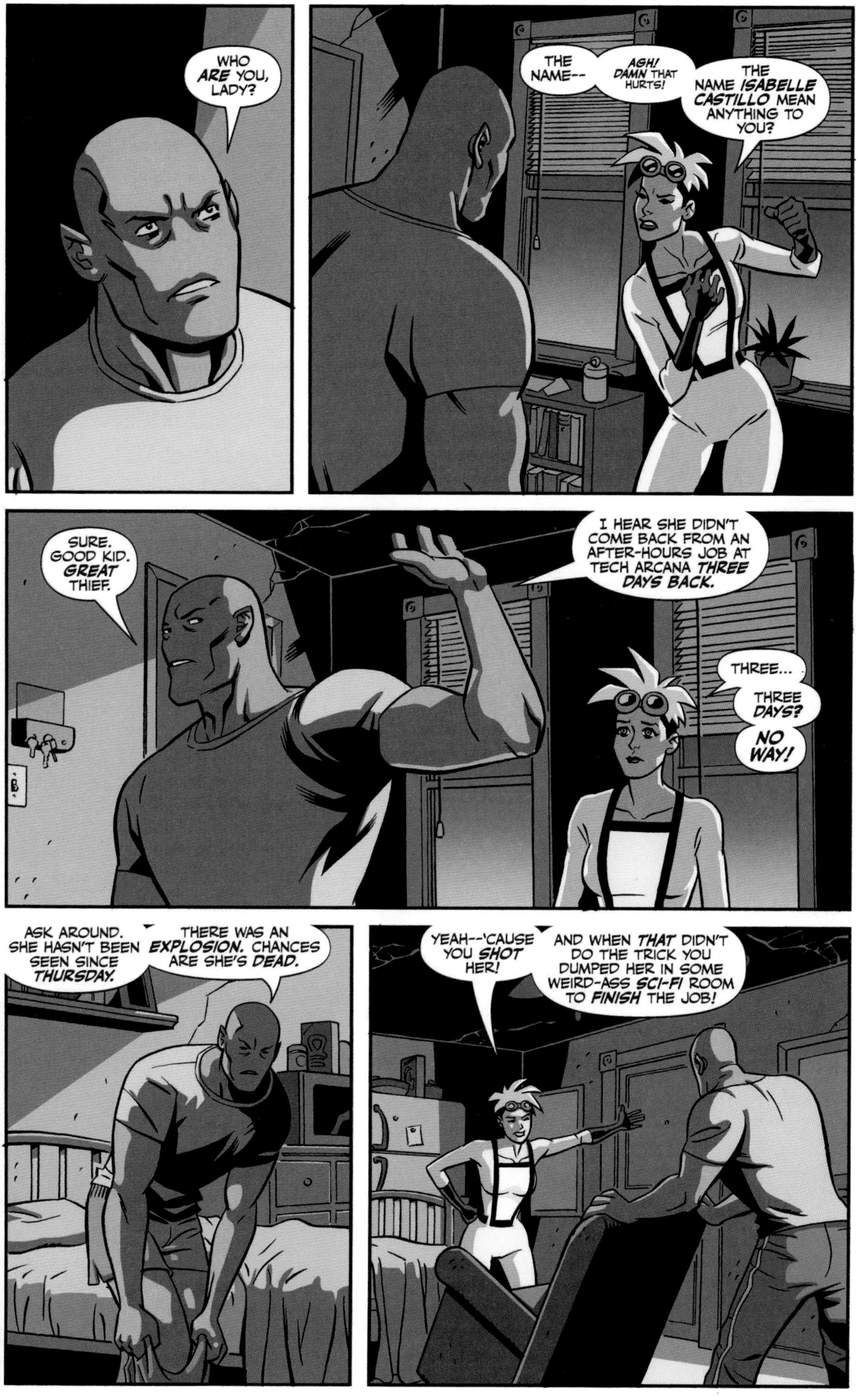
WHO ARE YOU, LADY?
THE NAME--
AGH! DAMN THAT HURTS!
THE NAME ISABELLE CASTILLO MEAN ANYTHING TO YOU?
SURE. GOOD KID. GREAT THIEF.
I HEAR SHE DIDN'T COME BACK FROM AN AFTER-HOURS JOB AT TECH ARCANA THREE DAYS BACK.
THREE...
THREE DAYS?
NO WAY!
ASK AROUND. SHE HASN'T BEEN SEEN SINCE THURSDAY.
THERE WAS AN EXPLOSION. CHANCES ARE SHE'S DEAD.
YEAH--'CAUSE YOU SHOT HER!
AND WHEN THAT DIDN'T DO THE TRICK YOU DUMPED HER IN SOME WEIRD-ASS SCI-FI ROOM TO FINISH THE JOB!

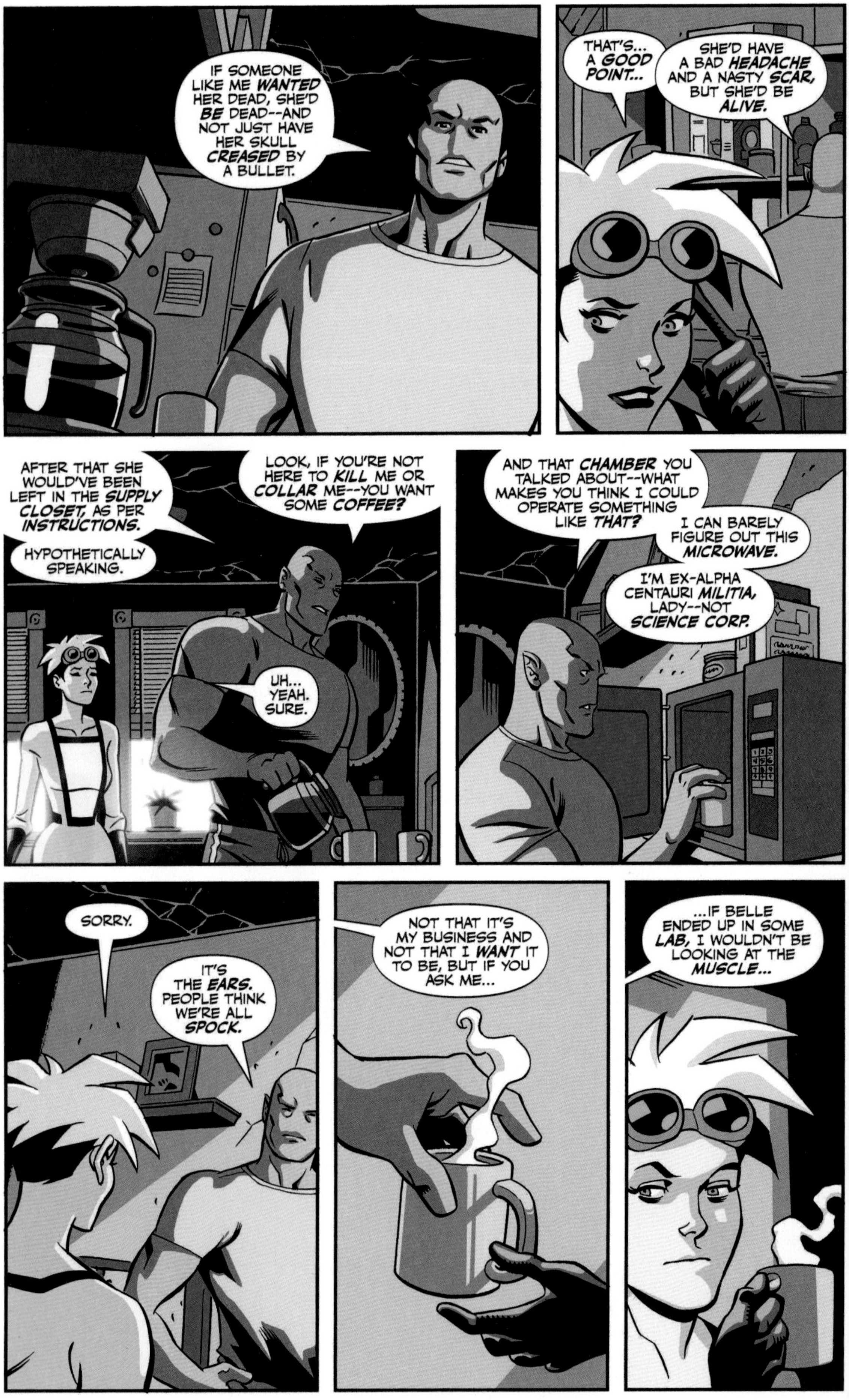
IF SOMEONE LIKE ME WANTED HER DEAD, SHE'D BE DEAD--AND NOT JUST HAVE HER SKULL CREASED BY A BULLET.
THAT'S... A GOOD POINT...
SHE'D HAVE A BAD HEADACHE AND A NASTY SCAR, BUT SHE'D BE ALIVE.
AFTER THAT SHE WOULD'VE BEEN LEFT IN THE SUPPLY CLOSET, AS PER INSTRUCTIONS.
HYPOTHETICALLY SPEAKING.
LOOK, IF YOU'RE NOT HERE TO KILL ME OR COLLAR ME--YOU WANT SOME COFFEE?
UH... YEAH. SURE.
AND THAT CHAMBER YOU TALKED ABOUT--WHAT MAKES YOU THINK I COULD OPERATE SOMETHING LIKE THAT?
I CAN BARELY FIGURE OUT THIS MICROWAVE.
I'M EX-ALPHA CENTAURI MILITIA, LADY--NOT SCIENCE CORP.
SORRY.
IT'S THE EARS. PEOPLE THINK WE'RE ALL SPOCK.
NOT THAT IT'S MY BUSINESS AND NOT THAT I WANT IT TO BE, BUT IF YOU ASK ME...
...IF BELLE ENDED UP IN SOME LAB, I WOULDN'T BE LOOKING AT THE MUSCLE...

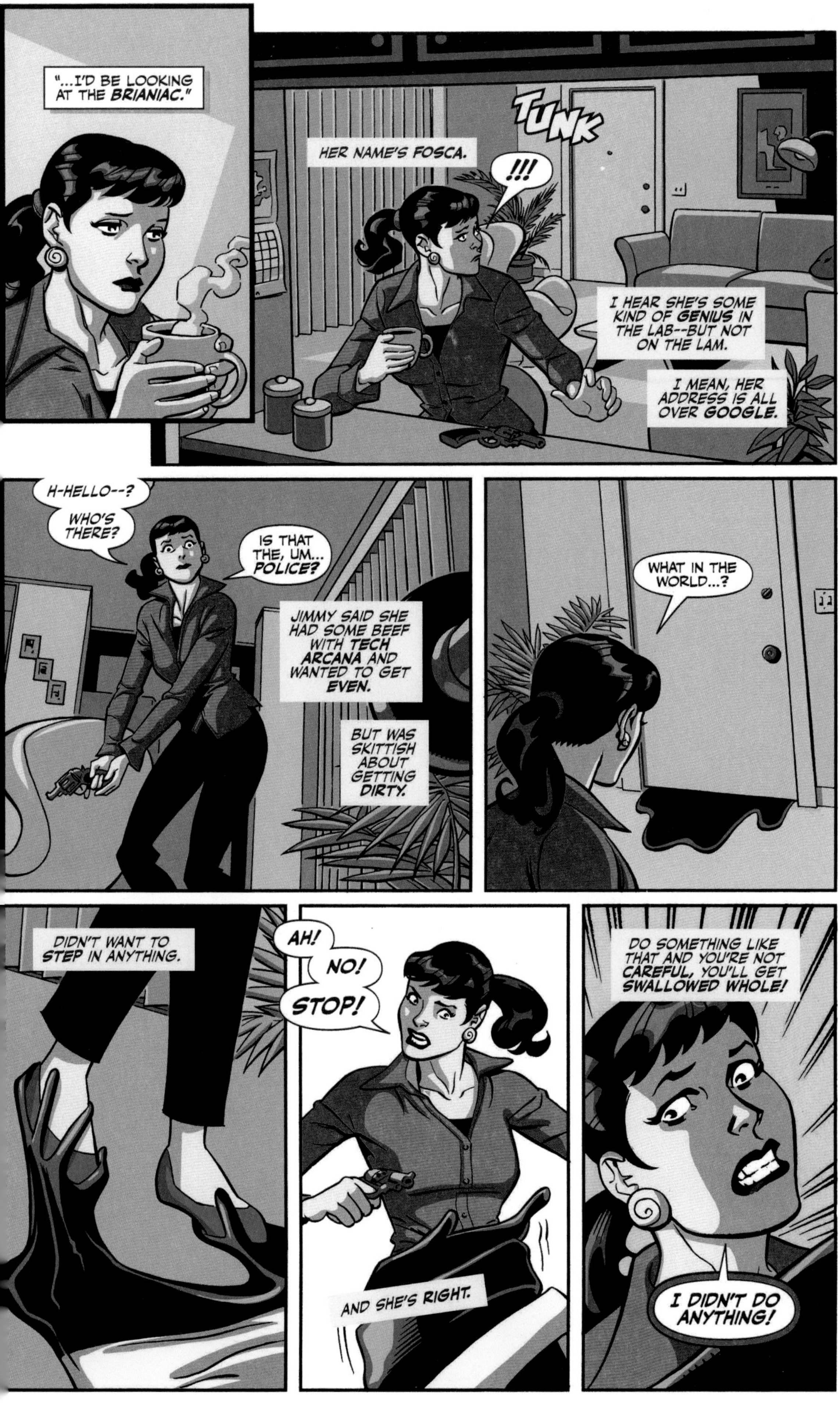
"...I'D BE LOOKING AT THE BRIANIAC."
HER NAME'S FOSCA.
TUNK
!!!
I HEAR SHE'S SOME KIND OF GENIUS IN THE LAB--BUT NOT ON THE LAM.
I MEAN, HER ADDRESS IS ALL OVER GOOGLE.
H-HELLO--?
WHO'S THERE?
IS THAT THE, UM... POLICE?
JIMMY SAID SHE HAD SOME BEEF WITH TECH ARCANA AND WANTED TO GET EVEN.
BUT WAS SKITTISH ABOUT GETTING DIRTY.
WHAT IN THE WORLD...?
DIDN'T WANT TO STEP IN ANYTHING.
AH!
NO!
STOP!
AND SHE'S RIGHT.
DO SOMETHING LIKE THAT AND YOU'RE NOT CAREFUL, YOU'LL GET SWALLOWED WHOLE!
I DIDN'T DO ANYTHING!

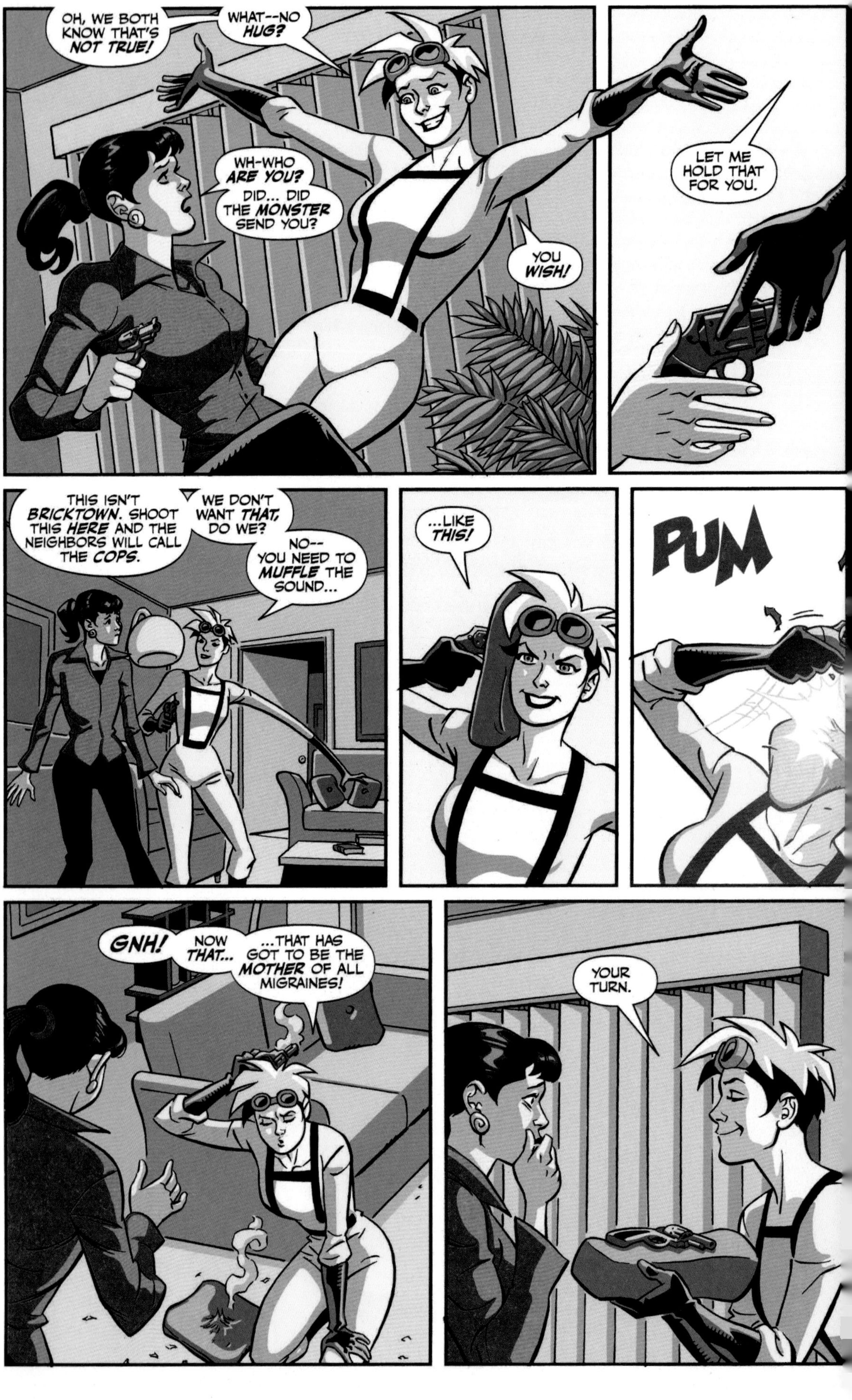
WHAT--NO HUG?
OH, WE BOTH KNOW THAT'S NOT TRUE!
WH-WHO ARE YOU? DID... DID THE MONSTER SEND YOU?
YOU WISH!
LET ME HOLD THAT FOR YOU.
THIS ISN'T BRICKTOWN. SHOOT THIS HERE AND THE NEIGHBORS WILL CALL THE COPS.
WE DON'T WANT THAT, DO WE?
NO-- YOU NEED TO MUFFLE THE SOUND...
...LIKE THIS!
PUM
GNH!
NOW THAT...
...THAT HAS GOT TO BE THE MOTHER OF ALL MIGRAINES!
YOUR TURN.

SCARED. GOOD.

SHE PICKED THE WRONG GIRL TO PLAY MAD SCIENTIST ON. IF SHE'D ONLY KNOWN...

BUT... SHE DIDN'T KNOW, DID SHE? WE'D NEVER MET.

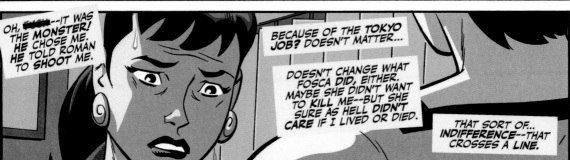

OH, ████--IT WAS THE MONSTER! HE CHOSE ME. HE TOLD ROMAN TO SHOOT ME.

BECAUSE OF THE TOKYO JOB? DOESN'T MATTER...

DOESN'T CHANGE WHAT FOSCA DID, EITHER. MAYBE SHE DIDN'T WANT TO KILL ME--BUT SHE SURE AS HELL DIDN'T CARE IF I LIVED OR DIED.

THAT SORT OF... INDIFFERENCE--THAT CROSSES A LINE.

AND SO DOES KILLING HER.

I WANT REVENGE, BUT DO I REALLY WANT THAT? I'M A THIEF, NOT A MURDERER!

COME ON, FOSCA-- GIVE ME SOMETHING! GROVEL... BEG...

WET YOURSELF WOULD BE NICE.

THEN IT ALL GOES TO HELL.

AGH!

I'M CUT? I'M BULLETPROOF BUT I'M CUT?! THAT'S IMPOSSIBLE!

AH! I SEE THERE'S A NEW GIRL IN TOWN.

SADLY, SHE WON'T BE STAYING LONG. AFTER ALL, SO FEW MAKE THE CUT...

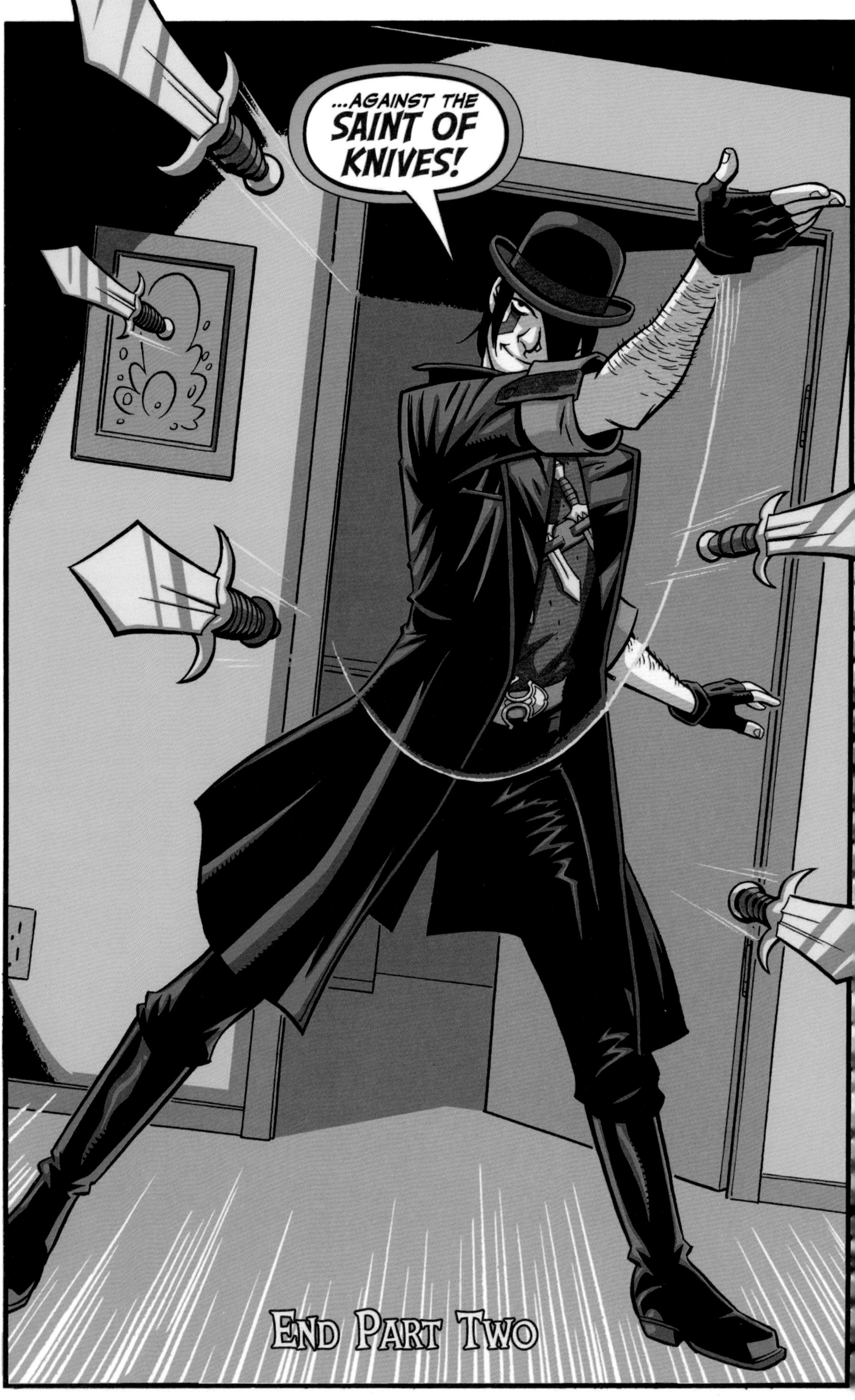
...AGAINST THE SAINT OF KNIVES!
END PART TWO

Part 3
"Yeah, That's Right—I'm a Superhero."

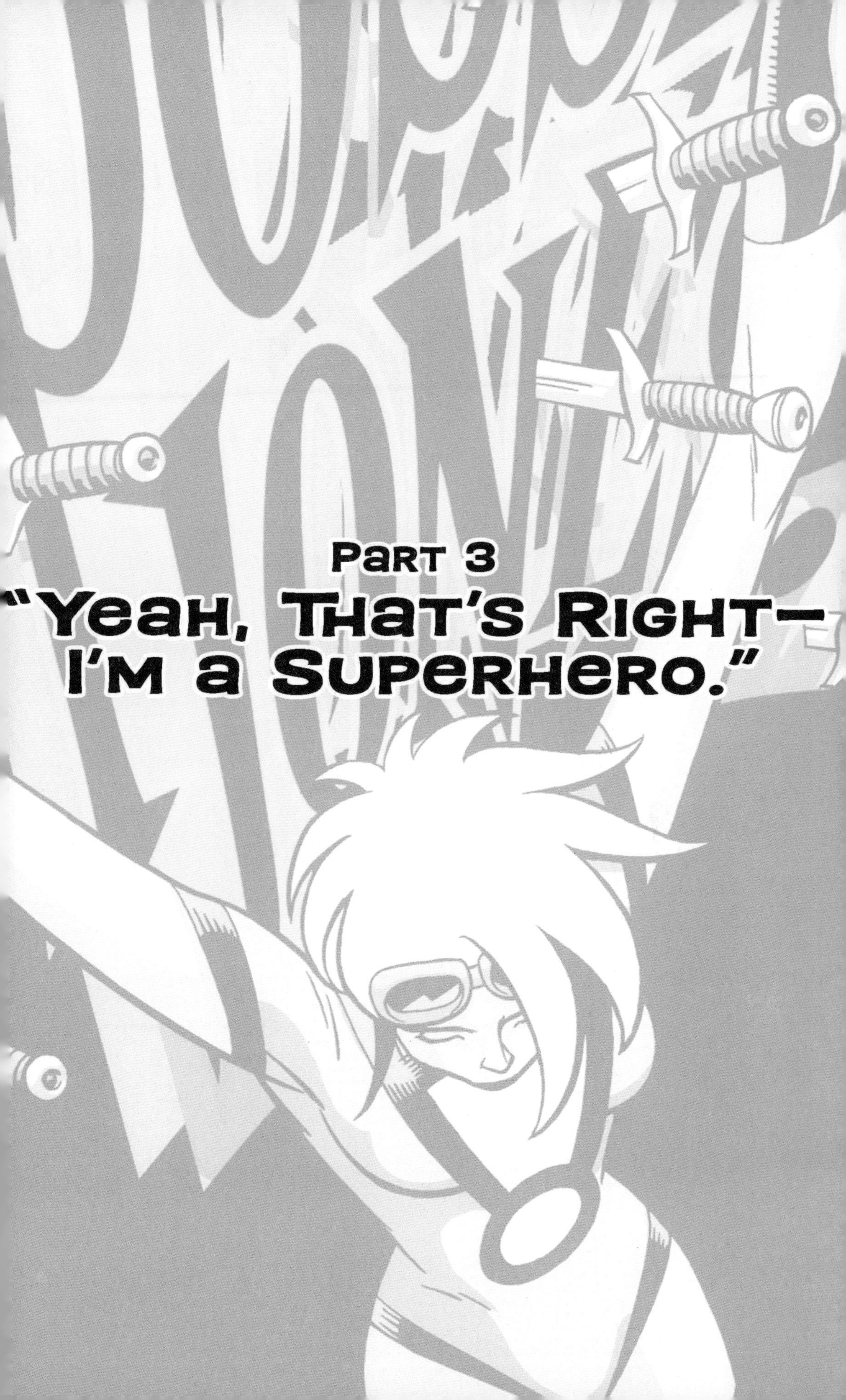

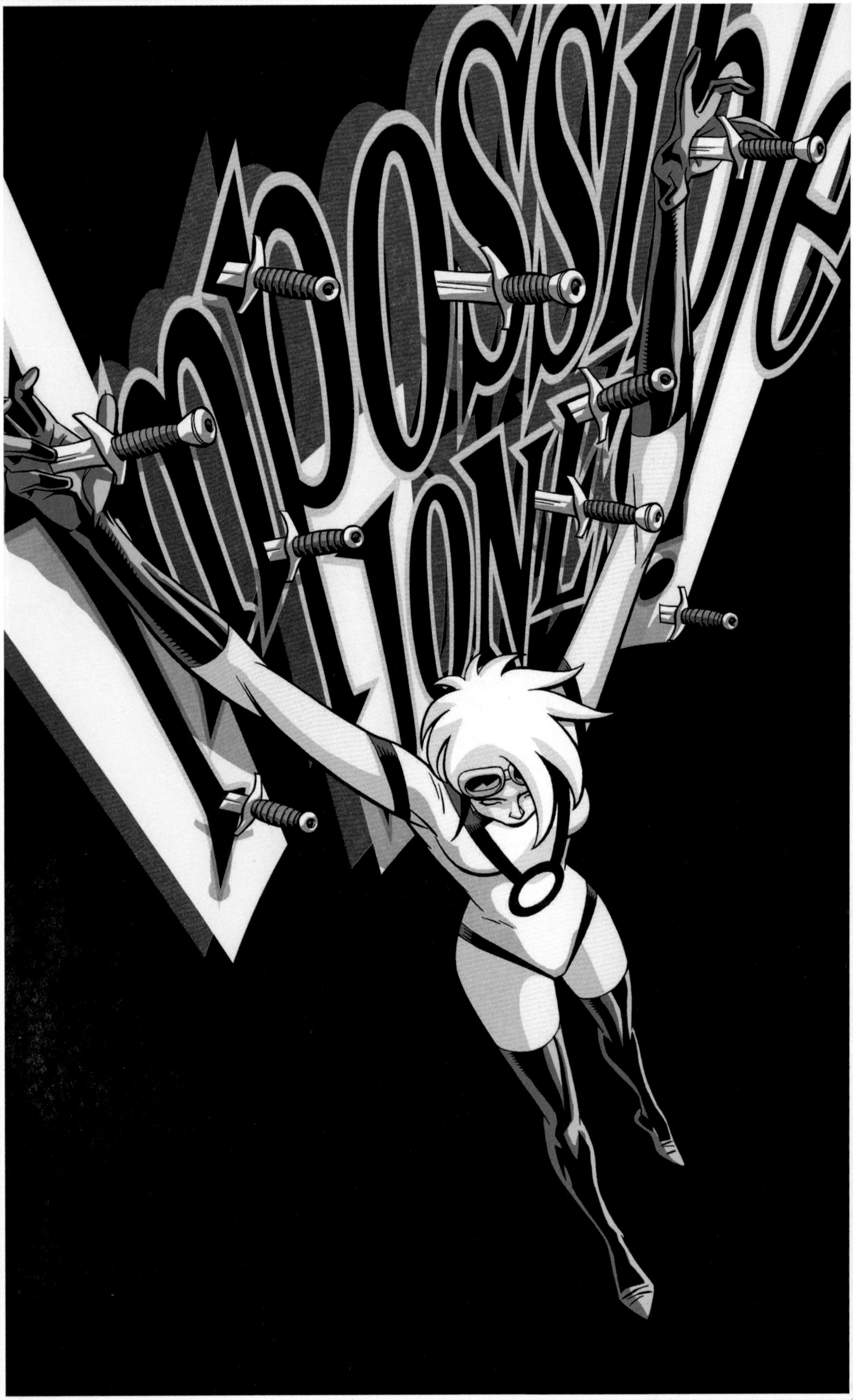
Impossible
Jones!

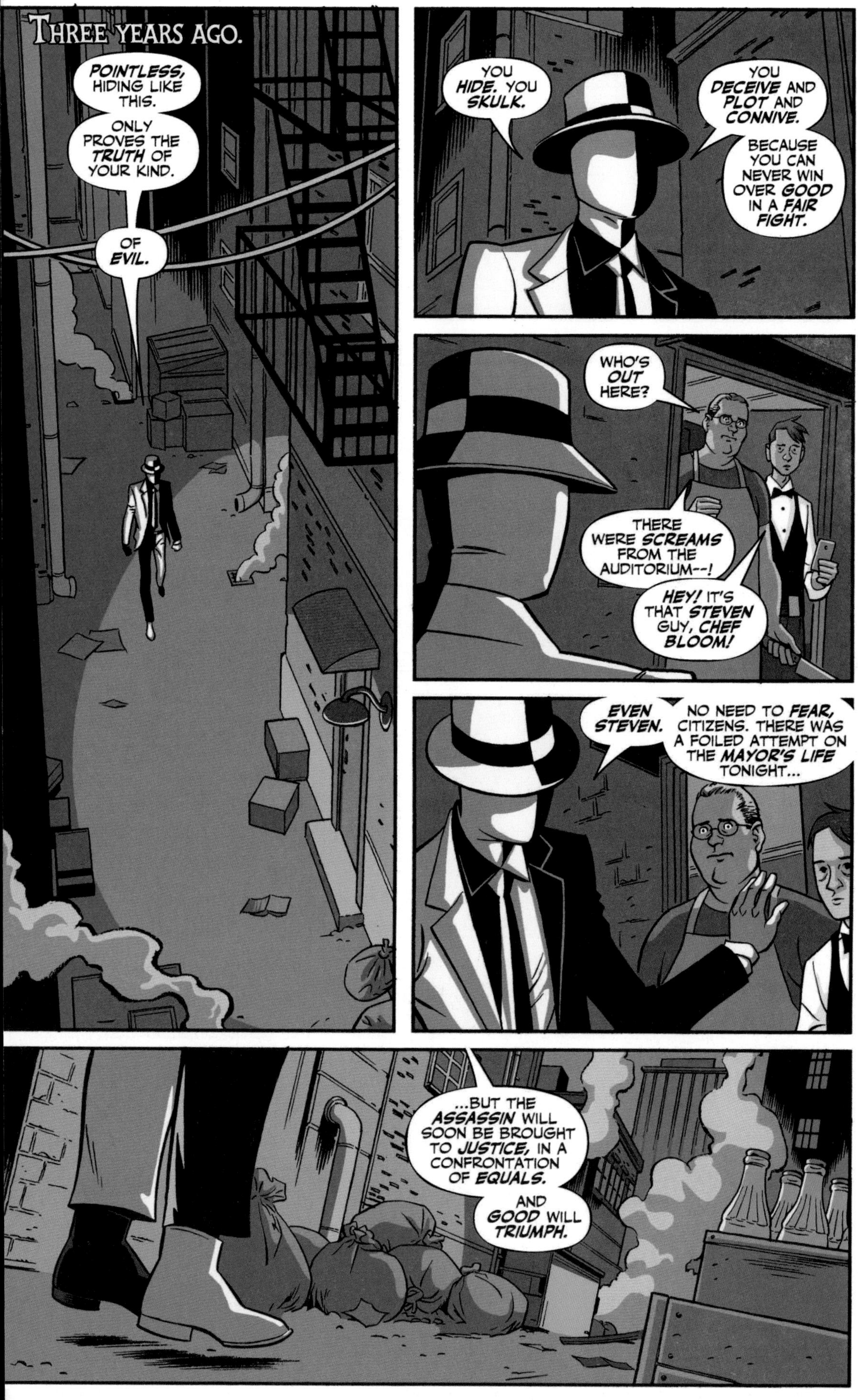
THREE YEARS AGO.
POINTLESS, HIDING LIKE THIS.
ONLY PROVES THE TRUTH OF YOUR KIND.
OF EVIL.
YOU HIDE. YOU SKULK.
YOU DECEIVE AND PLOT AND CONNIVE.
BECAUSE YOU CAN NEVER WIN OVER GOOD IN A FAIR FIGHT.
WHO'S OUT HERE?
THERE WERE SCREAMS FROM THE AUDITORIUM--!
HEY! IT'S THAT STEVEN GUY, CHEF BLOOM!
EVEN STEVEN.
NO NEED TO FEAR, CITIZENS. THERE WAS A FOILED ATTEMPT ON THE MAYOR'S LIFE TONIGHT...
...BUT THE ASSASSIN WILL SOON BE BROUGHT TO JUSTICE, IN A CONFRONTATION OF EQUALS.
AND GOOD WILL TRIUMPH.

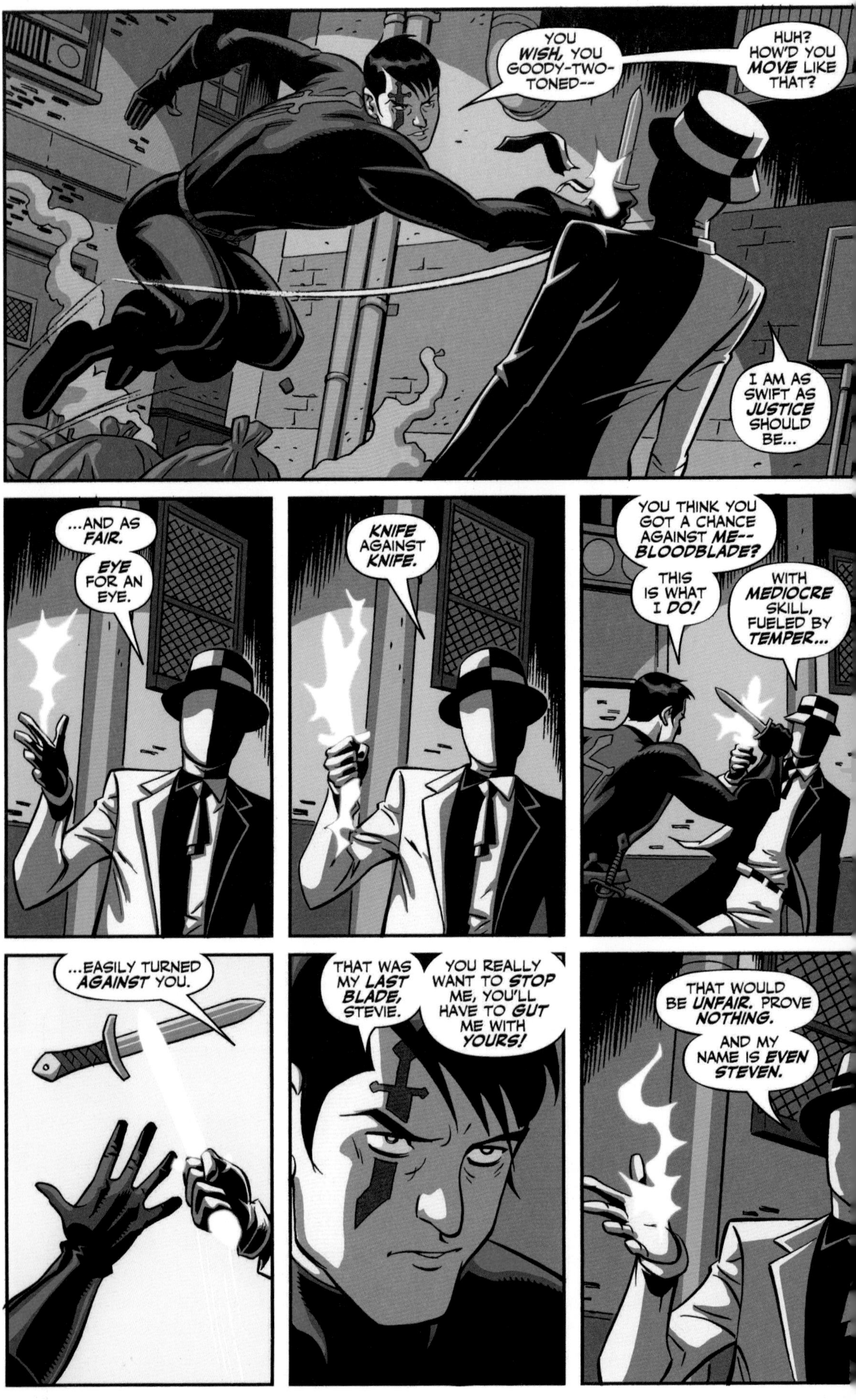
YOU WISH, YOU GOODY-TWO-TONED--
HUH? HOW'D YOU MOVE LIKE THAT?
I AM AS SWIFT AS JUSTICE SHOULD BE...
...AND AS FAIR.
EYE FOR AN EYE.
KNIFE AGAINST KNIFE.
YOU THINK YOU GOT A CHANCE AGAINST ME--BLOODBLADE?
THIS IS WHAT I DO!
WITH MEDIOCRE SKILL, FUELED BY TEMPER...
...EASILY TURNED AGAINST YOU.
THAT WAS MY LAST BLADE, STEVIE.
YOU REALLY WANT TO STOP ME, YOU'LL HAVE TO GUT ME WITH YOURS!
THAT WOULD BE UNFAIR. PROVE NOTHING.
AND MY NAME IS EVEN STEVEN.

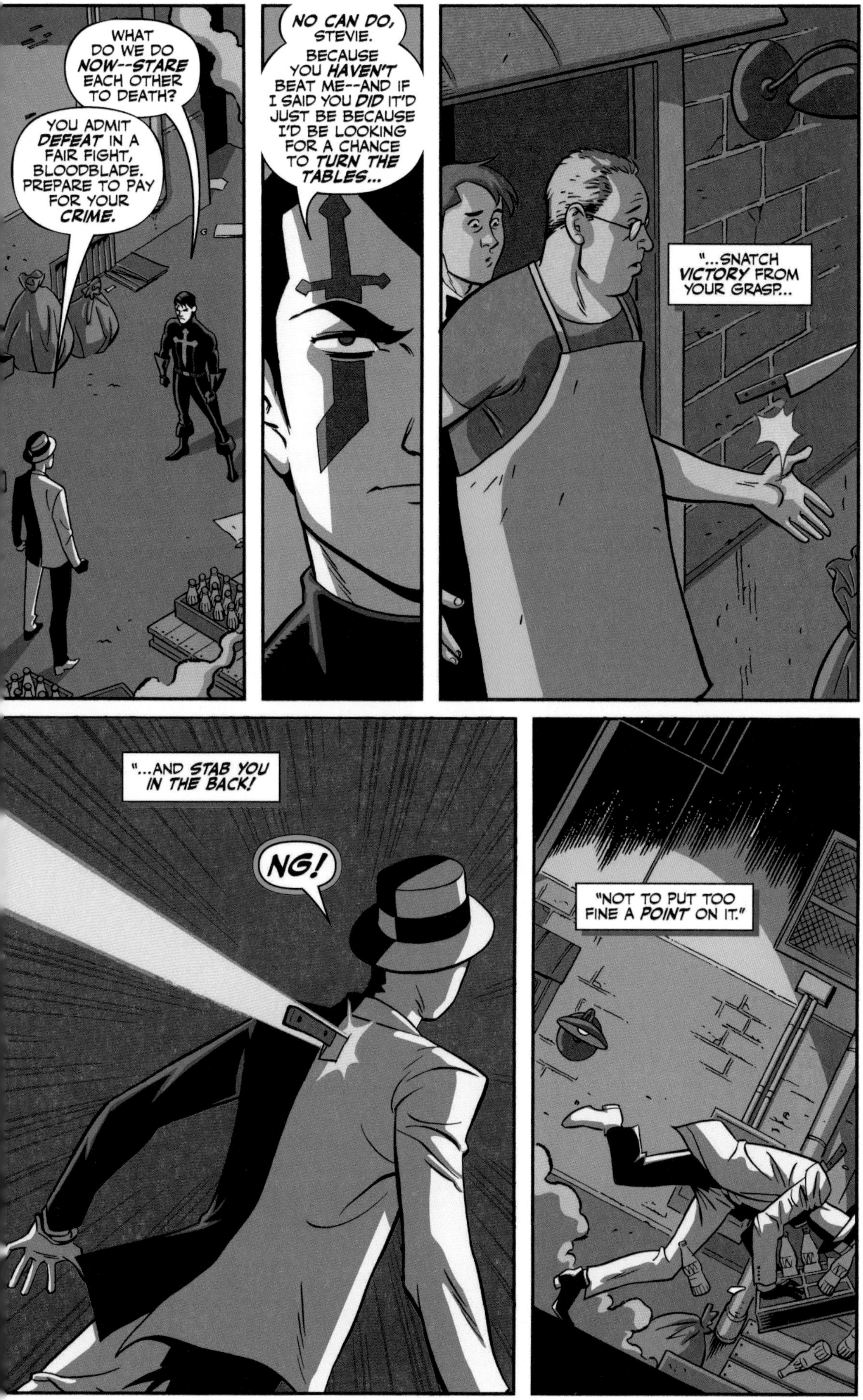
WHAT DO WE DO NOW--STARE EACH OTHER TO DEATH?
YOU ADMIT DEFEAT IN A FAIR FIGHT, BLOODBLADE. PREPARE TO PAY FOR YOUR CRIME.
NO CAN DO, STEVIE.
BECAUSE YOU HAVEN'T BEAT ME--AND IF I SAID YOU DID IT'D JUST BE BECAUSE I'D BE LOOKING FOR A CHANCE TO TURN THE TABLES...
"...SNATCH VICTORY FROM YOUR GRASP...
"...AND STAB YOU IN THE BACK!
NG!
"NOT TO PUT TOO FINE A POINT ON IT."

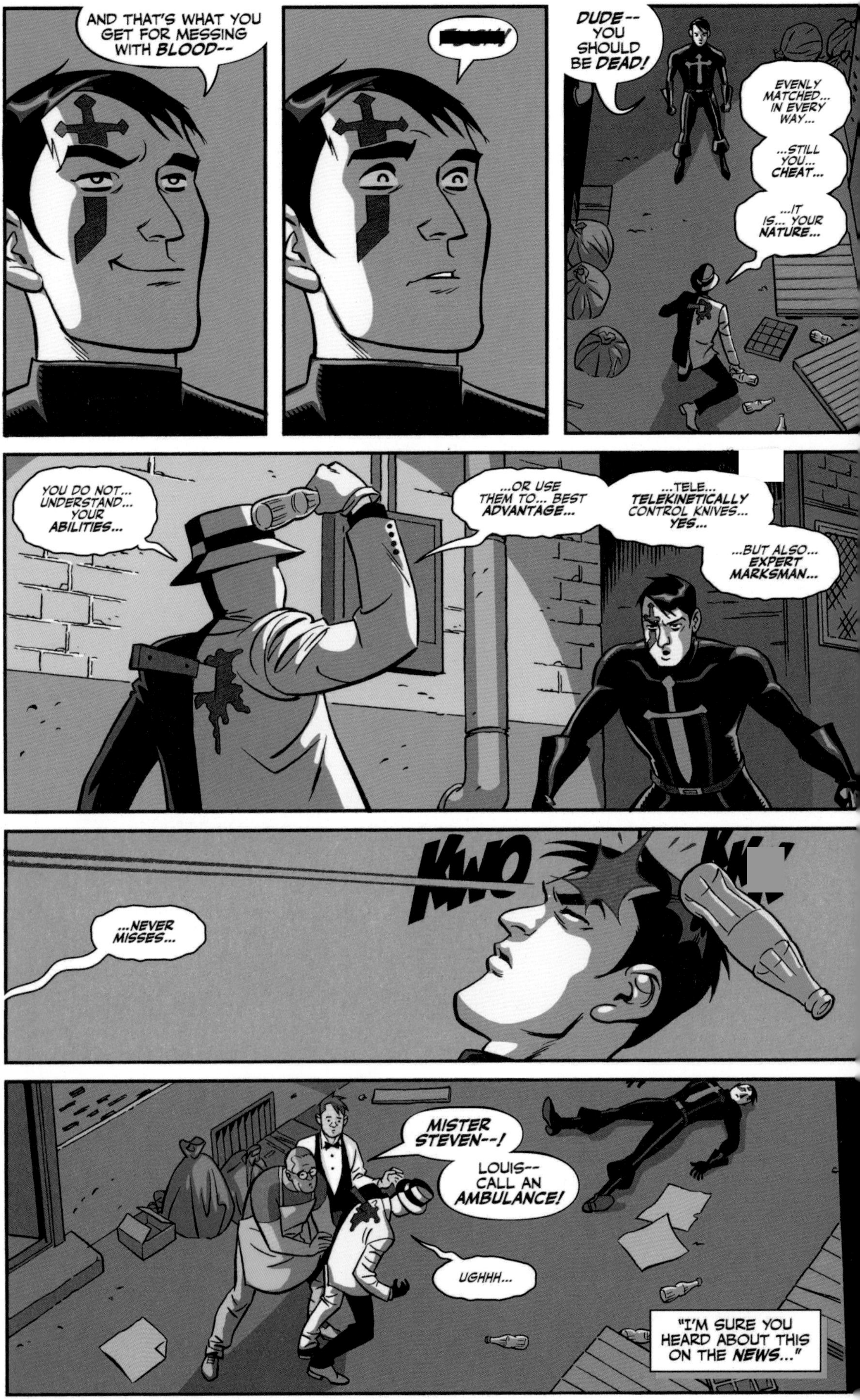
AND THAT'S WHAT YOU GET FOR MESSING WITH BLOOD--
[redacted]
DUDE-- YOU SHOULD BE DEAD!
EVENLY MATCHED... IN EVERY WAY...
...STILL YOU... CHEAT...
...IT IS... YOUR NATURE...
YOU DO NOT... UNDERSTAND... YOUR ABILITIES...
...OR USE THEM TO... BEST ADVANTAGE...
...TELE... TELEKINETICALLY CONTROL KNIVES... YES...
...BUT ALSO... EXPERT MARKSMAN...
KWO
...NEVER MISSES...
MISTER STEVEN--!
LOUIS-- CALL AN AMBULANCE!
UGHHH...
"I'M SURE YOU HEARD ABOUT THIS ON THE NEWS..."

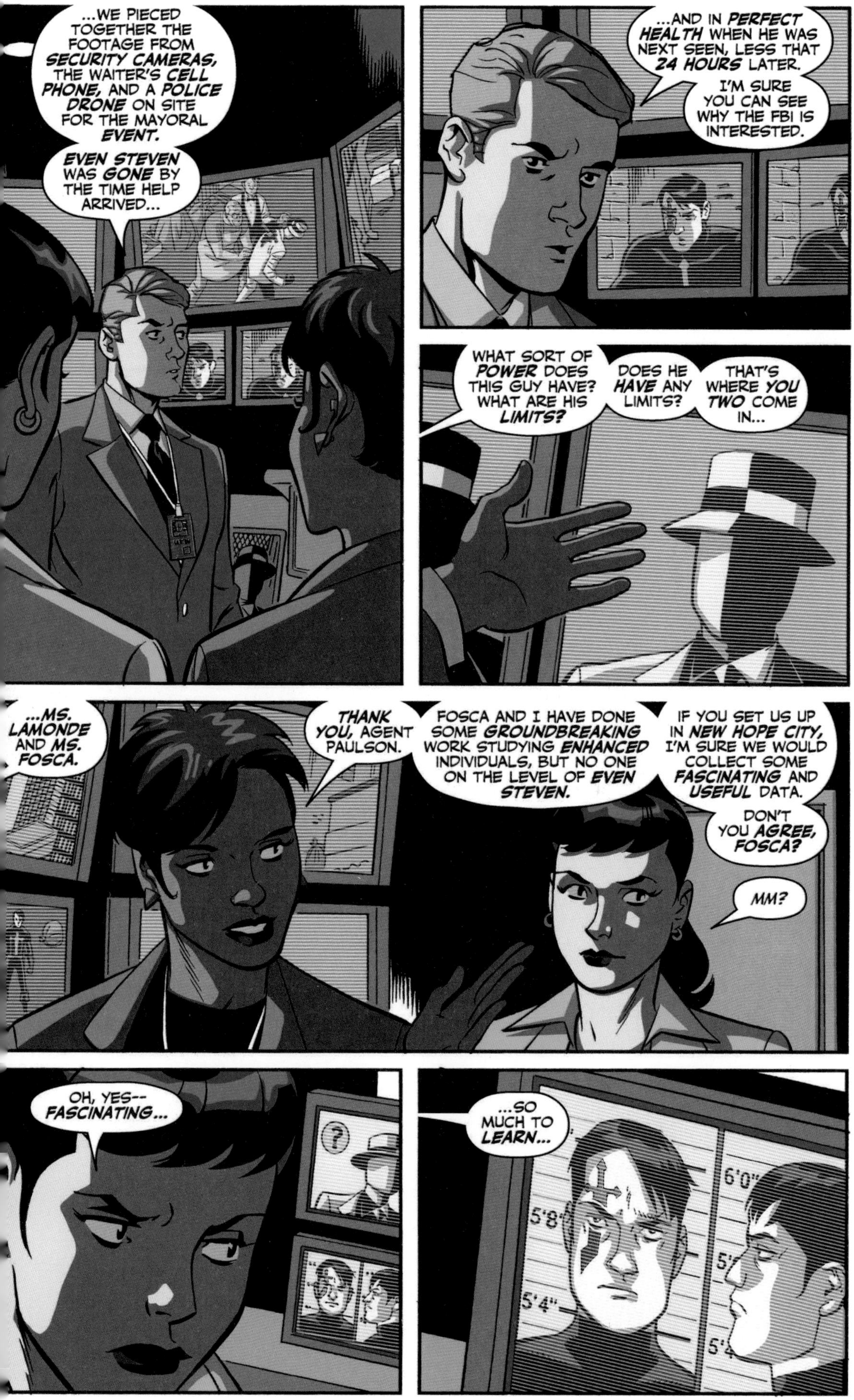
...WE PIECED TOGETHER THE FOOTAGE FROM SECURITY CAMERAS, THE WAITER'S CELL PHONE, AND A POLICE DRONE ON SITE FOR THE MAYORAL EVENT.
EVEN STEVEN WAS GONE BY THE TIME HELP ARRIVED...
...AND IN PERFECT HEALTH WHEN HE WAS NEXT SEEN, LESS THAT 24 HOURS LATER.
I'M SURE YOU CAN SEE WHY THE FBI IS INTERESTED.
WHAT SORT OF POWER DOES THIS GUY HAVE? WHAT ARE HIS LIMITS?
DOES HE HAVE ANY LIMITS?
THAT'S WHERE YOU TWO COME IN...
...MS. LAMONDE AND MS. FOSCA.
THANK YOU, AGENT PAULSON.
FOSCA AND I HAVE DONE SOME GROUNDBREAKING WORK STUDYING ENHANCED INDIVIDUALS, BUT NO ONE ON THE LEVEL OF EVEN STEVEN.
IF YOU SET US UP IN NEW HOPE CITY, I'M SURE WE WOULD COLLECT SOME FASCINATING AND USEFUL DATA.
DON'T YOU AGREE, FOSCA?
MM?
OH, YES-- FASCINATING...
...SO MUCH TO LEARN...
6'0"
5'8"
5'4"

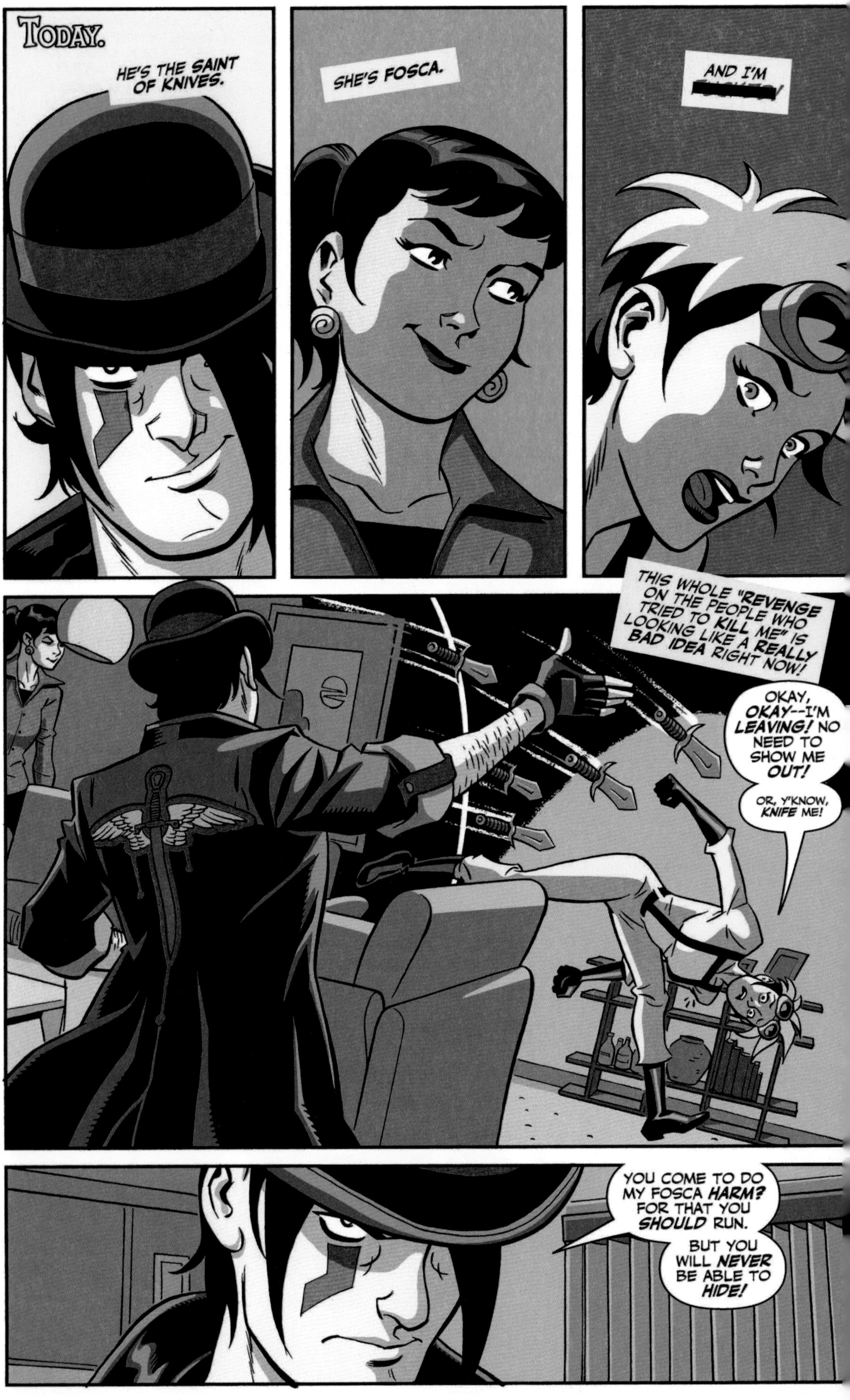
TODAY.
HE'S THE SAINT OF KNIVES.
SHE'S FOSCA.
AND I'M [redacted]
THIS WHOLE "REVENGE ON THE PEOPLE WHO TRIED TO KILL ME" IS LOOKING LIKE A REALLY BAD IDEA RIGHT NOW!
OKAY, OKAY--I'M LEAVING! NO NEED TO SHOW ME OUT!
OR, Y'KNOW, KNIFE ME!
YOU COME TO DO MY FOSCA HARM? FOR THAT YOU SHOULD RUN.
BUT YOU WILL NEVER BE ABLE TO HIDE!

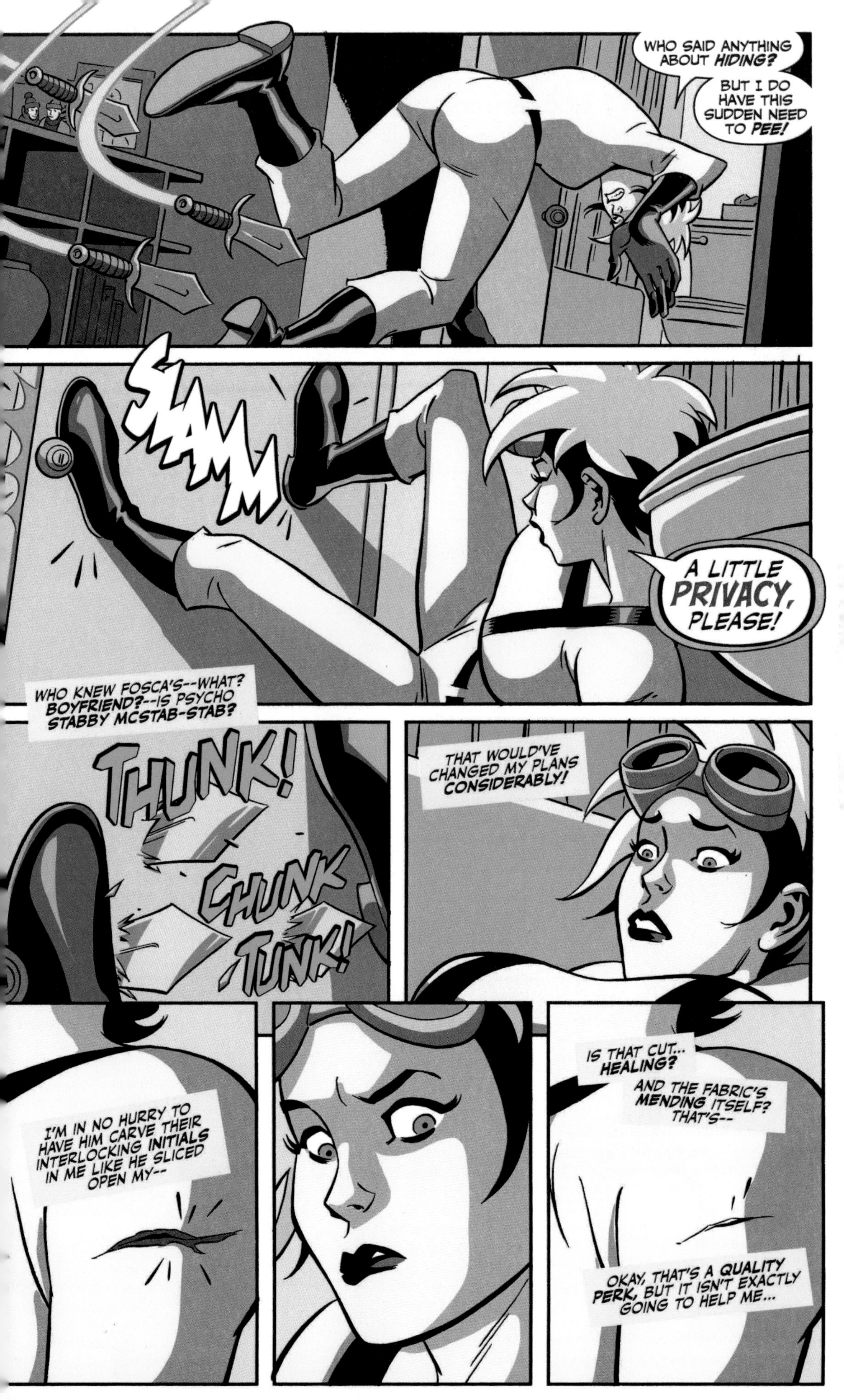
WHO SAID ANYTHING ABOUT HIDING?
BUT I DO HAVE THIS SUDDEN NEED TO PEE!
SLAMM
A LITTLE PRIVACY, PLEASE!
WHO KNEW FOSCA'S--WHAT? BOYFRIEND?--IS PSYCHO STABBY MCSTAB-STAB?
THUNK!
CHUNK
TUNK!
THAT WOULD'VE CHANGED MY PLANS CONSIDERABLY!
I'M IN NO HURRY TO HAVE HIM CARVE THEIR INTERLOCKING INITIALS IN ME LIKE HE SLICED OPEN MY--
IS THAT CUT... HEALING?
AND THE FABRIC'S MENDING ITSELF? THAT'S--
OKAY, THAT'S A QUALITY PERK, BUT IT ISN'T EXACTLY GOING TO HELP ME...

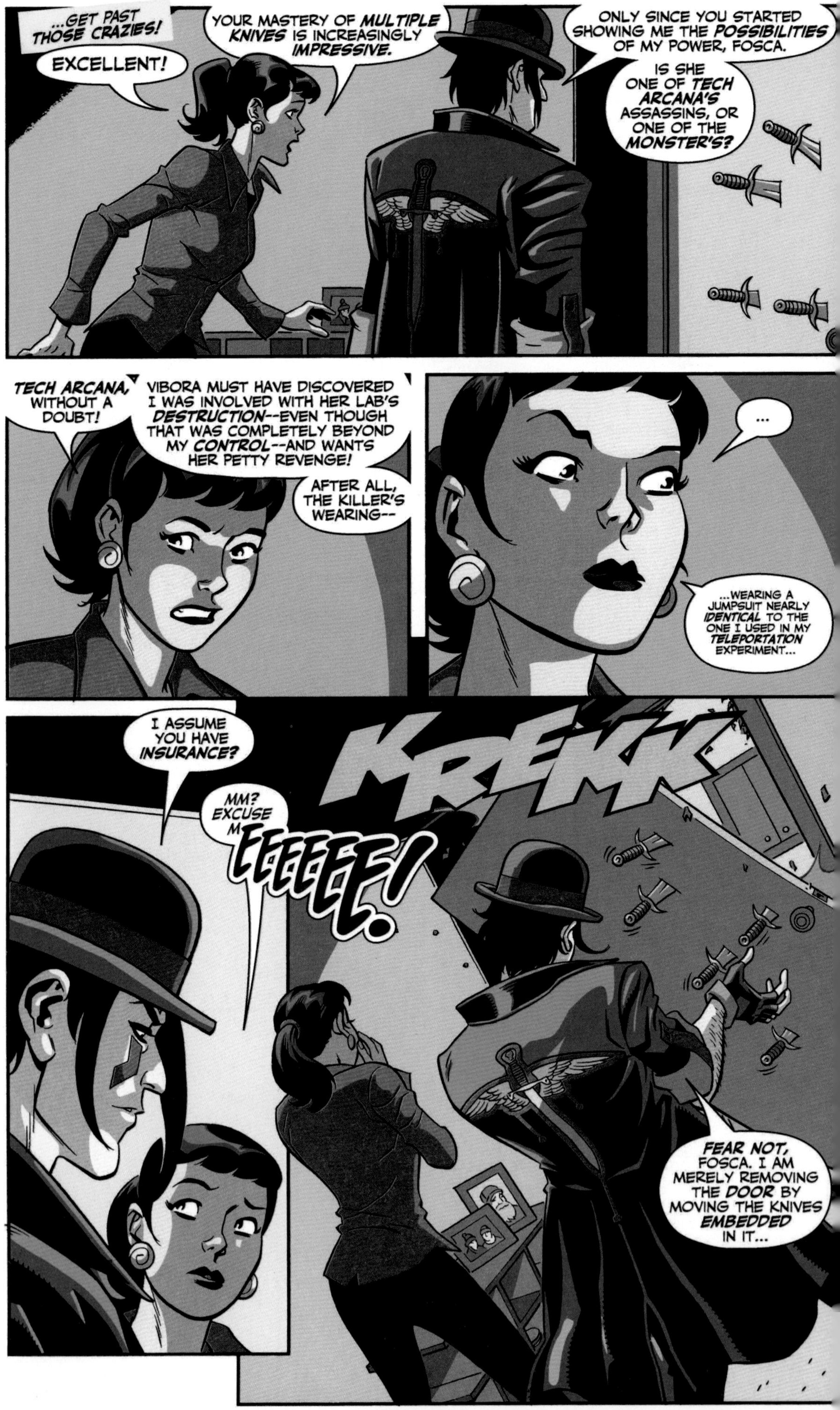

...GET PAST THOSE CRAZIES!
EXCELLENT!
YOUR MASTERY OF MULTIPLE KNIVES IS INCREASINGLY IMPRESSIVE.
ONLY SINCE YOU STARTED SHOWING ME THE POSSIBILITIES OF MY POWER, FOSCA.
IS SHE ONE OF TECH ARCANA'S ASSASSINS, OR ONE OF THE MONSTER'S?
TECH ARCANA, WITHOUT A DOUBT!
VIBORA MUST HAVE DISCOVERED I WAS INVOLVED WITH HER LAB'S DESTRUCTION--EVEN THOUGH THAT WAS COMPLETELY BEYOND MY CONTROL--AND WANTS HER PETTY REVENGE!
AFTER ALL, THE KILLER'S WEARING--
...
...WEARING A JUMPSUIT NEARLY IDENTICAL TO THE ONE I USED IN MY TELEPORTATION EXPERIMENT...
I ASSUME YOU HAVE INSURANCE?
MM? EXCUSE M
EEEEEE!
KREKK
FEAR NOT, FOSCA. I AM MERELY REMOVING THE DOOR BY MOVING THE KNIVES EMBEDDED IN IT...

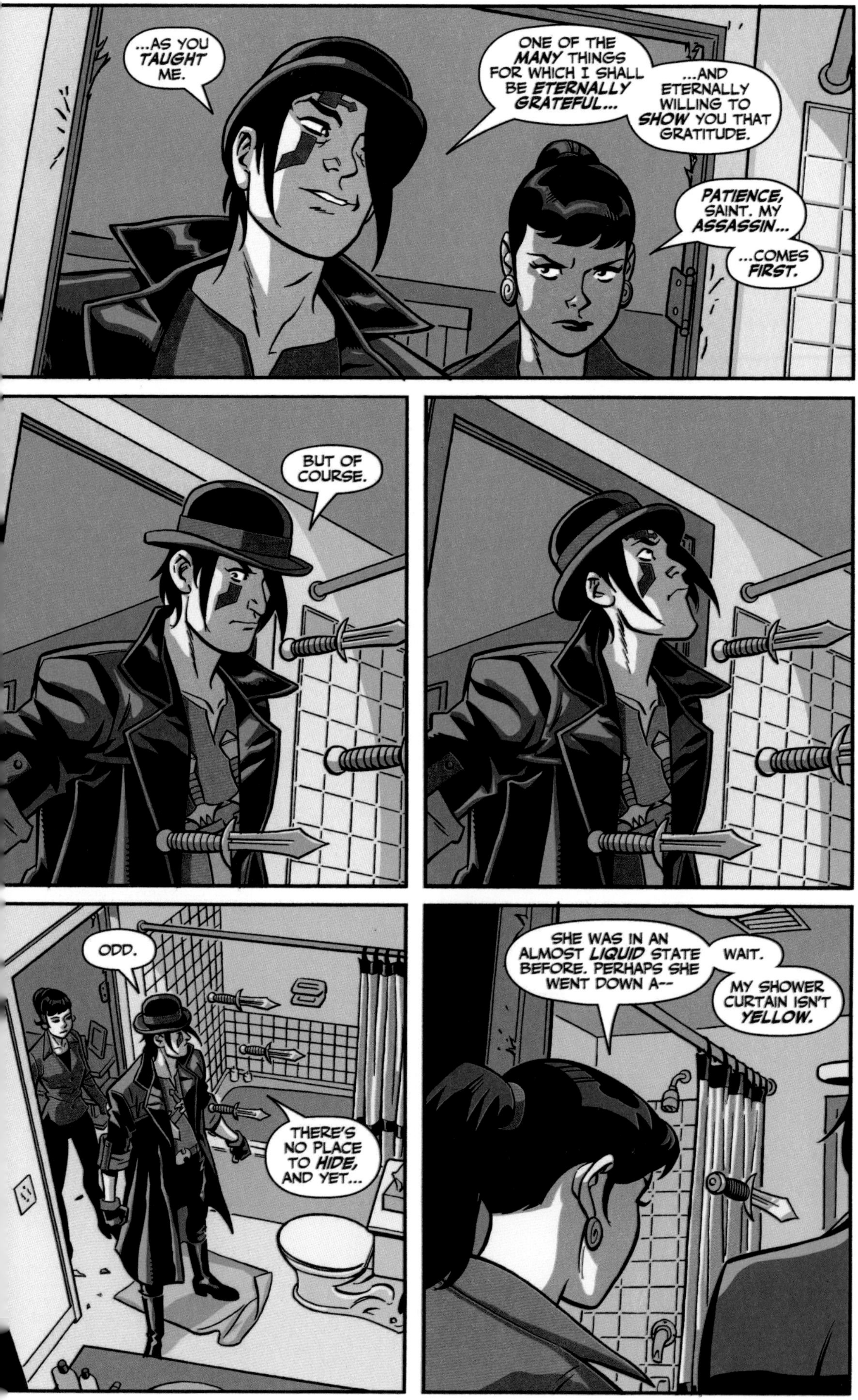
...AS YOU TAUGHT ME.
ONE OF THE MANY THINGS FOR WHICH I SHALL BE ETERNALLY GRATEFUL...
...AND ETERNALLY WILLING TO SHOW YOU THAT GRATITUDE.
PATIENCE, SAINT. MY ASSASSIN...
...COMES FIRST.
BUT OF COURSE.
ODD.
THERE'S NO PLACE TO HIDE, AND YET...
SHE WAS IN AN ALMOST LIQUID STATE BEFORE. PERHAPS SHE WENT DOWN A--
WAIT.
MY SHOWER CURTAIN ISN'T YELLOW.

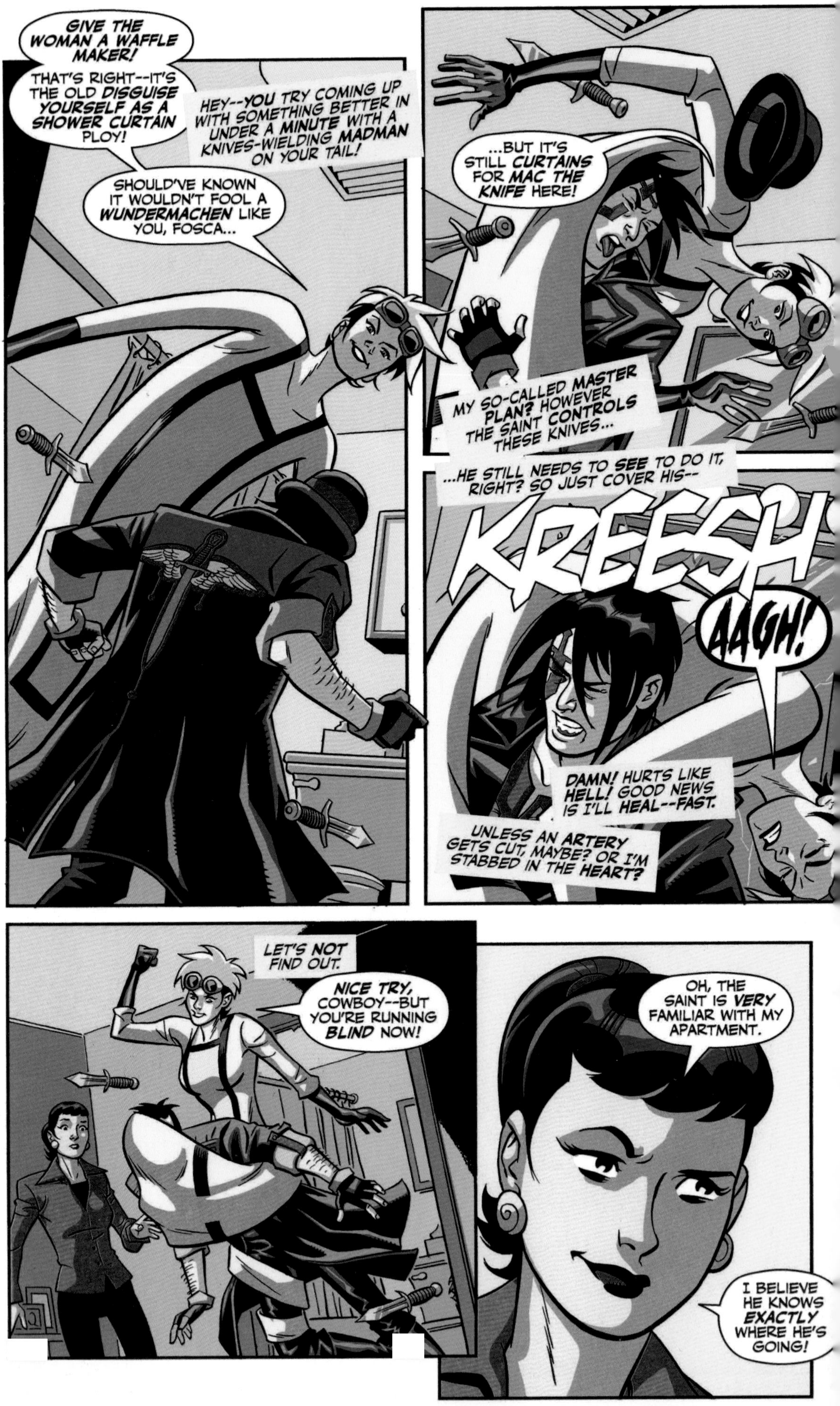
GIVE THE WOMAN A WAFFLE MAKER!
THAT'S RIGHT--IT'S THE OLD DISGUISE YOURSELF AS A SHOWER CURTAIN PLOY!
HEY--YOU TRY COMING UP WITH SOMETHING BETTER IN UNDER A MINUTE WITH A KNIVES-WIELDING MADMAN ON YOUR TAIL!
SHOULD'VE KNOWN IT WOULDN'T FOOL A WUNDERMACHEN LIKE YOU, FOSCA...
...BUT IT'S STILL CURTAINS FOR MAC THE KNIFE HERE!
MY SO-CALLED MASTER PLAN? HOWEVER THE SAINT CONTROLS THESE KNIVES...
...HE STILL NEEDS TO SEE TO DO IT, RIGHT? SO JUST COVER HIS--
KREESH
AAGH!
DAMN! HURTS LIKE HELL! GOOD NEWS IS I'LL HEAL--FAST.
UNLESS AN ARTERY GETS CUT, MAYBE? OR I'M STABBED IN THE HEART?
LET'S NOT FIND OUT.
NICE TRY, COWBOY--BUT YOU'RE RUNNING BLIND NOW!
OH, THE SAINT IS VERY FAMILIAR WITH MY APARTMENT.
I BELIEVE HE KNOWS EXACTLY WHERE HE'S GOING!

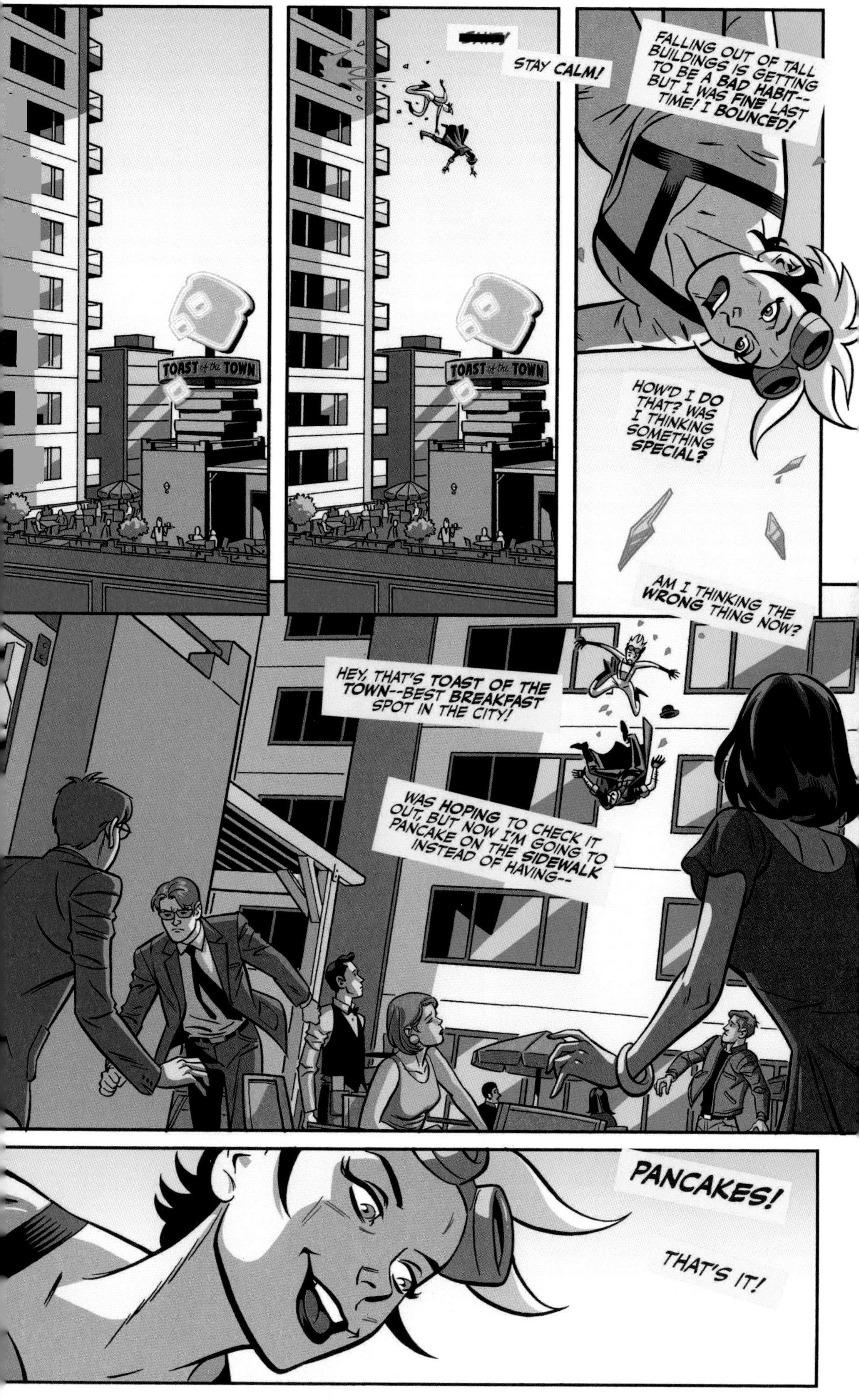

[redacted]
STAY CALM!
FALLING OUT OF TALL BUILDINGS IS GETTING TO BE A BAD HABIT-- BUT I WAS FINE LAST TIME! I BOUNCED!
HOW'D I DO THAT? WAS I THINKING SOMETHING SPECIAL?
AM I THINKING THE WRONG THING NOW?
TOAST of the TOWN
HEY, THAT'S TOAST OF THE TOWN--BEST BREAKFAST SPOT IN THE CITY!
WAS HOPING TO CHECK IT OUT, BUT NOW I'M GOING TO PANCAKE ON THE SIDEWALK INSTEAD OF HAVING--
PANCAKES!
THAT'S IT!

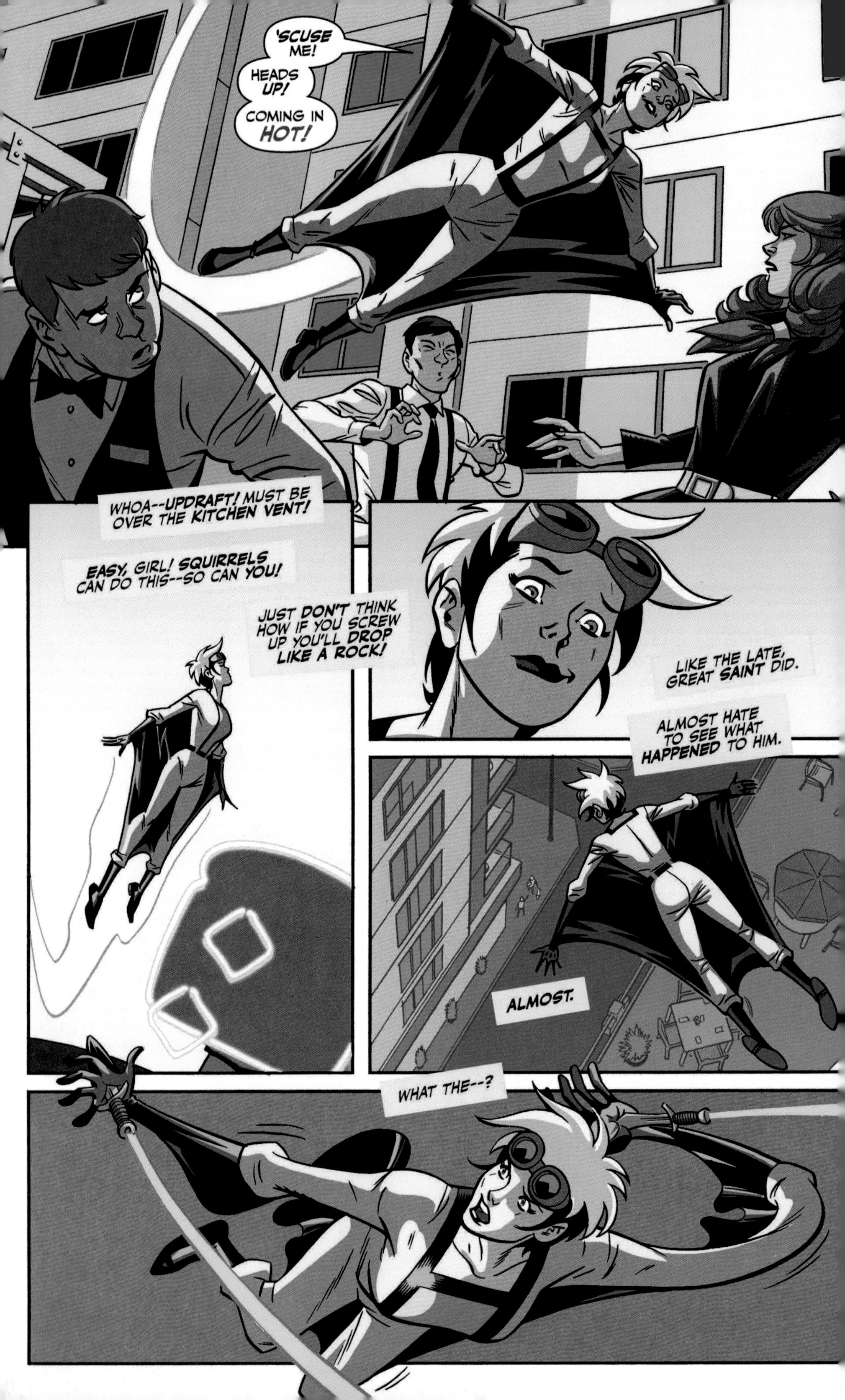
'SCUSE ME!
HEADS UP!
COMING IN HOT!
WHOA--UPDRAFT! MUST BE OVER THE KITCHEN VENT!
EASY, GIRL! SQUIRRELS CAN DO THIS--SO CAN YOU!
JUST DON'T THINK HOW IF YOU SCREW UP YOU'LL DROP LIKE A ROCK!
LIKE THE LATE, GREAT SAINT DID.
ALMOST HATE TO SEE WHAT HAPPENED TO HIM.
ALMOST.
WHAT THE--?

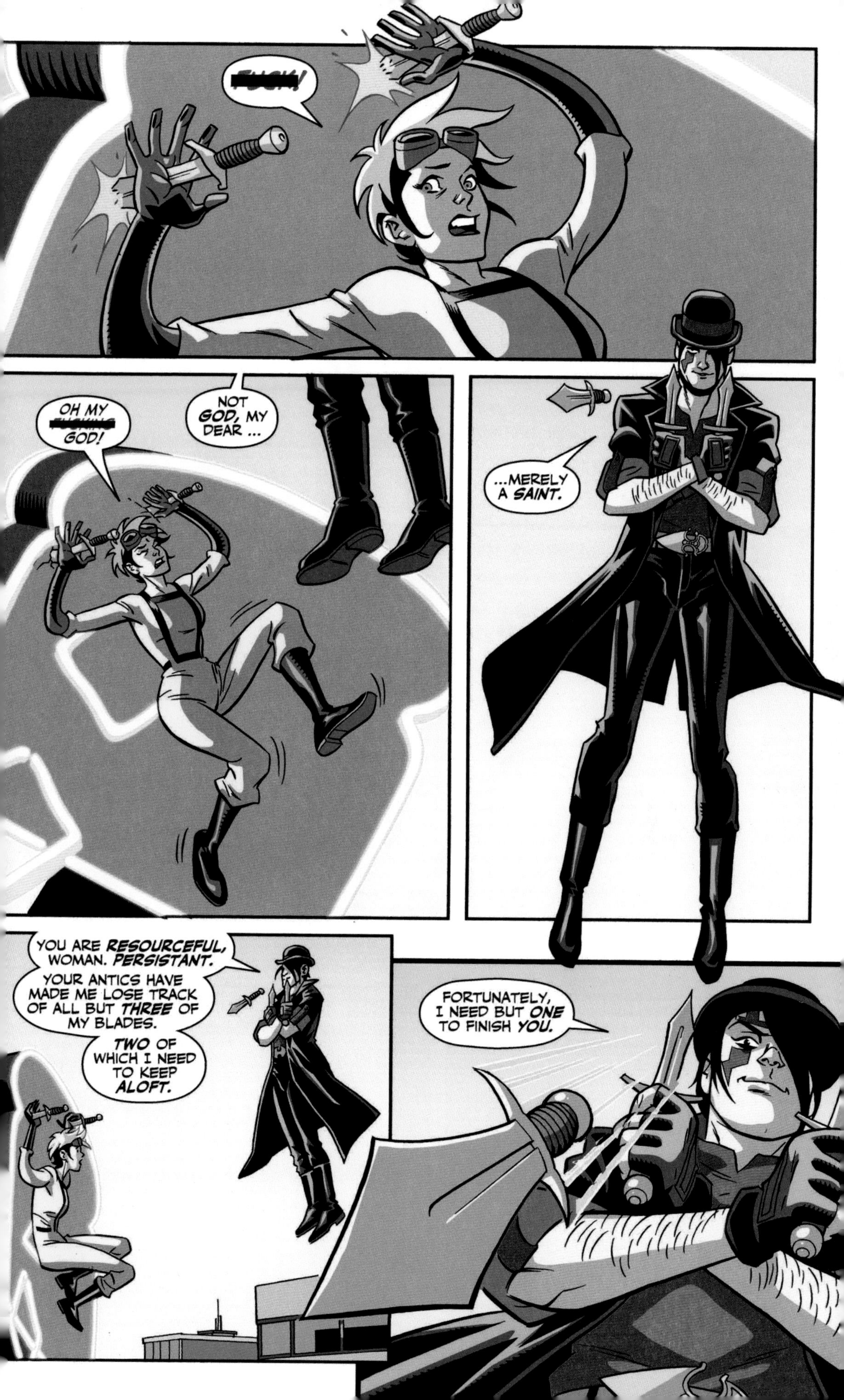
[redacted]!
OH MY [redacted] GOD!
NOT GOD, MY DEAR ...
...MERELY A SAINT.
YOU ARE RESOURCEFUL, WOMAN. PERSISTANT.
YOUR ANTICS HAVE MADE ME LOSE TRACK OF ALL BUT THREE OF MY BLADES.
TWO OF WHICH I NEED TO KEEP ALOFT.
FORTUNATELY, I NEED BUT ONE TO FINISH YOU.

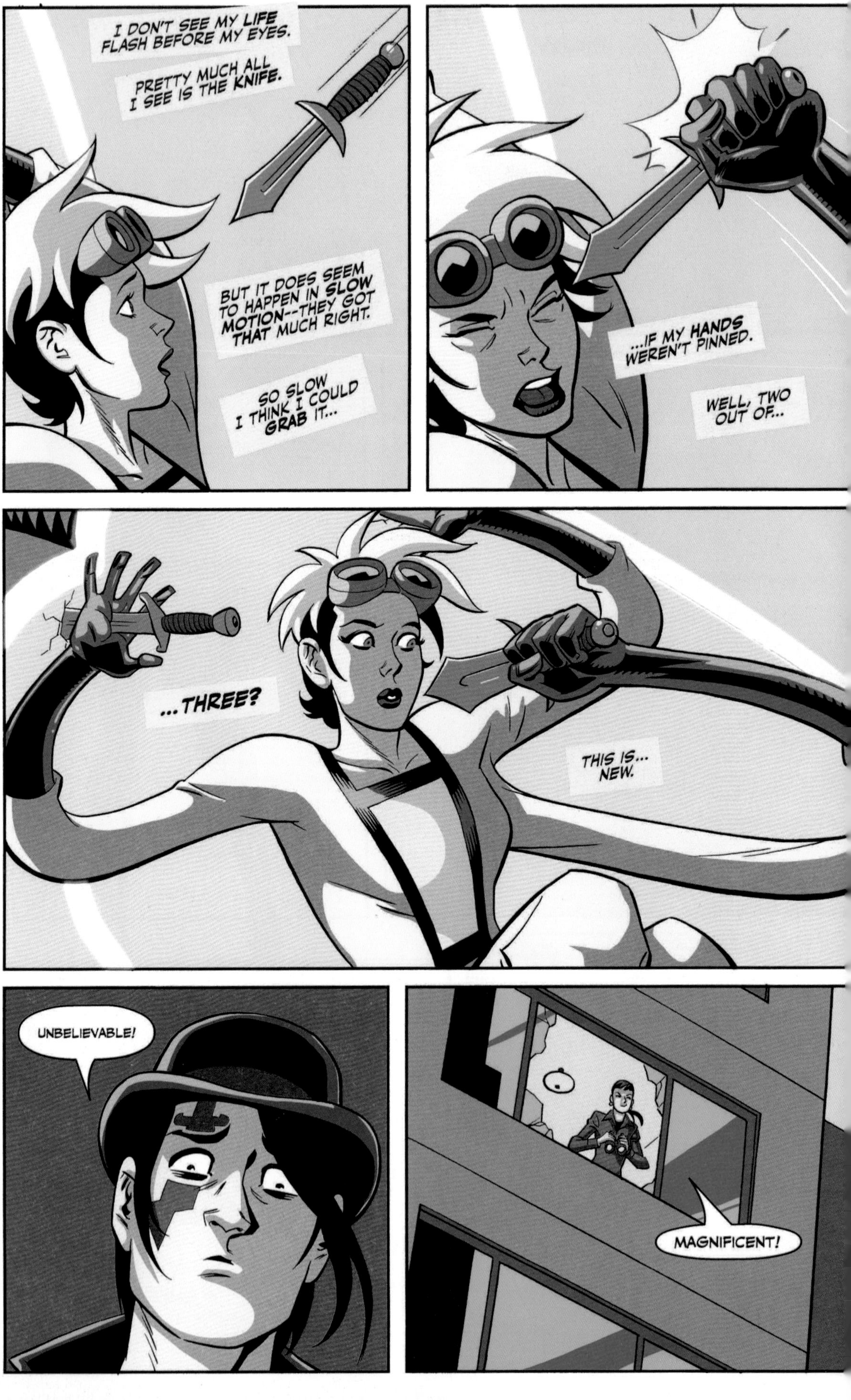
I DON'T SEE MY LIFE FLASH BEFORE MY EYES.
PRETTY MUCH ALL I SEE IS THE KNIFE.
BUT IT DOES SEEM TO HAPPEN IN SLOW MOTION--THEY GOT THAT MUCH RIGHT.
SO SLOW I THINK I COULD GRAB IT...
...IF MY HANDS WEREN'T PINNED.
WELL, TWO OUT OF...
...THREE?
THIS IS... NEW.
UNBELIEVABLE!
MAGNIFICENT!

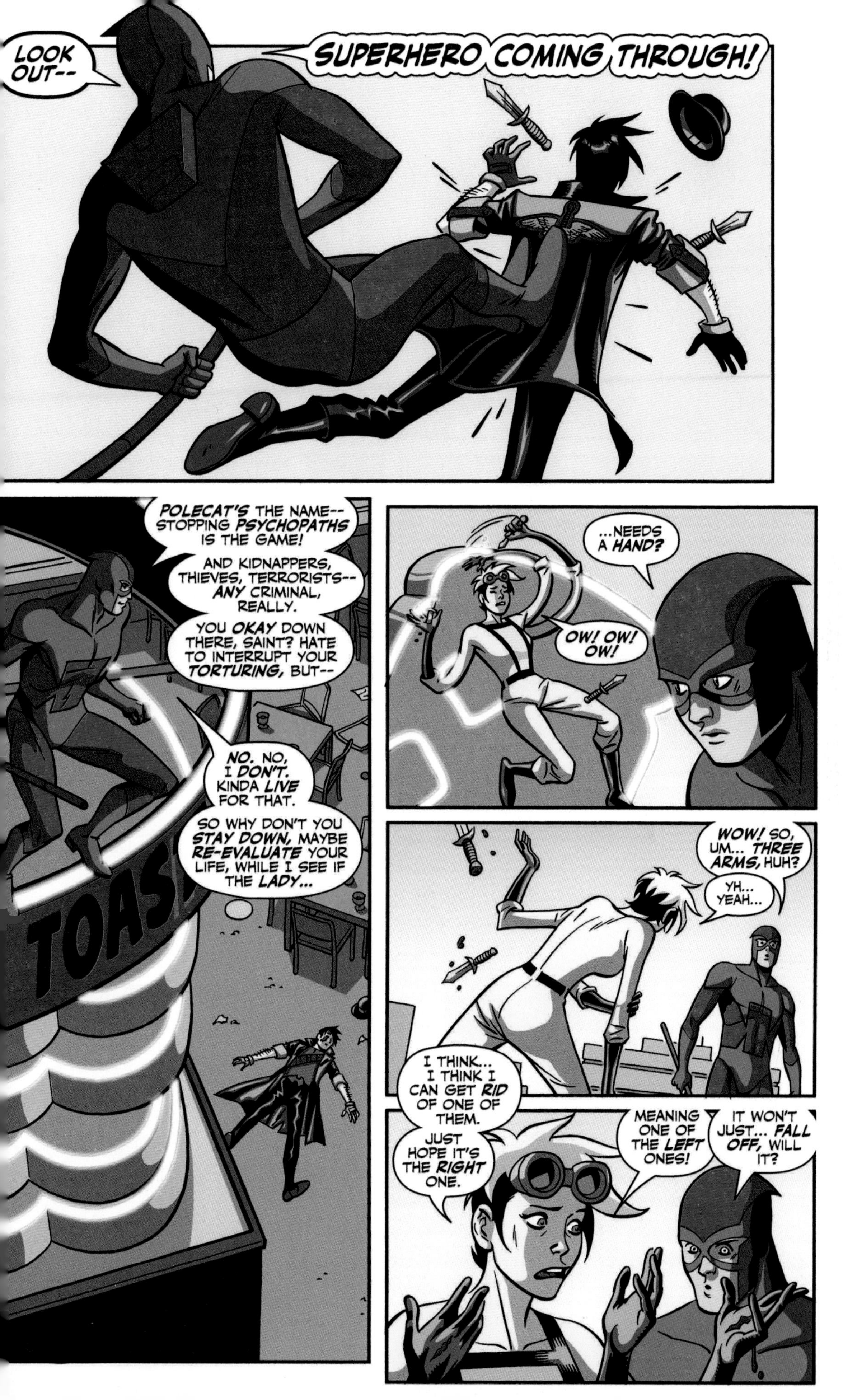
LOOK OUT--
SUPERHERO COMING THROUGH!
POLECAT'S THE NAME-- STOPPING PSYCHOPATHS IS THE GAME!
AND KIDNAPPERS, THIEVES, TERRORISTS-- ANY CRIMINAL, REALLY.
YOU OKAY DOWN THERE, SAINT? HATE TO INTERRUPT YOUR TORTURING, BUT--
NO. NO, I DON'T. KINDA LIVE FOR THAT.
SO WHY DON'T YOU STAY DOWN, MAYBE RE-EVALUATE YOUR LIFE, WHILE I SEE IF THE LADY...
TOAS
...NEEDS A HAND?
OW! OW! OW!
WOW! SO, UM... THREE ARMS, HUH?
YH... YEAH...
I THINK... I THINK I CAN GET RID OF ONE OF THEM.
JUST HOPE IT'S THE RIGHT ONE.
MEANING ONE OF THE LEFT ONES!
IT WON'T JUST... FALL OFF, WILL IT?

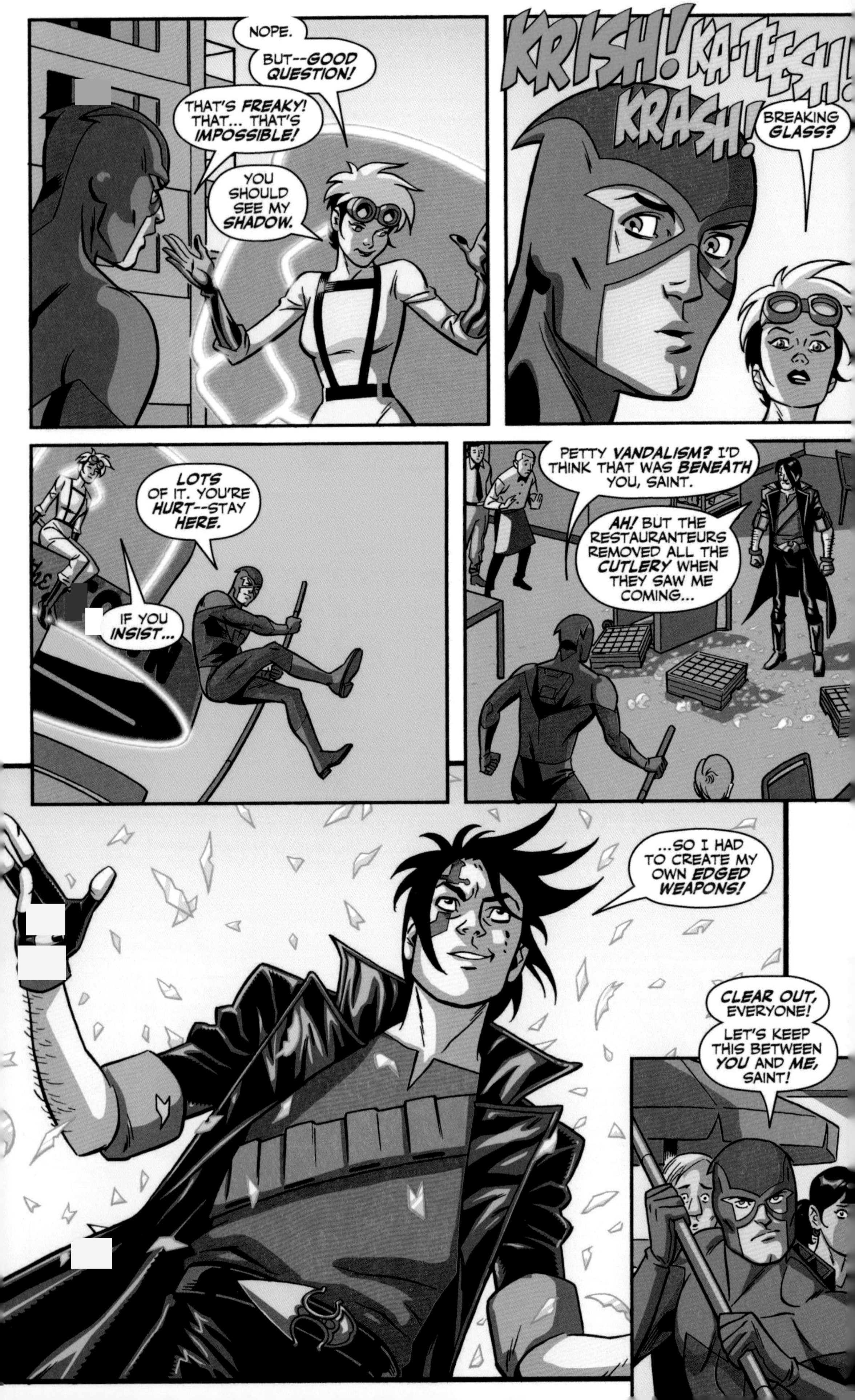

NOPE.
BUT--GOOD QUESTION!
THAT'S FREAKY! THAT... THAT'S IMPOSSIBLE!
YOU SHOULD SEE MY SHADOW.
KRISH! KA-TESH! KRASH!
BREAKING GLASS?
LOTS OF IT. YOU'RE HURT--STAY HERE.
IF YOU INSIST...
PETTY VANDALISM? I'D THINK THAT WAS BENEATH YOU, SAINT.
AH! BUT THE RESTAURANTEURS REMOVED ALL THE CUTLERY WHEN THEY SAW ME COMING...
...SO I HAD TO CREATE MY OWN EDGED WEAPONS!
CLEAR OUT, EVERYONE!
LET'S KEEP THIS BETWEEN YOU AND ME, SAINT!

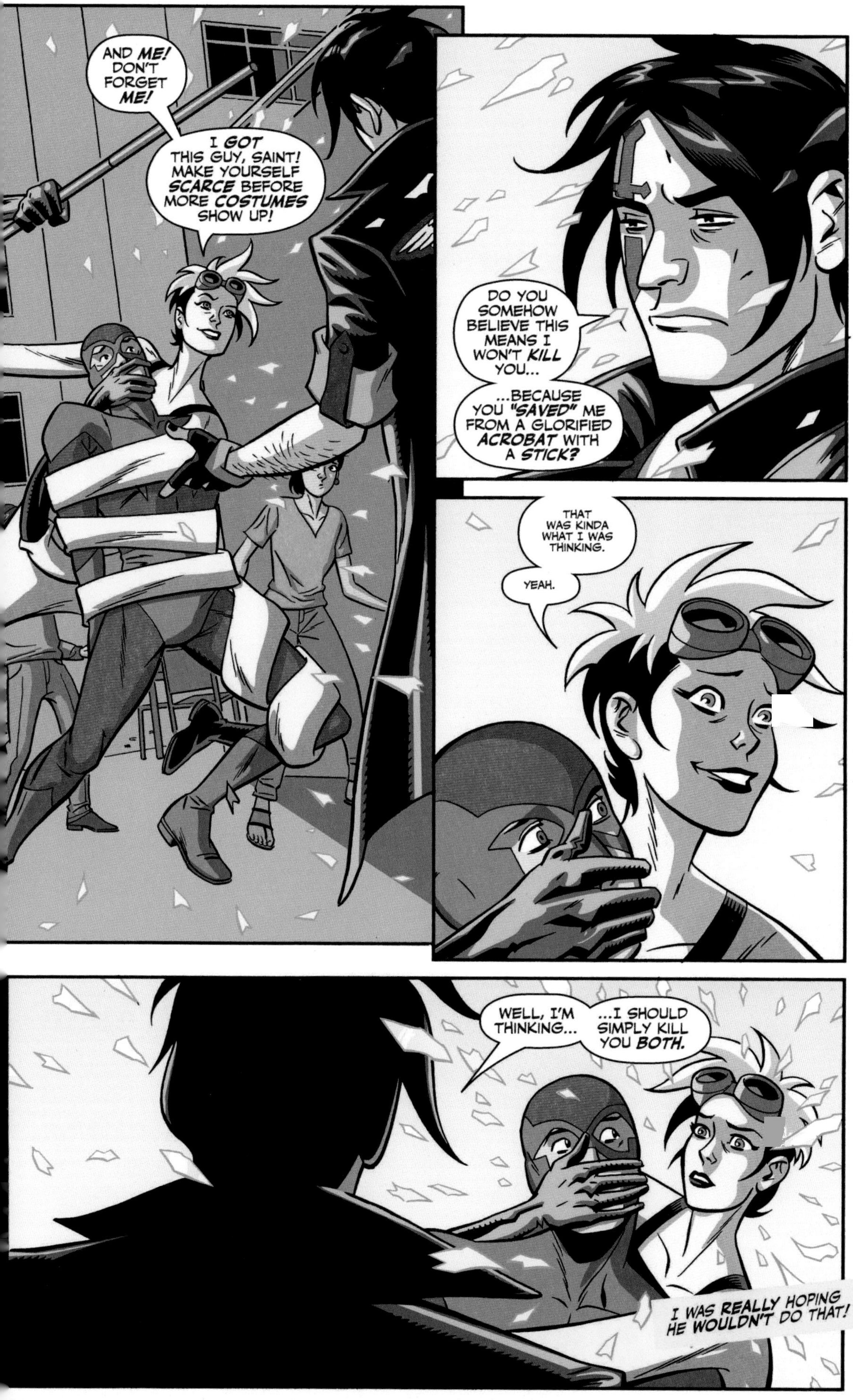
AND ME! DON'T FORGET ME!
I GOT THIS GUY, SAINT! MAKE YOURSELF SCARCE BEFORE MORE COSTUMES SHOW UP!
DO YOU SOMEHOW BELIEVE THIS MEANS I WON'T KILL YOU...
...BECAUSE YOU "SAVED" ME FROM A GLORIFIED ACROBAT WITH A STICK?
THAT WAS KINDA WHAT I WAS THINKING.
YEAH.
WELL, I'M THINKING...
...I SHOULD SIMPLY KILL YOU BOTH.
I WAS REALLY HOPING HE WOULDN'T DO THAT!

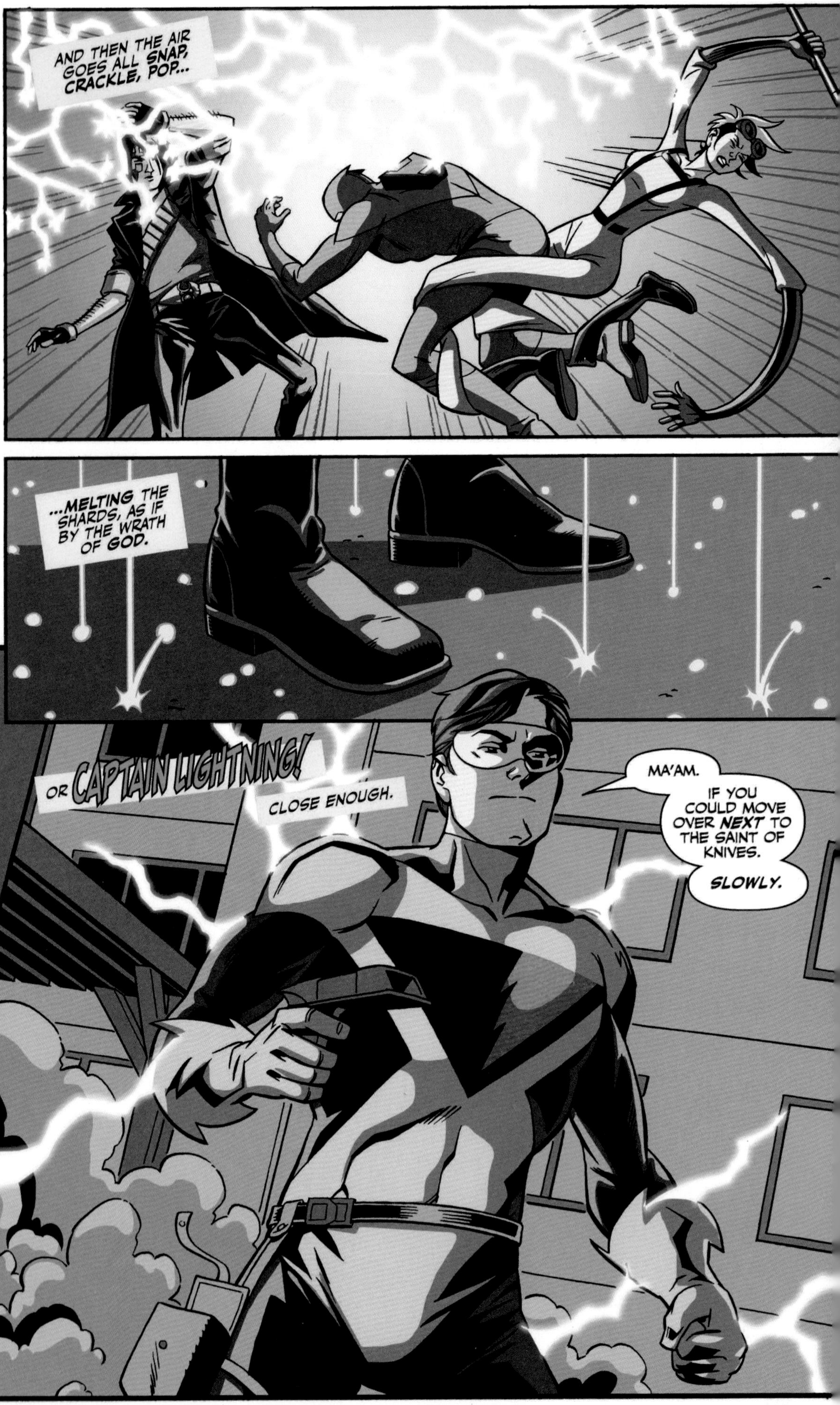

AND THEN THE AIR GOES ALL SNAP, CRACKLE, POP...
...MELTING THE SHARDS, AS IF BY THE WRATH OF GOD.
OR CAPTAIN LIGHTNING!
CLOSE ENOUGH.
MA'AM.
IF YOU COULD MOVE OVER NEXT TO THE SAINT OF KNIVES.
SLOWLY.

YOU *ALL RIGHT,* POLECAT?

OH, YOU KNOW *ME*--KNOCKED *DOWN,* MADE *SMALL,* TREATED LIKE A *RUBBER BALL.*

BUT I ALWAYS *BOUNCE BACK!*

YOU'RE *NEW* IN TOWN, MA'AM. WHAT'S YOUR *NAME?*

BELLE.

ER, I MEAN, UMMM...*POSSIBLE.* BELLE'S SHORT FOR *IMPOSSIBLE.*

YEAH, PEOPLE BEEN CALLING ME "IMPOSSIBLE" MY *WHOLE LIFE...*

CUT HER SOME *SLACK,* CAP.

SHE *ATTACKED* YOU. TOOK YOUR *WEAPON.*

THE SAINT WAS TRYING TO *KILL HER...*

...SHE WAS *BLUFFING!* BUYING *TIME!*

I'M NOT SO SURE-- SEEMS MORE LIKE A *FALLING OUT AMONG THIEVES...*

THE ONE THING I GOT *GOING* FOR ME-- BESIDES THOSE TWO TALKING LIKE AN OLD *MARRIED COUPLE*--

--IS THE SAINT THINKS I'M AN ASSASSIN, TOO.

WHICH I GUESS I KINDA *AM*--BUT THE POINT IS WHEN HE GIVES ME *"THE LOOK"* I KNOW SOMETHING'S UP.

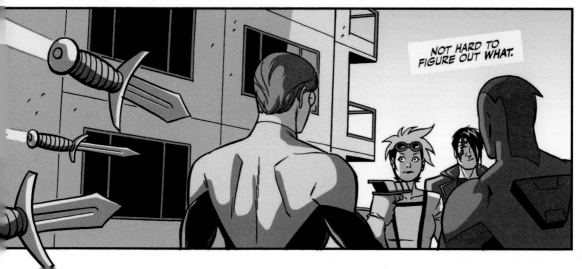

NOT HARD TO FIGURE OUT *WHAT.*

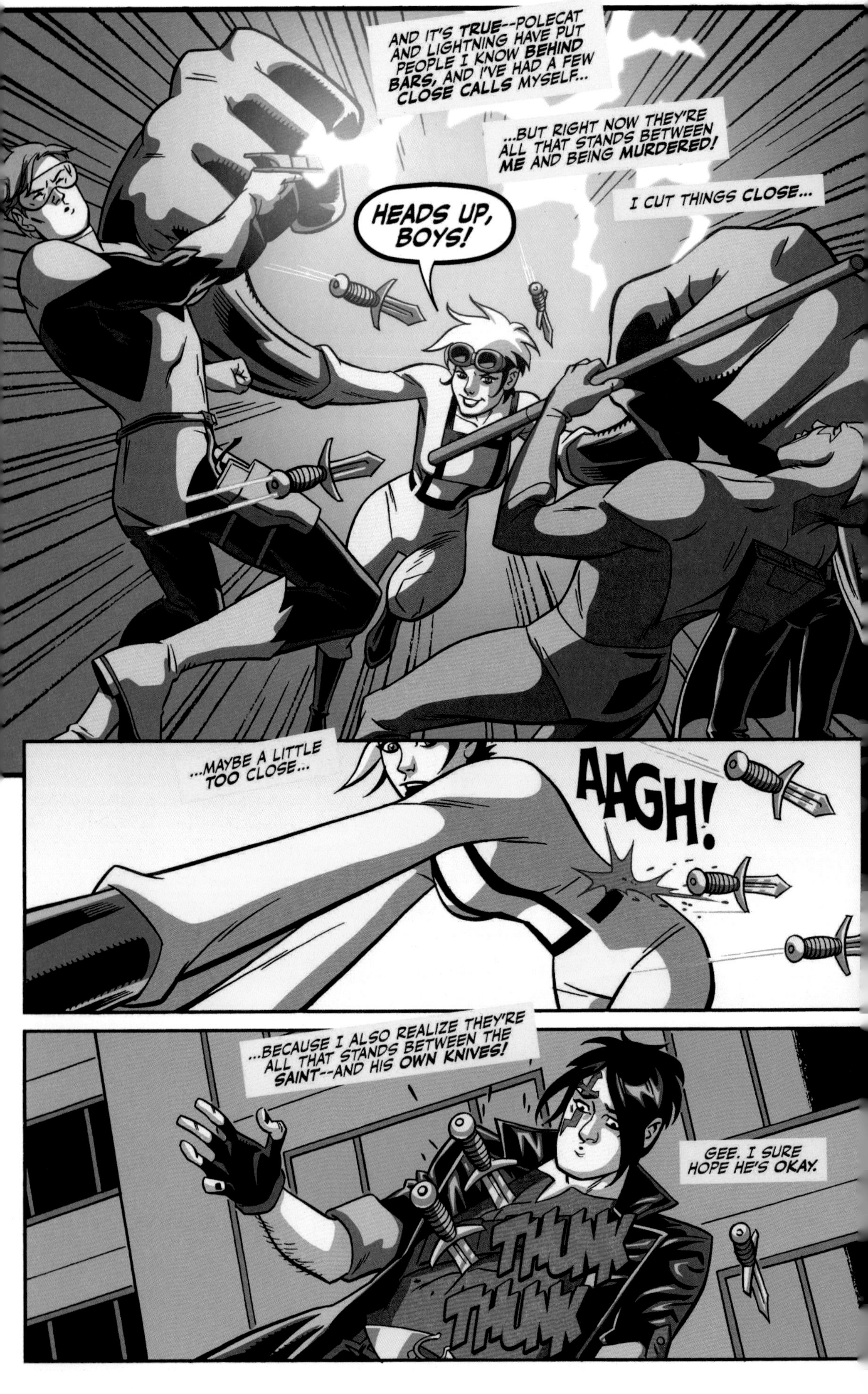
AND IT'S TRUE--POLECAT AND LIGHTNING HAVE PUT PEOPLE I KNOW BEHIND BARS, AND I'VE HAD A FEW CLOSE CALLS MYSELF...
...BUT RIGHT NOW THEY'RE ALL THAT STANDS BETWEEN ME AND BEING MURDERED!
I CUT THINGS CLOSE...
HEADS UP, BOYS!
...MAYBE A LITTLE TOO CLOSE...
AAGH!
...BECAUSE I ALSO REALIZE THEY'RE ALL THAT STANDS BETWEEN THE SAINT--AND HIS OWN KNIVES!
GEE. I SURE HOPE HE'S OKAY.
THUNK
THUNK

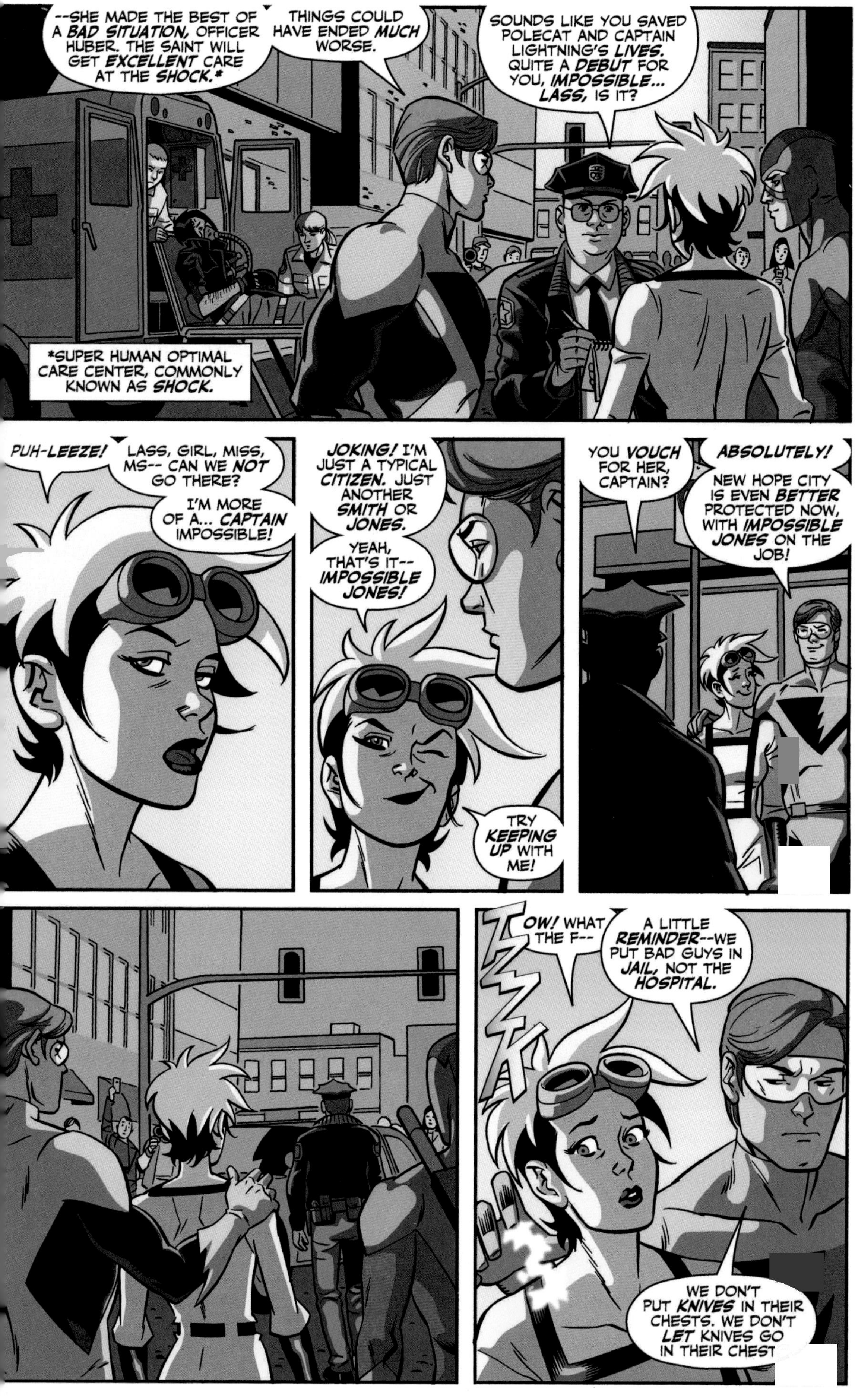

--SHE MADE THE BEST OF A BAD SITUATION, OFFICER HUBER. THE SAINT WILL GET EXCELLENT CARE AT THE SHOCK.*
THINGS COULD HAVE ENDED MUCH WORSE.
SOUNDS LIKE YOU SAVED POLECAT AND CAPTAIN LIGHTNING'S LIVES. QUITE A DEBUT FOR YOU, IMPOSSIBLE... LASS, IS IT?
*SUPER HUMAN OPTIMAL CARE CENTER, COMMONLY KNOWN AS SHOCK.
PUH-LEEZE!
LASS, GIRL, MISS, MS-- CAN WE NOT GO THERE?
I'M MORE OF A... CAPTAIN IMPOSSIBLE!
JOKING! I'M JUST A TYPICAL CITIZEN. JUST ANOTHER SMITH OR JONES.
YEAH, THAT'S IT-- IMPOSSIBLE JONES!
TRY KEEPING UP WITH ME!
YOU VOUCH FOR HER, CAPTAIN?
ABSOLUTELY!
NEW HOPE CITY IS EVEN BETTER PROTECTED NOW, WITH IMPOSSIBLE JONES ON THE JOB!
OW! WHAT THE F--
A LITTLE REMINDER--WE PUT BAD GUYS IN JAIL, NOT THE HOSPITAL.
WE DON'T PUT KNIVES IN THEIR CHESTS. WE DON'T LET KNIVES GO IN THEIR CHEST

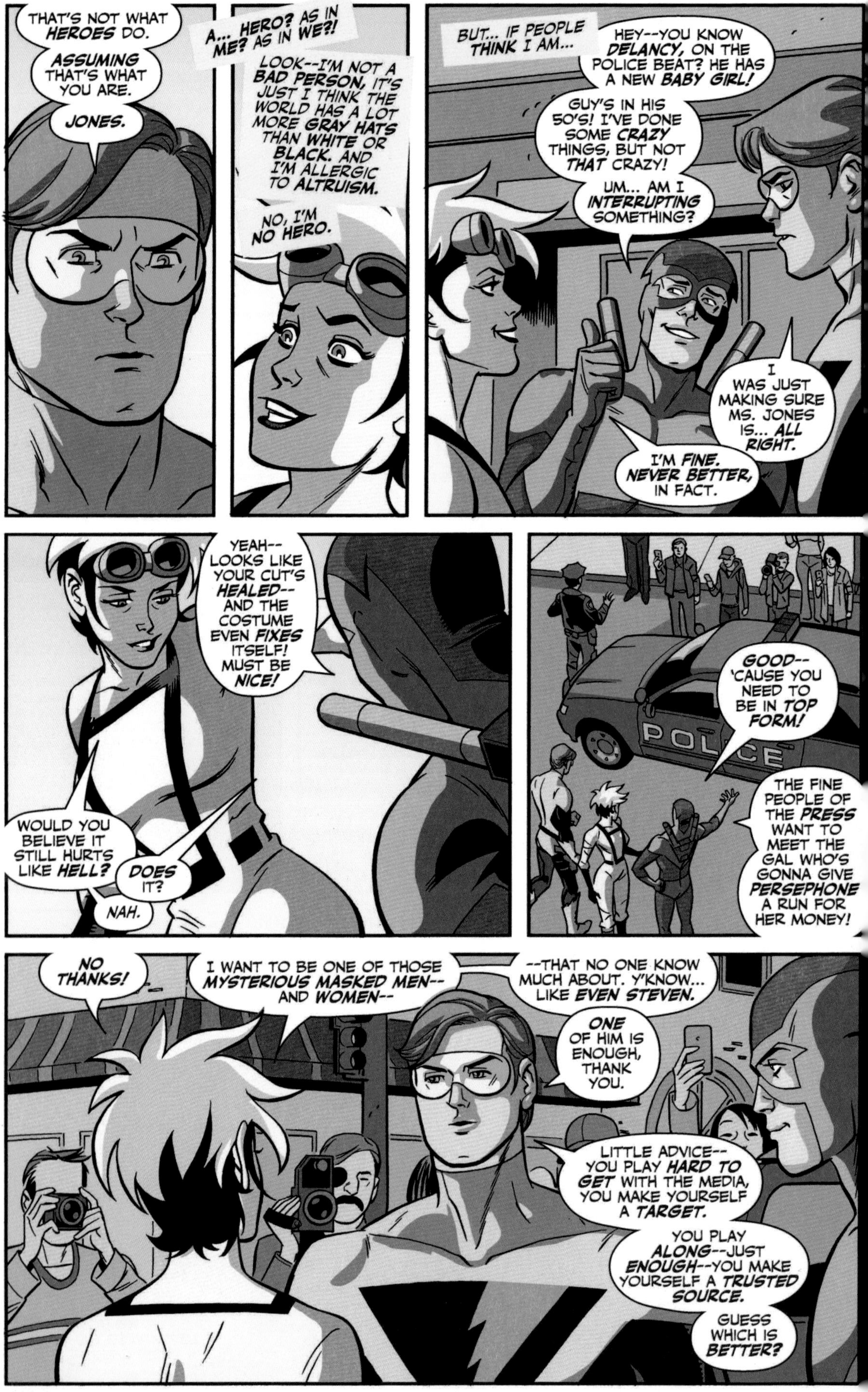

THAT'S NOT WHAT HEROES DO.
ASSUMING THAT'S WHAT YOU ARE.
JONES.
A... HERO? AS IN ME? AS IN WE?!
LOOK--I'M NOT A BAD PERSON, IT'S JUST I THINK THE WORLD HAS A LOT MORE GRAY HATS THAN WHITE OR BLACK. AND I'M ALLERGIC TO ALTRUISM.
NO, I'M NO HERO.
BUT... IF PEOPLE THINK I AM...
HEY--YOU KNOW DELANCY, ON THE POLICE BEAT? HE HAS A NEW BABY GIRL!
GUY'S IN HIS 50'S! I'VE DONE SOME CRAZY THINGS, BUT NOT THAT CRAZY!
UM... AM I INTERRUPTING SOMETHING?
I WAS JUST MAKING SURE MS. JONES IS... ALL RIGHT.
I'M FINE. NEVER BETTER, IN FACT.
YEAH--LOOKS LIKE YOUR CUT'S HEALED--AND THE COSTUME EVEN FIXES ITSELF! MUST BE NICE!
WOULD YOU BELIEVE IT STILL HURTS LIKE HELL?
DOES IT?
NAH.
POLICE
GOOD--'CAUSE YOU NEED TO BE IN TOP FORM!
THE FINE PEOPLE OF THE PRESS WANT TO MEET THE GAL WHO'S GONNA GIVE PERSEPHONE A RUN FOR HER MONEY!
NO THANKS!
I WANT TO BE ONE OF THOSE MYSTERIOUS MASKED MEN--AND WOMEN--
--THAT NO ONE KNOW MUCH ABOUT. Y'KNOW... LIKE EVEN STEVEN.
ONE OF HIM IS ENOUGH, THANK YOU.
LITTLE ADVICE--YOU PLAY HARD TO GET WITH THE MEDIA, YOU MAKE YOURSELF A TARGET.
YOU PLAY ALONG--JUST ENOUGH--YOU MAKE YOURSELF A TRUSTED SOURCE.
GUESS WHICH IS BETTER?

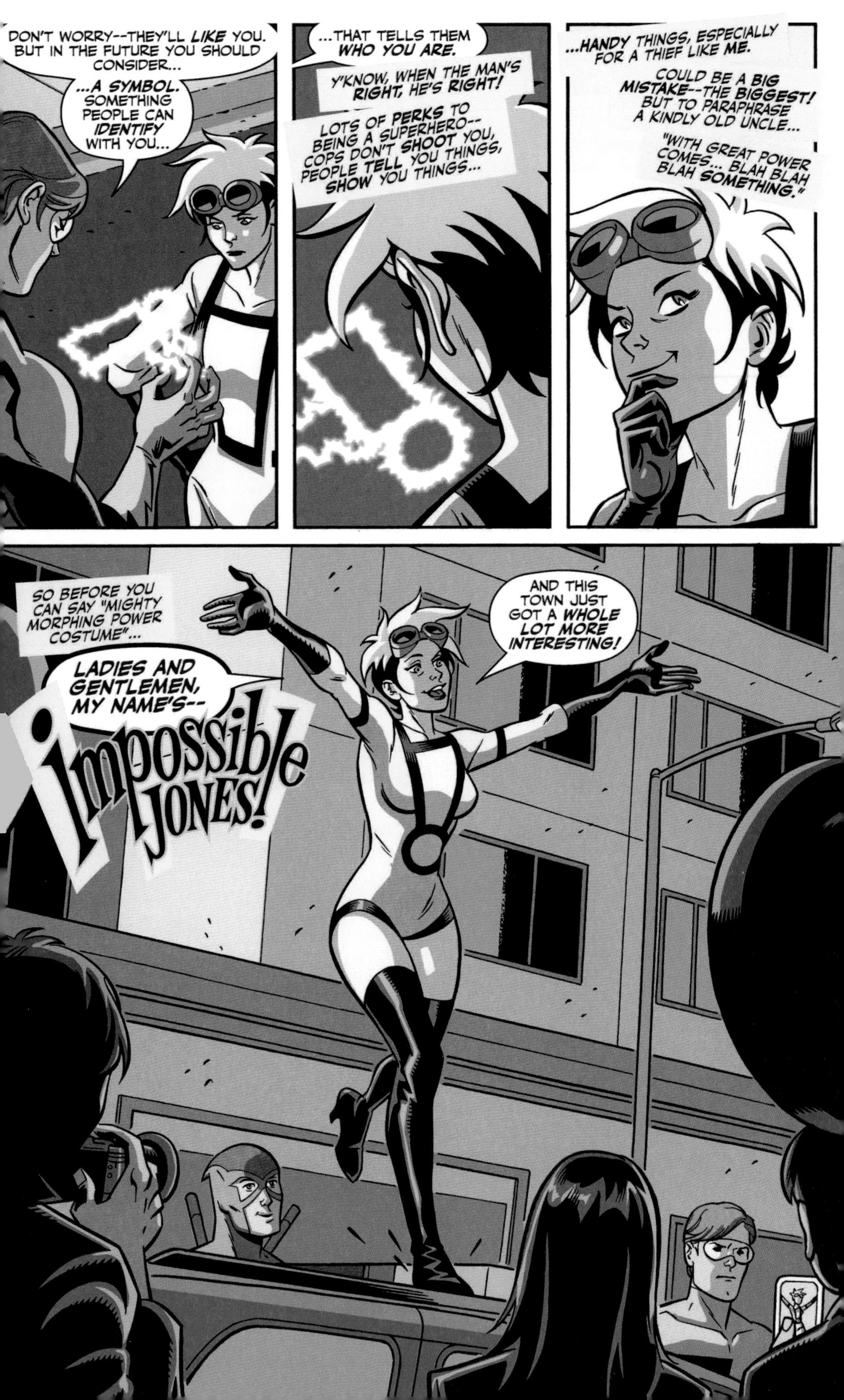
DON'T WORRY--THEY'LL LIKE YOU. BUT IN THE FUTURE YOU SHOULD CONSIDER...
...A SYMBOL. SOMETHING PEOPLE CAN IDENTIFY WITH YOU...
...THAT TELLS THEM WHO YOU ARE.
Y'KNOW, WHEN THE MAN'S RIGHT, HE'S RIGHT!
LOTS OF PERKS TO BEING A SUPERHERO-- COPS DON'T SHOOT YOU, PEOPLE TELL YOU THINGS, SHOW YOU THINGS...
...HANDY THINGS, ESPECIALLY FOR A THIEF LIKE ME.
COULD BE A BIG MISTAKE--THE BIGGEST! BUT TO PARAPHRASE A KINDLY OLD UNCLE...
"WITH GREAT POWER COMES... BLAH BLAH BLAH SOMETHING."
SO BEFORE YOU CAN SAY "MIGHTY MORPHING POWER COSTUME"...
LADIES AND GENTLEMEN, MY NAME'S--
impossible JONES!
AND THIS TOWN JUST GOT A WHOLE LOT MORE INTERESTING!

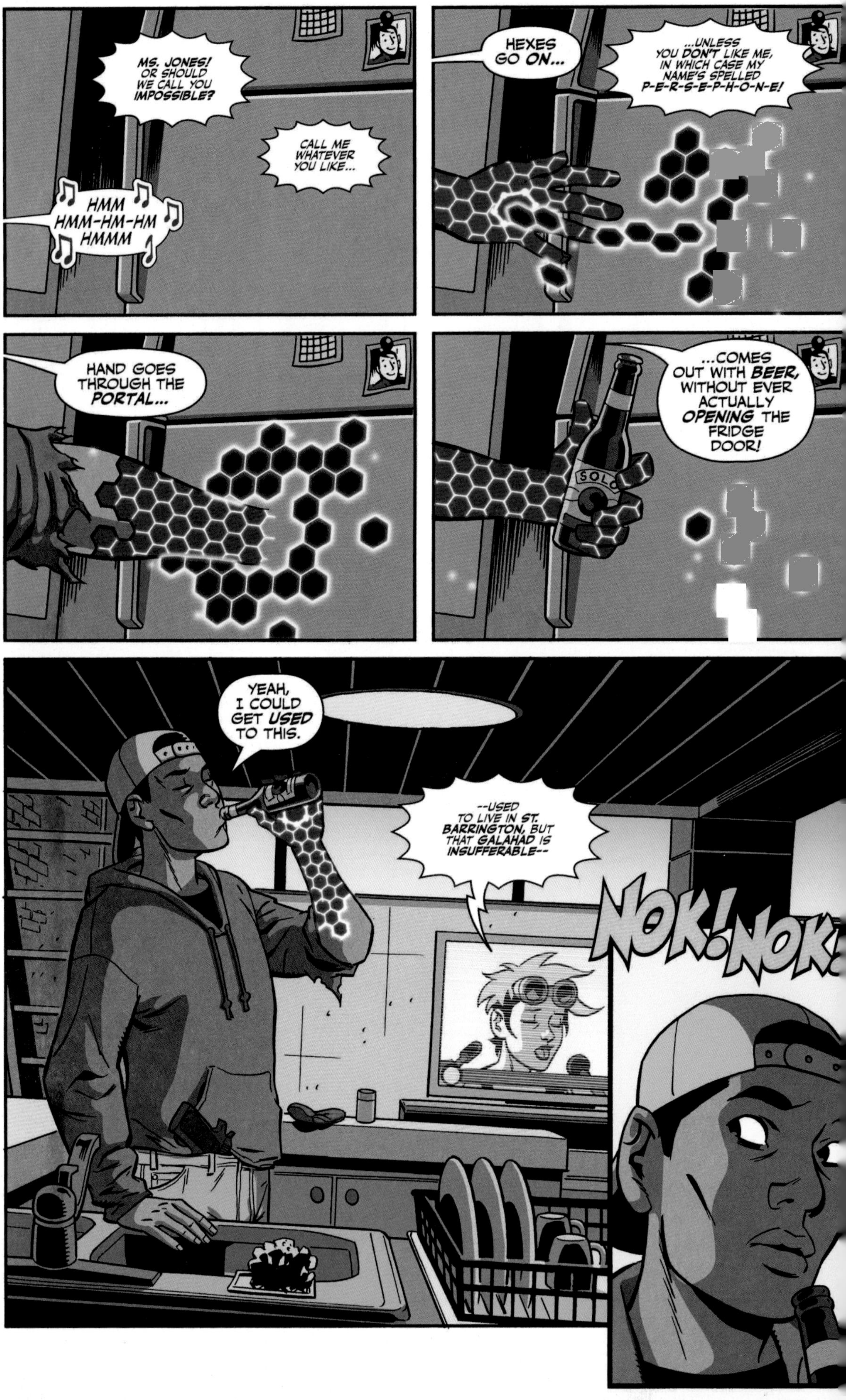
MS. JONES! OR SHOULD WE CALL YOU IMPOSSIBLE?
CALL ME WHATEVER YOU LIKE...
HMM HMM-HM-HM HMMM
HEXES GO ON...
...UNLESS YOU DON'T LIKE ME, IN WHICH CASE MY NAME'S SPELLED P-E-R-S-E-P-H-O-N-E!
HAND GOES THROUGH THE PORTAL...
...COMES OUT WITH BEER, WITHOUT EVER ACTUALLY OPENING THE FRIDGE DOOR!
SOLO
YEAH, I COULD GET USED TO THIS.
--USED TO LIVE IN ST. BARRINGTON, BUT THAT GALAHAD IS INSUFFERABLE--
NOK! NOK!

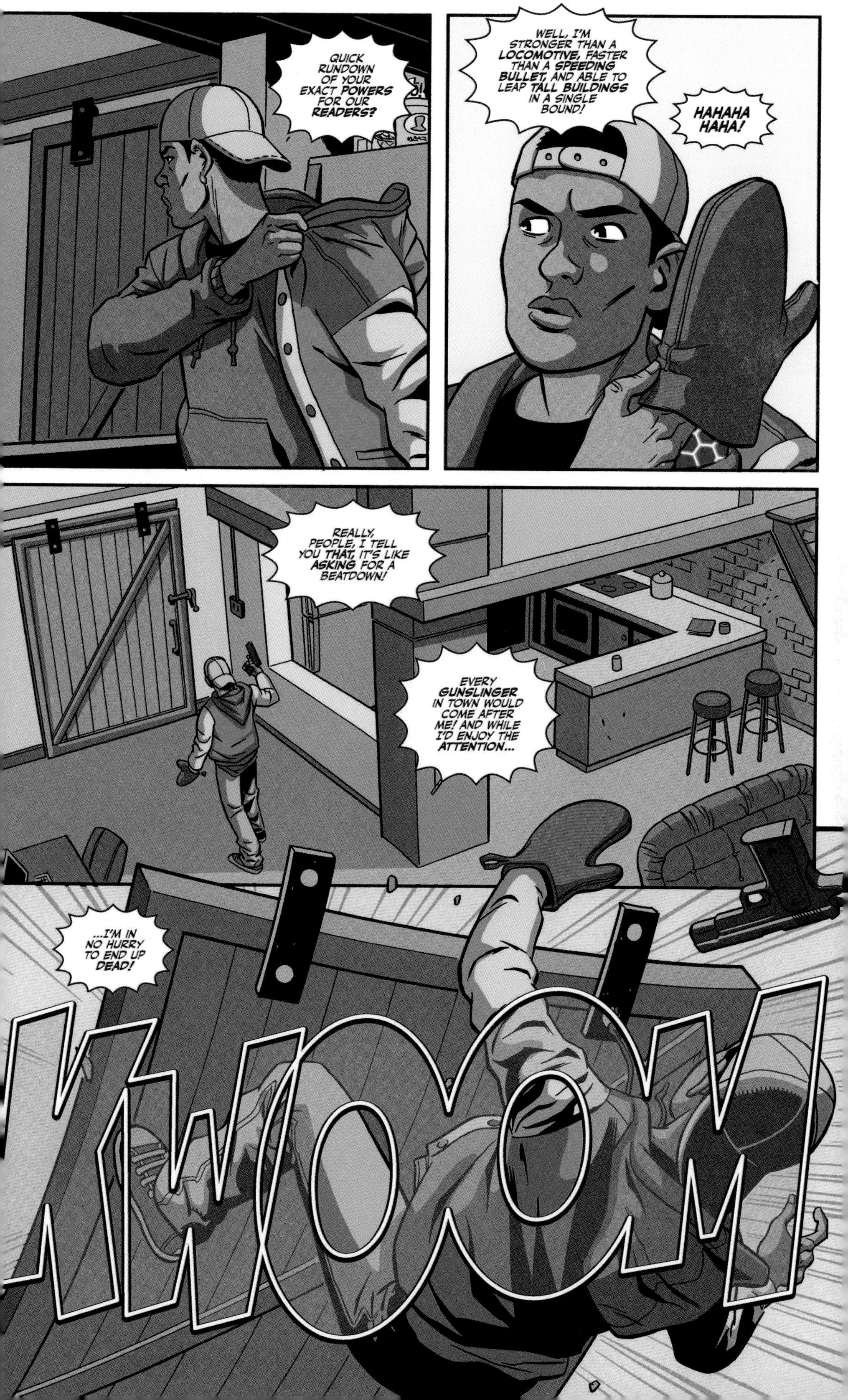
QUICK RUNDOWN OF YOUR EXACT POWERS FOR OUR READERS?
WELL, I'M STRONGER THAN A LOCOMOTIVE, FASTER THAN A SPEEDING BULLET, AND ABLE TO LEAP TALL BUILDINGS IN A SINGLE BOUND!
HAHAHA HAHA!
REALLY, PEOPLE, I TELL YOU THAT, IT'S LIKE ASKING FOR A BEATDOWN!
EVERY GUNSLINGER IN TOWN WOULD COME AFTER ME! AND WHILE I'D ENJOY THE ATTENTION...
...I'M IN NO HURRY TO END UP DEAD!
KWOOM

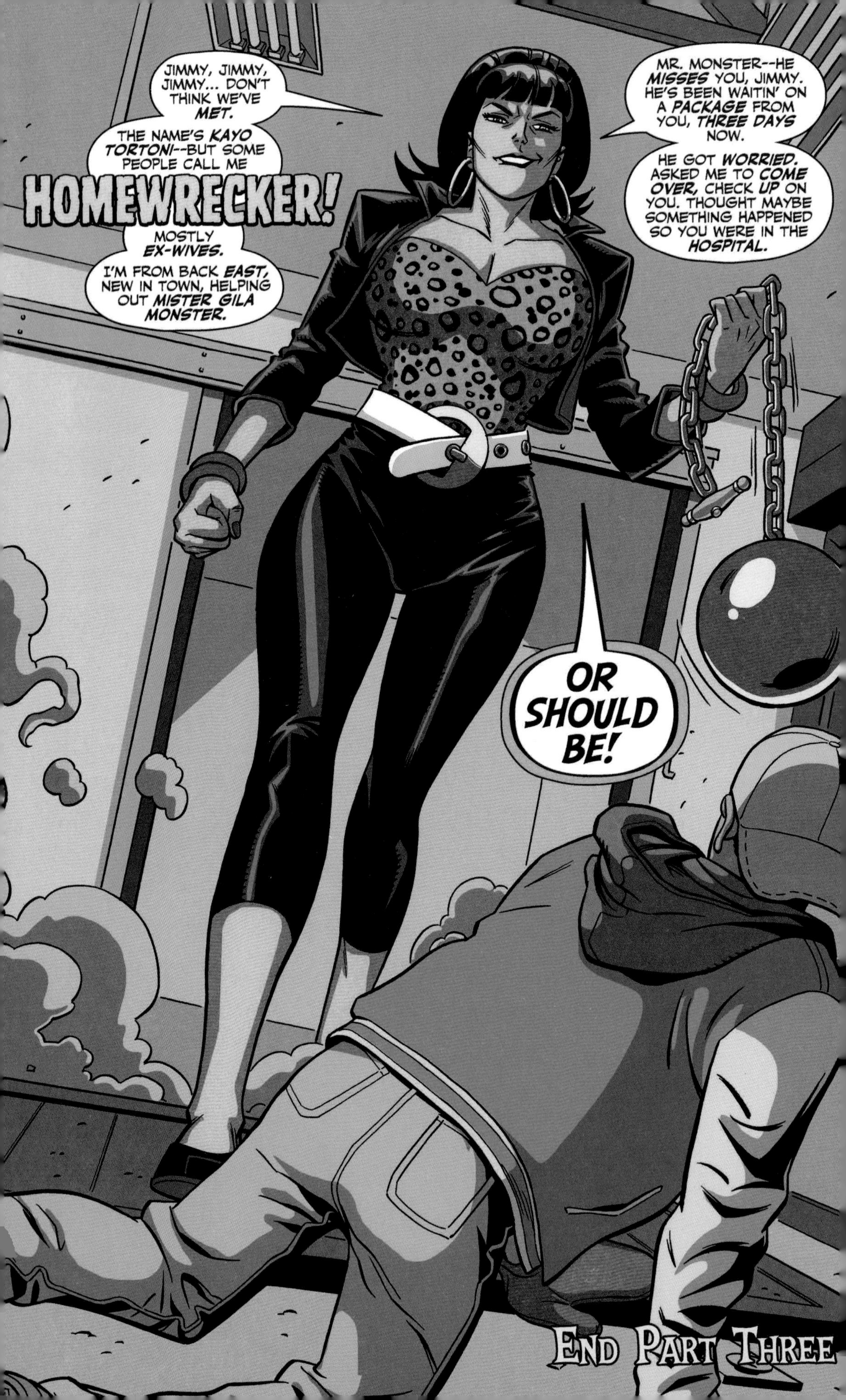
JIMMY, JIMMY, JIMMY... DON'T THINK WE'VE MET.
THE NAME'S KAYO TORTONI--BUT SOME PEOPLE CALL ME
HOMEWRECKER!
MOSTLY EX-WIVES.
I'M FROM BACK EAST, NEW IN TOWN, HELPING OUT MISTER GILA MONSTER.
MR. MONSTER--HE MISSES YOU, JIMMY. HE'S BEEN WAITIN' ON A PACKAGE FROM YOU, THREE DAYS NOW.
HE GOT WORRIED. ASKED ME TO COME OVER, CHECK UP ON YOU. THOUGHT MAYBE SOMETHING HAPPENED SO YOU WERE IN THE HOSPITAL.
OR SHOULD BE!
END PART THREE

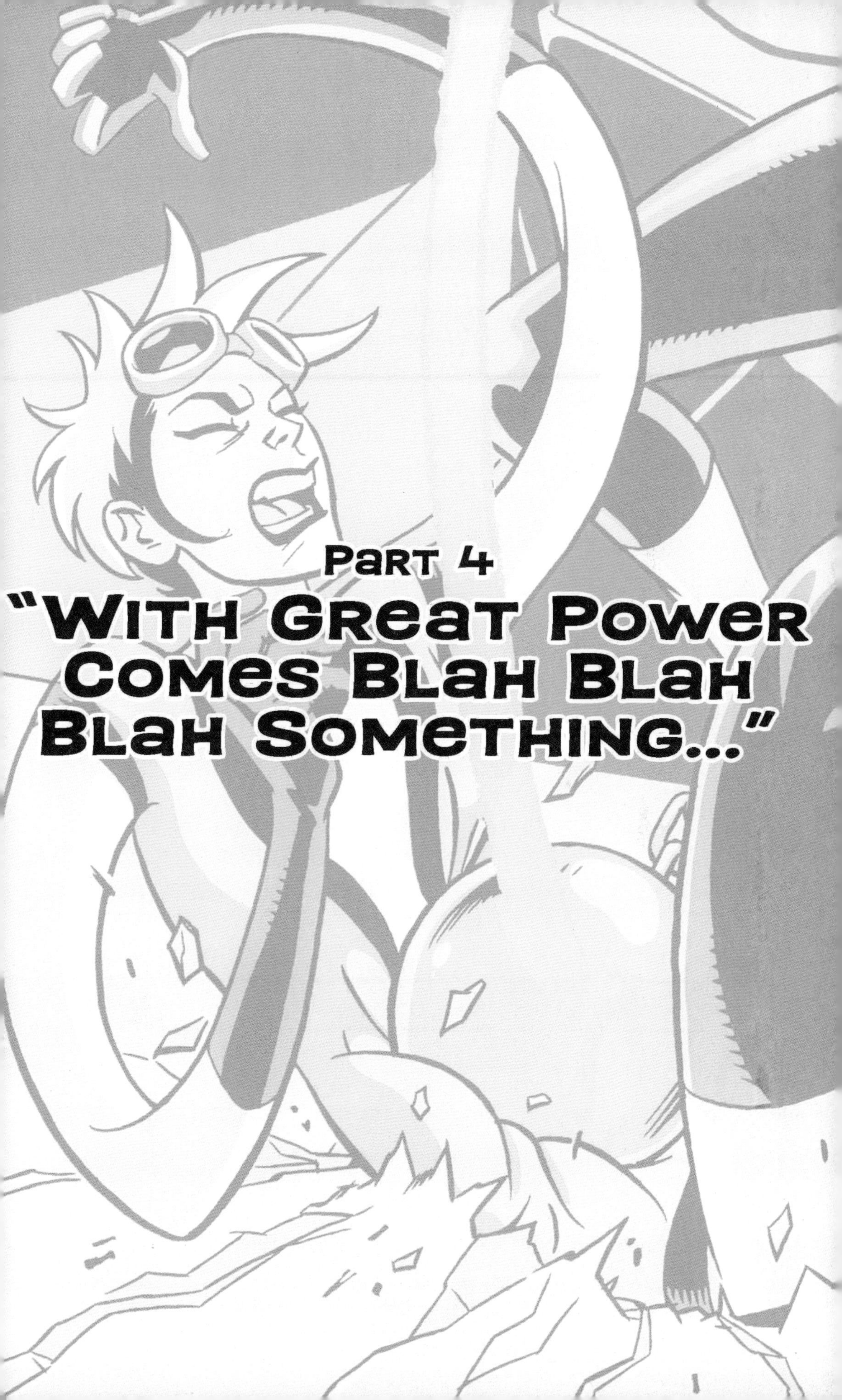

Part 4

"With Great Power Comes Blah Blah Blah Something..."

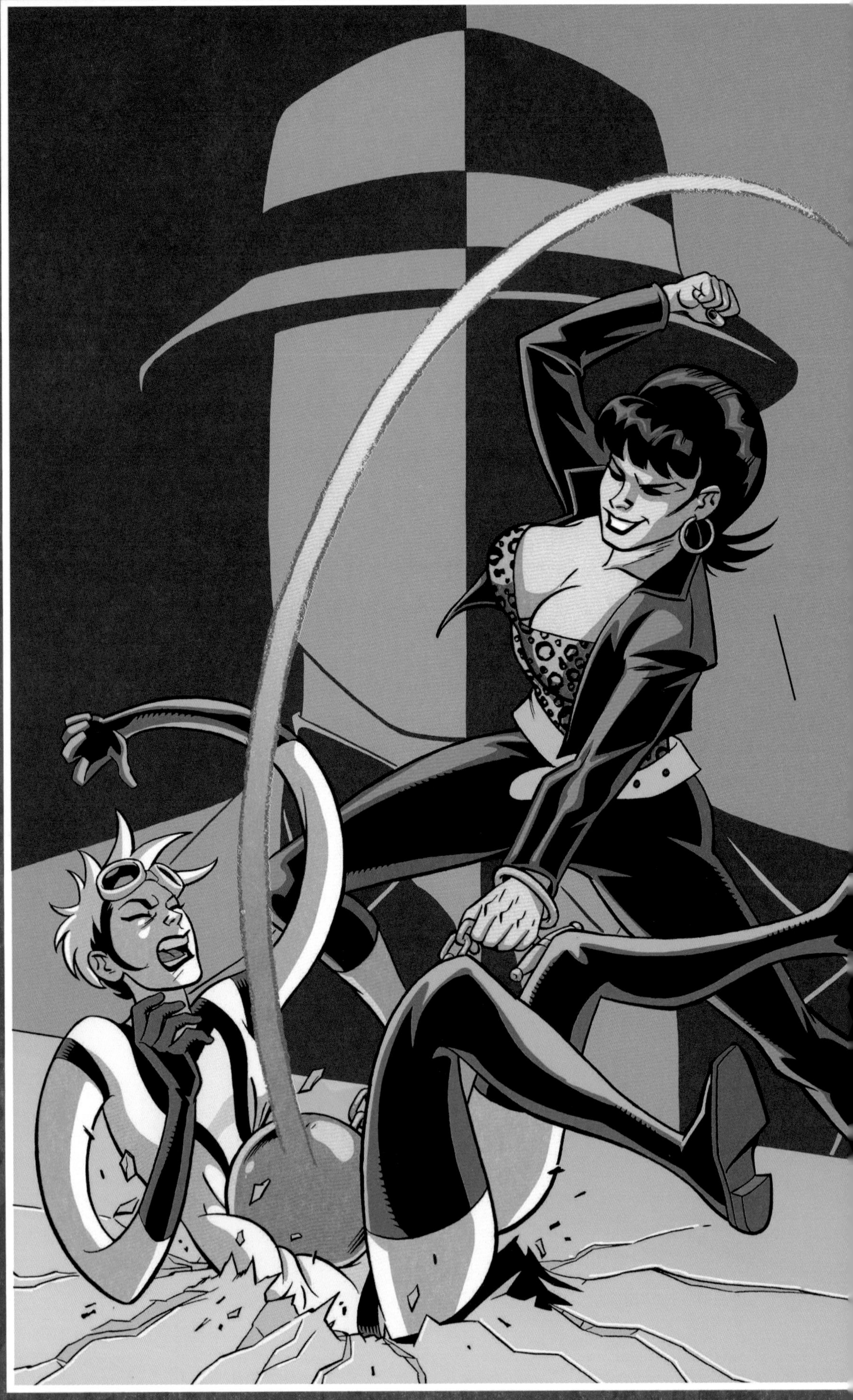

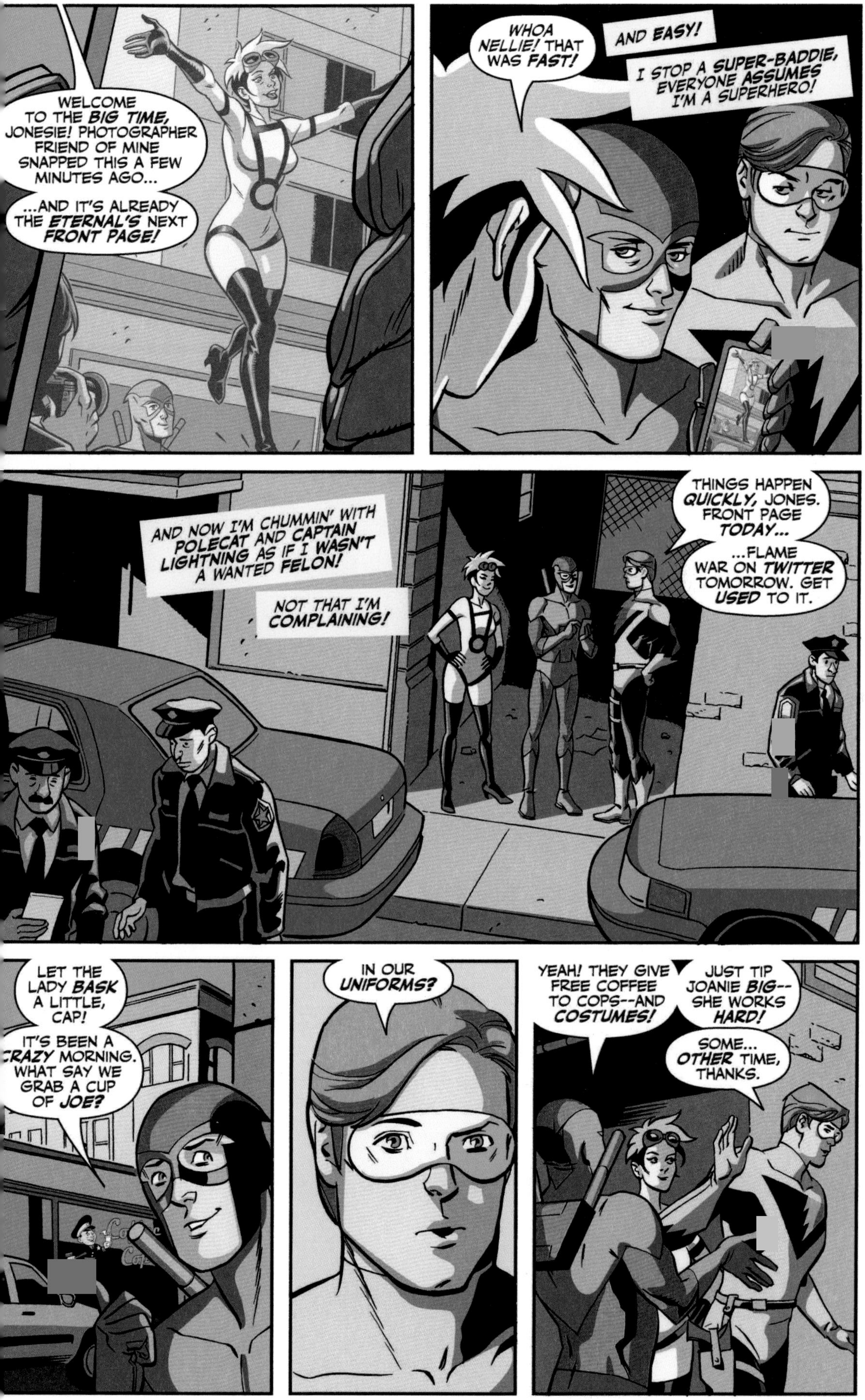
WELCOME TO THE BIG TIME, JONESIE! PHOTOGRAPHER FRIEND OF MINE SNAPPED THIS A FEW MINUTES AGO...
...AND IT'S ALREADY THE ETERNAL'S NEXT FRONT PAGE!
WHOA NELLIE! THAT WAS FAST!
AND EASY!
I STOP A SUPER-BADDIE, EVERYONE ASSUMES I'M A SUPERHERO!
AND NOW I'M CHUMMIN' WITH POLECAT AND CAPTAIN LIGHTNING AS IF I WASN'T A WANTED FELON!
NOT THAT I'M COMPLAINING!
THINGS HAPPEN QUICKLY, JONES. FRONT PAGE TODAY...
...FLAME WAR ON TWITTER TOMORROW. GET USED TO IT.
LET THE LADY BASK A LITTLE, CAP!
IT'S BEEN A CRAZY MORNING. WHAT SAY WE GRAB A CUP OF JOE?
IN OUR UNIFORMS?
YEAH! THEY GIVE FREE COFFEE TO COPS--AND COSTUMES!
JUST TIP JOANIE BIG-- SHE WORKS HARD!
SOME... OTHER TIME, THANKS.

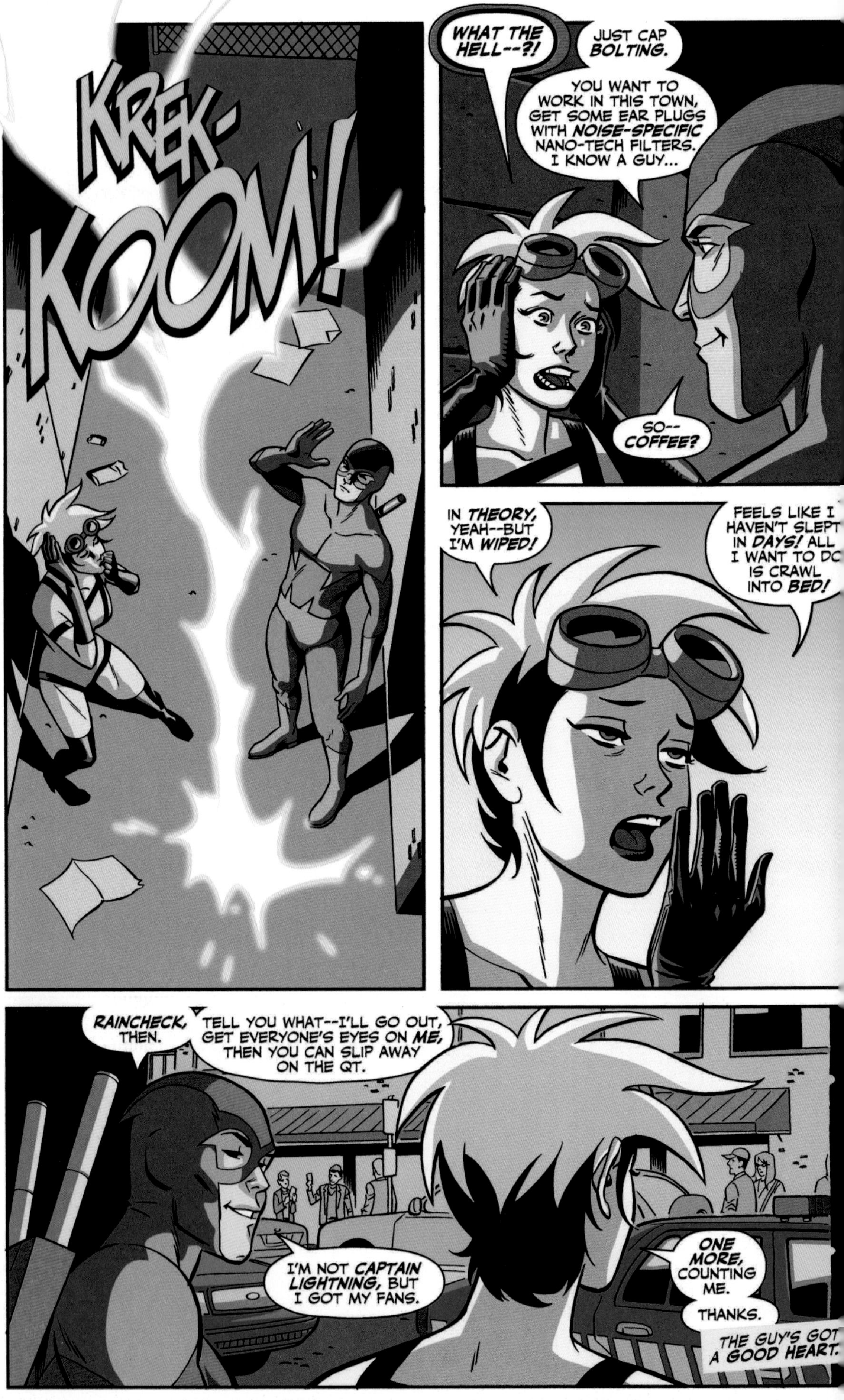
KREK-KOOM!
WHAT THE HELL--?!
JUST CAP BOLTING.
YOU WANT TO WORK IN THIS TOWN, GET SOME EAR PLUGS WITH NOISE-SPECIFIC NANO-TECH FILTERS. I KNOW A GUY...
SO--COFFEE?
IN THEORY, YEAH--BUT I'M WIPED!
FEELS LIKE I HAVEN'T SLEPT IN DAYS! ALL I WANT TO DO IS CRAWL INTO BED!
RAINCHECK, THEN.
TELL YOU WHAT--I'LL GO OUT, GET EVERYONE'S EYES ON ME, THEN YOU CAN SLIP AWAY ON THE QT.
I'M NOT CAPTAIN LIGHTNING, BUT I GOT MY FANS.
ONE MORE, COUNTING ME.
THANKS.
THE GUY'S GOT A GOOD HEART.

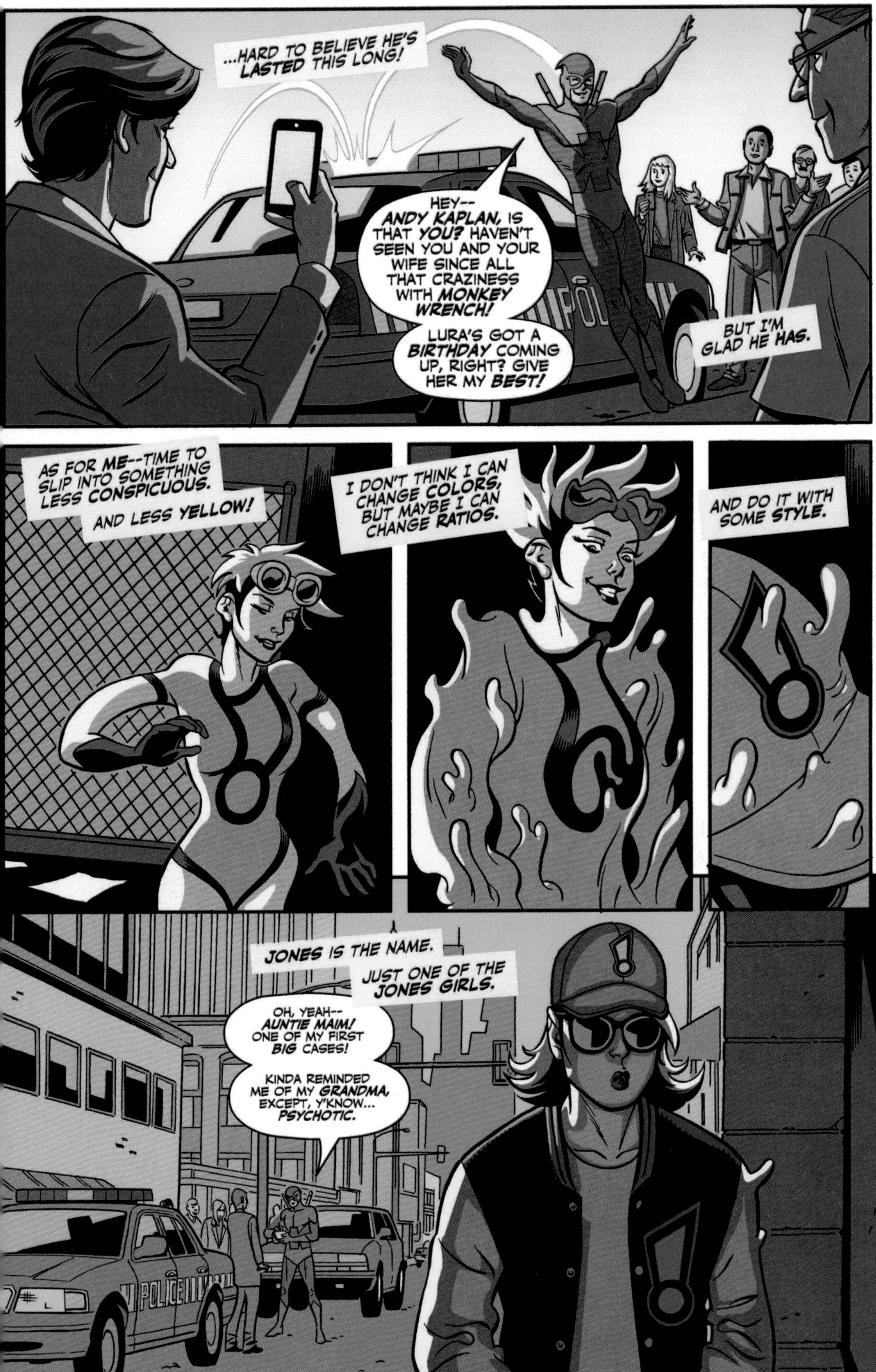
...HARD TO BELIEVE HE'S LASTED THIS LONG!
HEY-- ANDY KAPLAN, IS THAT YOU? HAVEN'T SEEN YOU AND YOUR WIFE SINCE ALL THAT CRAZINESS WITH MONKEY WRENCH!
LURA'S GOT A BIRTHDAY COMING UP, RIGHT? GIVE HER MY BEST!
POLICE
BUT I'M GLAD HE HAS.
AS FOR ME--TIME TO SLIP INTO SOMETHING LESS CONSPICUOUS.
AND LESS YELLOW!
I DON'T THINK I CAN CHANGE COLORS, BUT MAYBE I CAN CHANGE RATIOS.
AND DO IT WITH SOME STYLE.
JONES IS THE NAME.
JUST ONE OF THE JONES GIRLS.
OH, YEAH-- AUNTIE MAIM! ONE OF MY FIRST BIG CASES!
KINDA REMINDED ME OF MY GRANDMA, EXCEPT, Y'KNOW... PSYCHOTIC.
POLICE

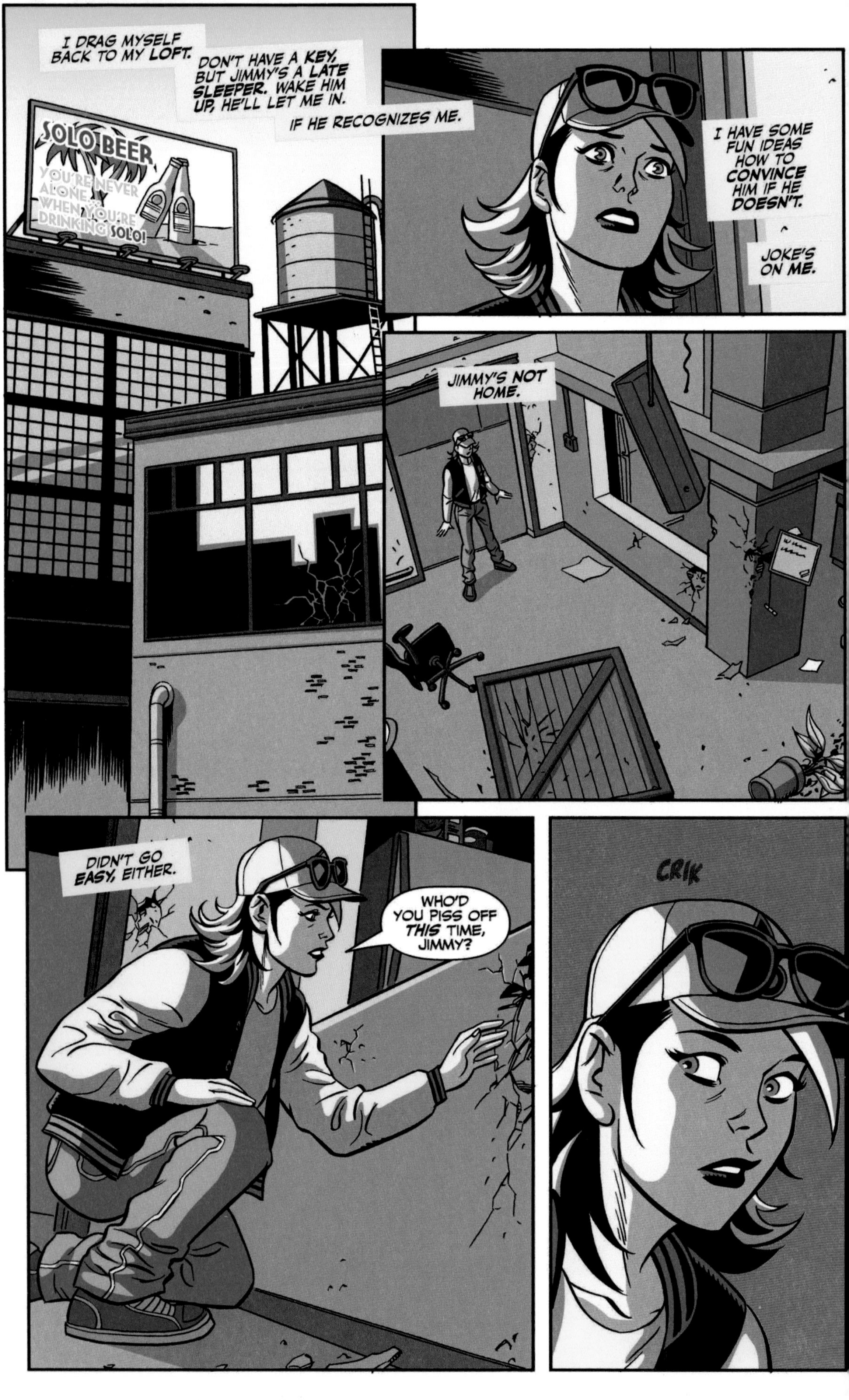

I DRAG MYSELF BACK TO MY LOFT.
DON'T HAVE A KEY, BUT JIMMY'S A LATE SLEEPER. WAKE HIM UP, HE'LL LET ME IN.
IF HE RECOGNIZES ME.
SOLO BEER
YOU'RE NEVER ALONE... WHEN YOU'RE DRINKING SOLO!
I HAVE SOME FUN IDEAS HOW TO CONVINCE HIM IF HE DOESN'T.
JOKE'S ON ME.
JIMMY'S NOT HOME.
DIDN'T GO EASY, EITHER.
WHO'D YOU PISS OFF THIS TIME, JIMMY?
CRIK

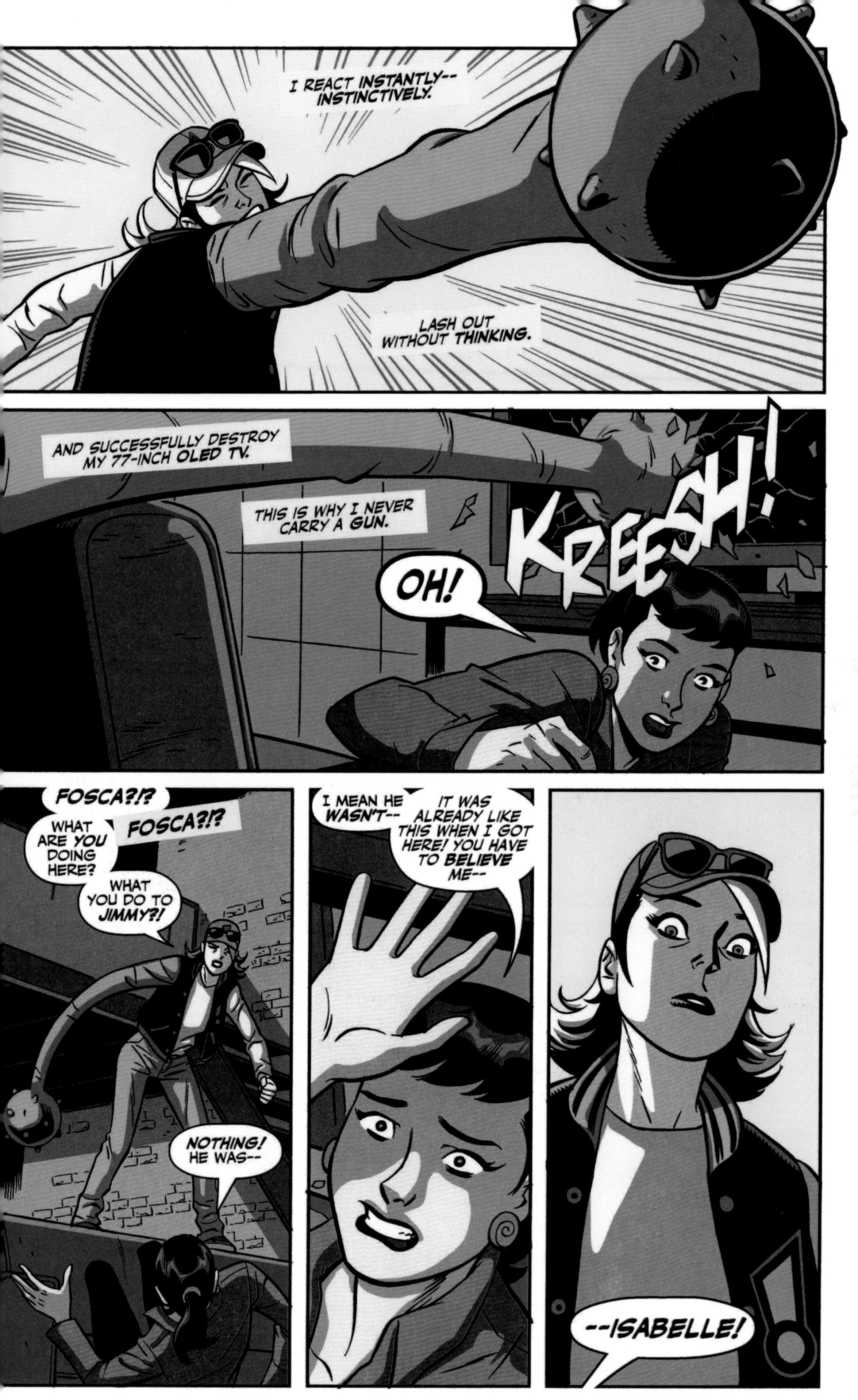

I REACT INSTANTLY--
INSTINCTIVELY.
LASH OUT WITHOUT THINKING.
AND SUCCESSFULLY DESTROY MY 77-INCH OLED TV.
THIS IS WHY I NEVER CARRY A GUN.
KREESH!
OH!
FOSCA?!?
WHAT ARE YOU DOING HERE?
FOSCA?!?
WHAT YOU DO TO JIMMY?!
NOTHING! HE WAS--
I MEAN HE WASN'T--
IT WAS ALREADY LIKE THIS WHEN I GOT HERE! YOU HAVE TO BELIEVE ME--
--ISABELLE!

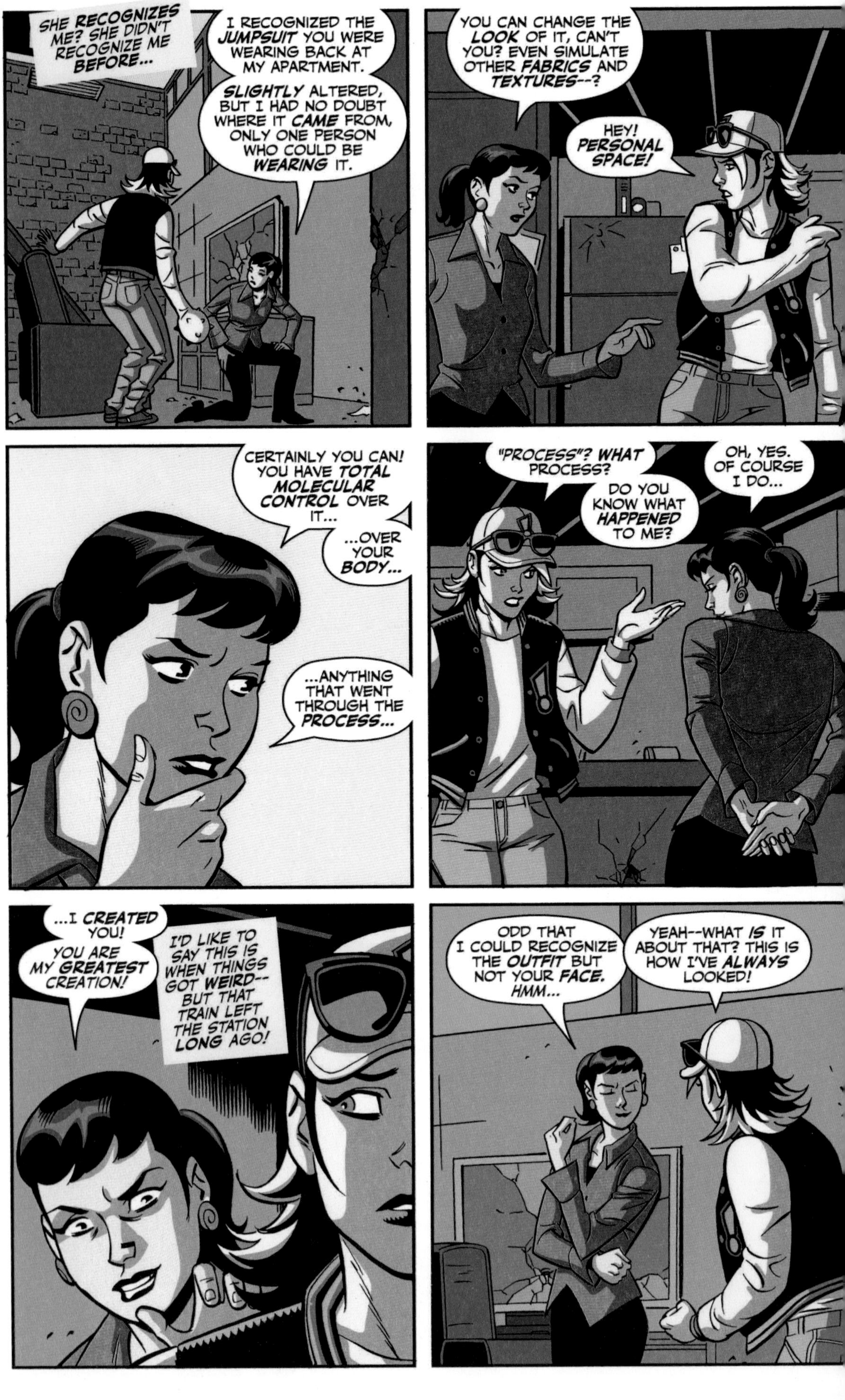
SHE RECOGNIZES ME? SHE DIDN'T RECOGNIZE ME BEFORE...
I RECOGNIZED THE JUMPSUIT YOU WERE WEARING BACK AT MY APARTMENT.
SLIGHTLY ALTERED, BUT I HAD NO DOUBT WHERE IT CAME FROM, ONLY ONE PERSON WHO COULD BE WEARING IT.
YOU CAN CHANGE THE LOOK OF IT, CAN'T YOU? EVEN SIMULATE OTHER FABRICS AND TEXTURES--?
HEY! PERSONAL SPACE!
CERTAINLY YOU CAN! YOU HAVE TOTAL MOLECULAR CONTROL OVER IT...
...OVER YOUR BODY...
...ANYTHING THAT WENT THROUGH THE PROCESS...
"PROCESS"? WHAT PROCESS?
DO YOU KNOW WHAT HAPPENED TO ME?
OH, YES. OF COURSE I DO...
...I CREATED YOU!
YOU ARE MY GREATEST CREATION!
I'D LIKE TO SAY THIS IS WHEN THINGS GOT WEIRD-- BUT THAT TRAIN LEFT THE STATION LONG AGO!
ODD THAT I COULD RECOGNIZE THE OUTFIT BUT NOT YOUR FACE. HMM...
YEAH--WHAT IS IT ABOUT THAT? THIS IS HOW I'VE ALWAYS LOOKED!

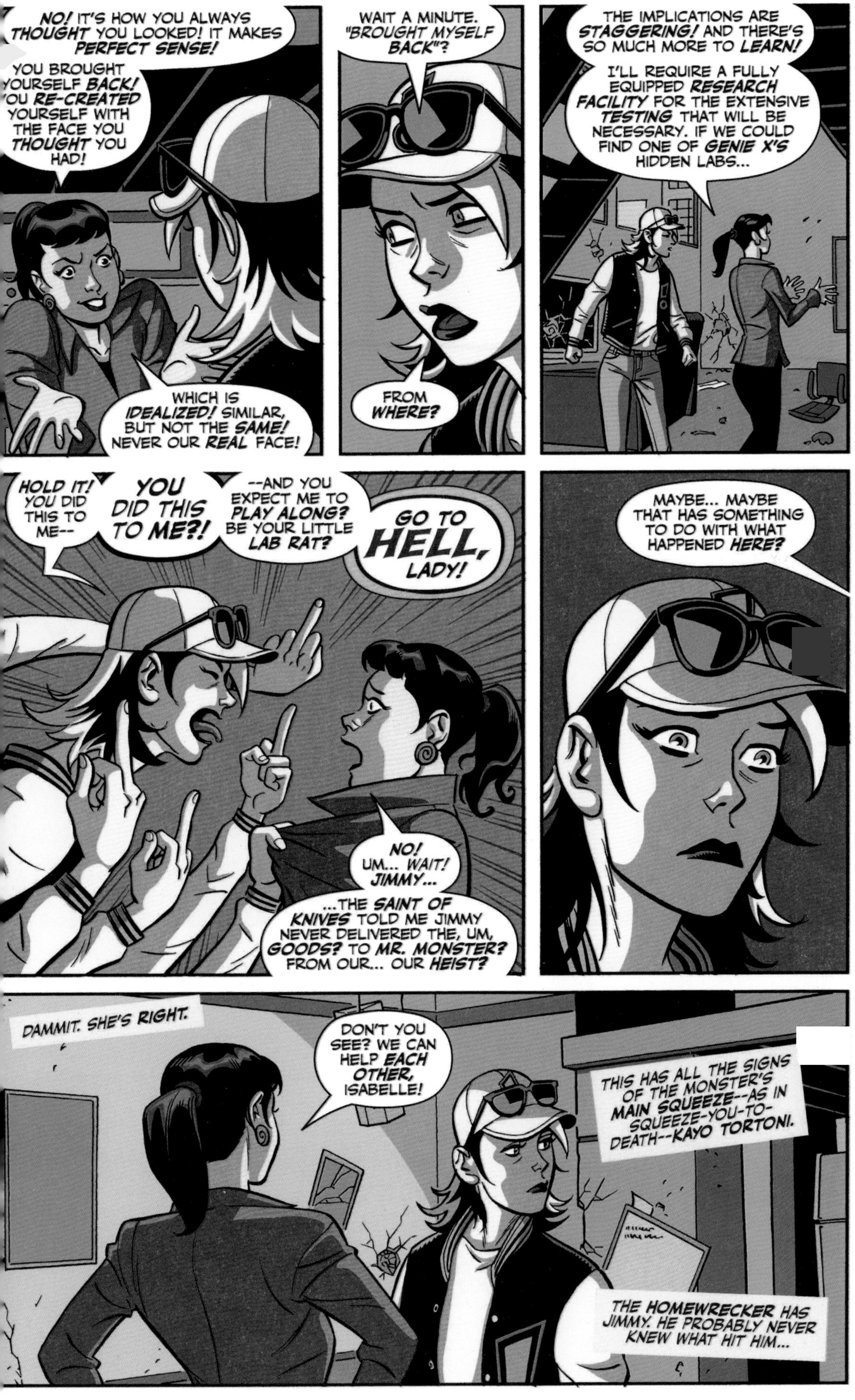
NO! IT'S HOW YOU ALWAYS THOUGHT YOU LOOKED! IT MAKES PERFECT SENSE!
YOU BROUGHT YOURSELF BACK! YOU RE-CREATED YOURSELF WITH THE FACE YOU THOUGHT YOU HAD!
WHICH IS IDEALIZED! SIMILAR, BUT NOT THE SAME! NEVER OUR REAL FACE!
WAIT A MINUTE. "BROUGHT MYSELF BACK"?
FROM WHERE?
THE IMPLICATIONS ARE STAGGERING! AND THERE'S SO MUCH MORE TO LEARN!
I'LL REQUIRE A FULLY EQUIPPED RESEARCH FACILITY FOR THE EXTENSIVE TESTING THAT WILL BE NECESSARY. IF WE COULD FIND ONE OF GENIE X'S HIDDEN LABS...
HOLD IT! YOU DID THIS TO ME--
YOU DID THIS TO ME?!
--AND YOU EXPECT ME TO PLAY ALONG? BE YOUR LITTLE LAB RAT?
GO TO HELL, LADY!
NO! UM... WAIT! JIMMY...
...THE SAINT OF KNIVES TOLD ME JIMMY NEVER DELIVERED THE, UM, GOODS? TO MR. MONSTER? FROM OUR... OUR HEIST?
MAYBE... MAYBE THAT HAS SOMETHING TO DO WITH WHAT HAPPENED HERE?
DAMMIT. SHE'S RIGHT.
DON'T YOU SEE? WE CAN HELP EACH OTHER, ISABELLE!
THIS HAS ALL THE SIGNS OF THE MONSTER'S MAIN SQUEEZE--AS IN SQUEEZE-YOU-TO-DEATH--KAYO TORTONI.
THE HOMEWRECKER HAS JIMMY. HE PROBABLY NEVER KNEW WHAT HIT HIM...

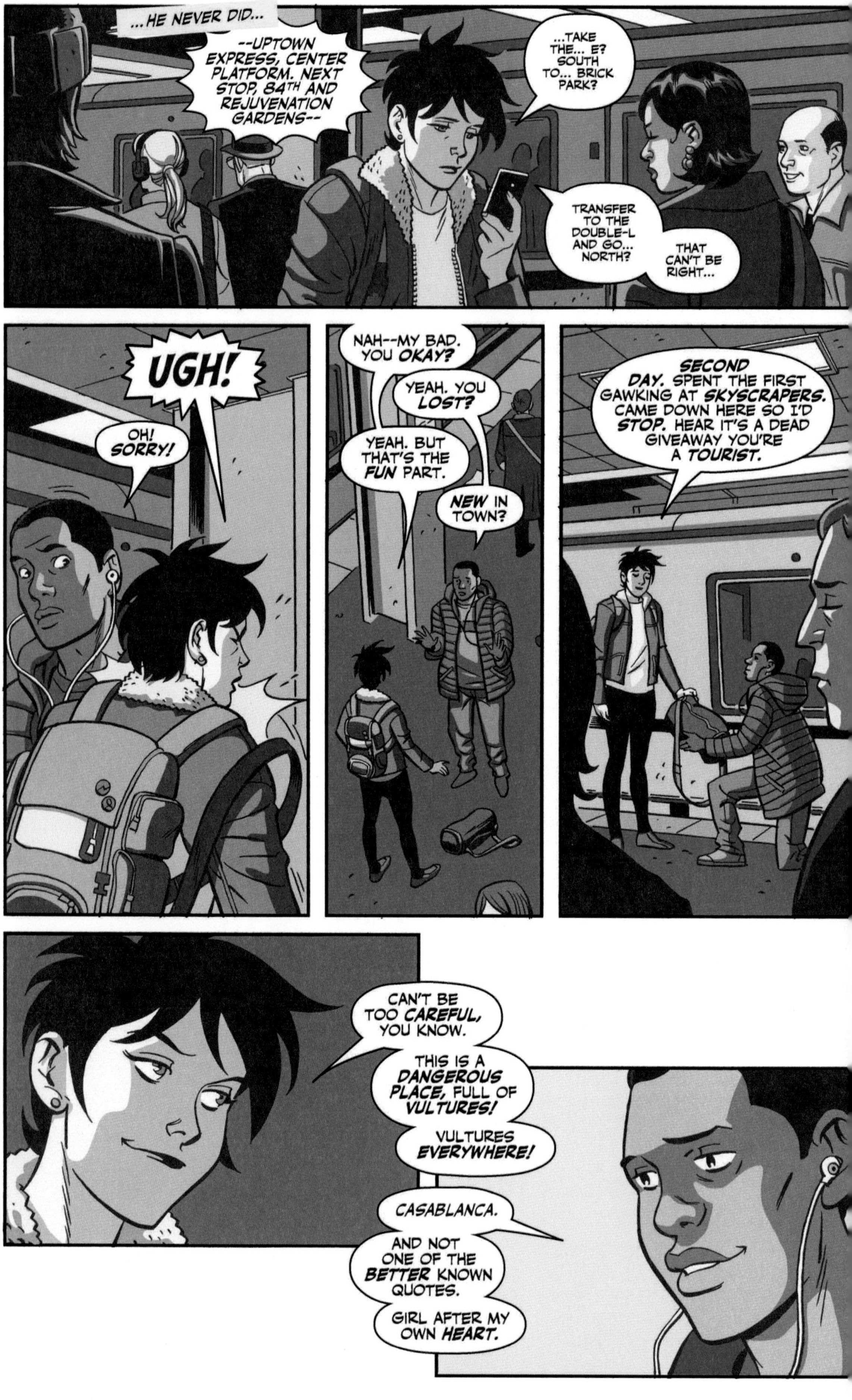
...HE NEVER DID...
--UPTOWN EXPRESS, CENTER PLATFORM. NEXT STOP, 84TH AND REJUVENATION GARDENS--
...TAKE THE... E? SOUTH TO... BRICK PARK?
TRANSFER TO THE DOUBLE-L AND GO... NORTH?
THAT CAN'T BE RIGHT...
UGH!
OH! SORRY!
NAH--MY BAD. YOU OKAY?
YEAH. YOU LOST?
YEAH. BUT THAT'S THE FUN PART.
NEW IN TOWN?
SECOND DAY. SPENT THE FIRST GAWKING AT SKYSCRAPERS. CAME DOWN HERE SO I'D STOP. HEAR IT'S A DEAD GIVEAWAY YOU'RE A TOURIST.
CAN'T BE TOO CAREFUL, YOU KNOW.
THIS IS A DANGEROUS PLACE, FULL OF VULTURES!
VULTURES EVERYWHERE!
CASABLANCA.
AND NOT ONE OF THE BETTER KNOWN QUOTES.
GIRL AFTER MY OWN HEART.

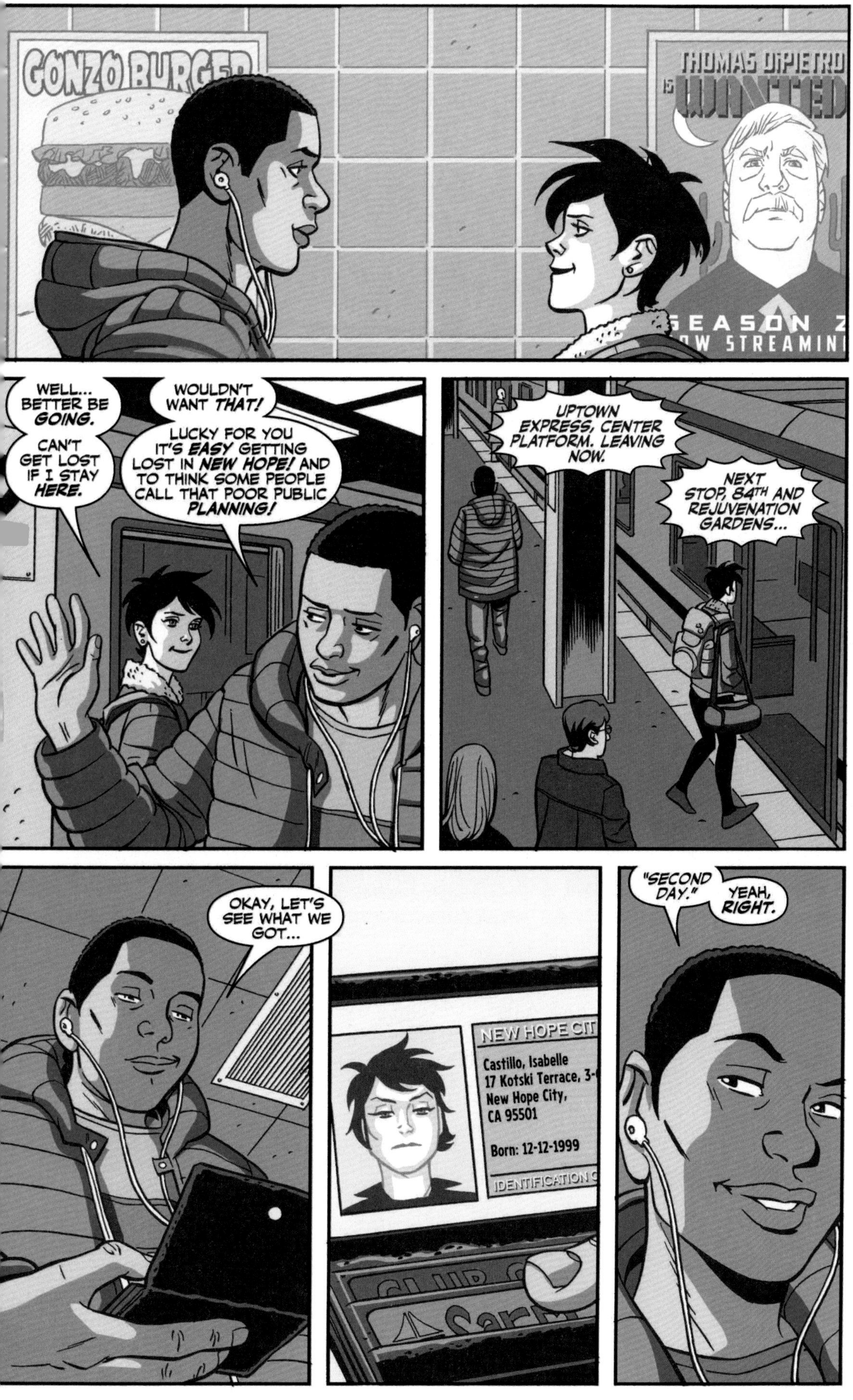
GONZO BURGER
THOMAS DIPIETRO IS WANTED
SEASON 2
NOW STREAMING
WELL... BETTER BE GOING.
CAN'T GET LOST IF I STAY HERE.
WOULDN'T WANT THAT!
LUCKY FOR YOU IT'S EASY GETTING LOST IN NEW HOPE! AND TO THINK SOME PEOPLE CALL THAT POOR PUBLIC PLANNING!
UPTOWN EXPRESS, CENTER PLATFORM. LEAVING NOW.
NEXT STOP, 84TH AND REJUVENATION GARDENS...
OKAY, LET'S SEE WHAT WE GOT...
NEW HOPE CIT
Castillo, Isabelle
17 Kotski Terrace, 3-
New Hope City,
CA 95501
Born: 12-12-1999
IDENTIFICATION C
"SECOND DAY."
YEAH, RIGHT.

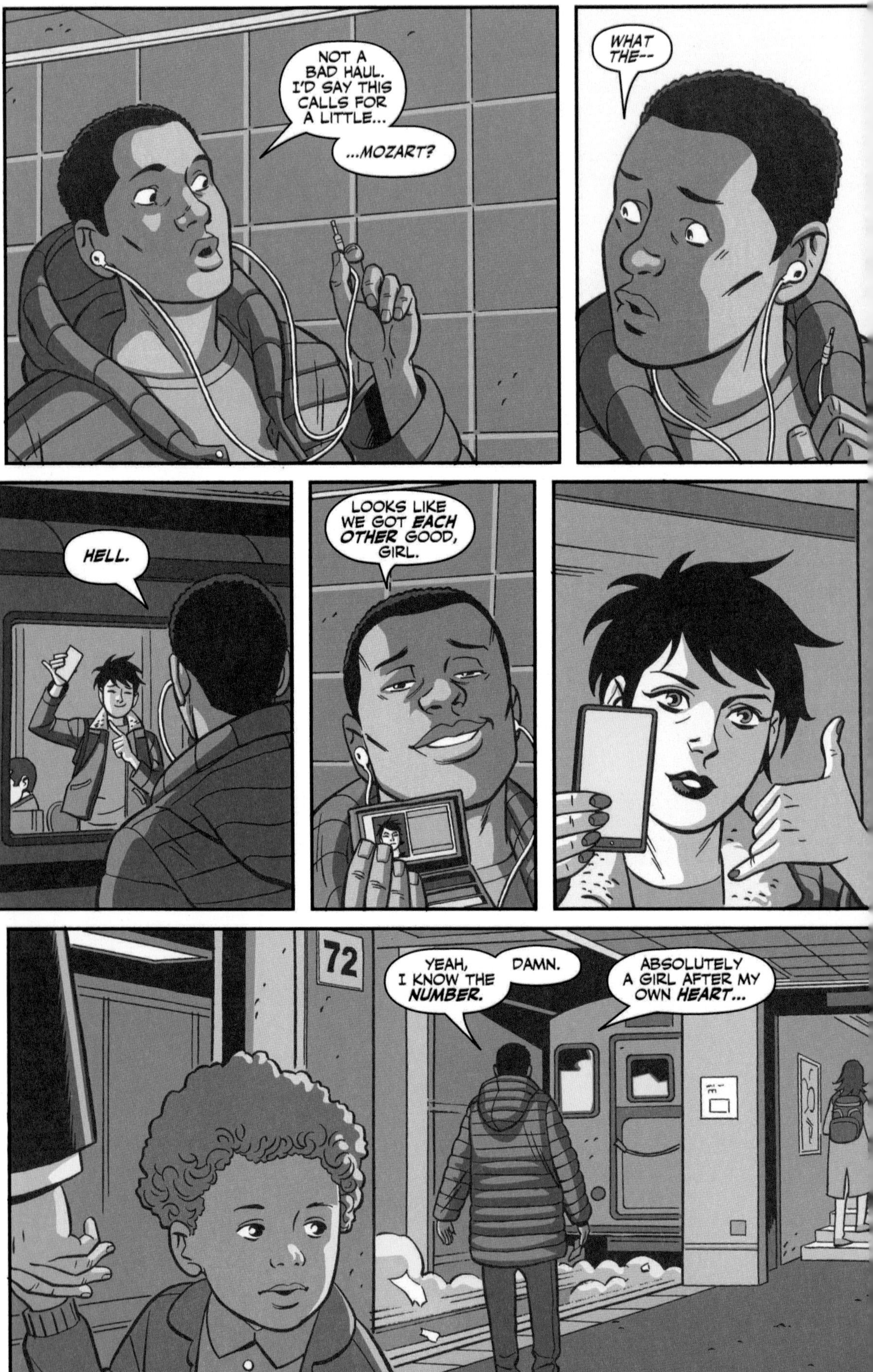
NOT A BAD HAUL. I'D SAY THIS CALLS FOR A LITTLE...
...MOZART?
WHAT THE--
HELL.
LOOKS LIKE WE GOT *EACH OTHER* GOOD, GIRL.
YEAH, I KNOW THE *NUMBER.*
DAMN.
ABSOLUTELY A GIRL AFTER MY OWN *HEART...*
72

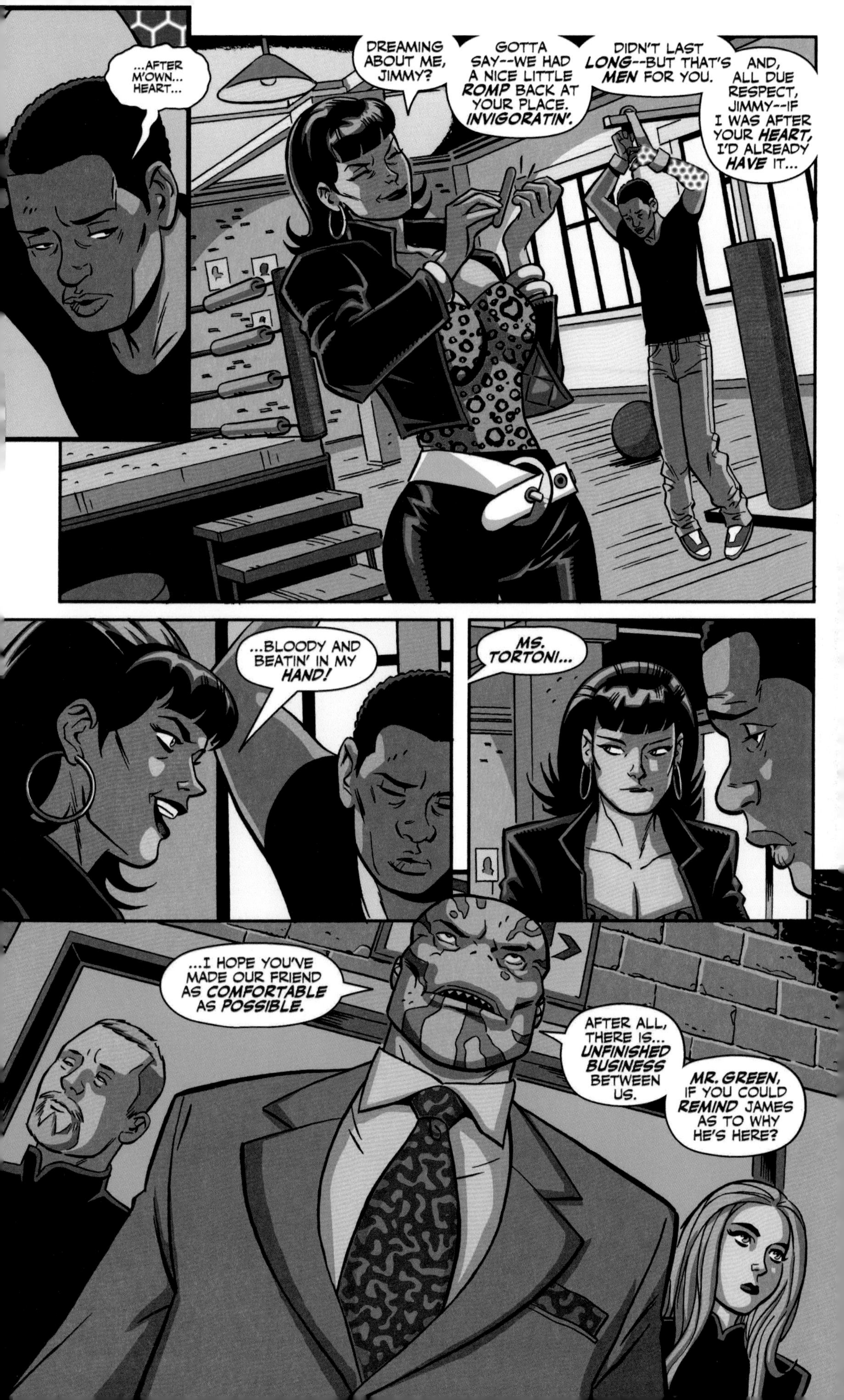
...AFTER M'OWN... HEART...
DREAMING ABOUT ME, JIMMY?
GOTTA SAY--WE HAD A NICE LITTLE ROMP BACK AT YOUR PLACE. INVIGORATIN'.
DIDN'T LAST LONG--BUT THAT'S MEN FOR YOU.
AND, ALL DUE RESPECT, JIMMY--IF I WAS AFTER YOUR HEART, I'D ALREADY HAVE IT...
...BLOODY AND BEATIN' IN MY HAND!
MS. TORTONI...
...I HOPE YOU'VE MADE OUR FRIEND AS COMFORTABLE AS POSSIBLE.
AFTER ALL, THERE IS... UNFINISHED BUSINESS BETWEEN US.
MR. GREEN, IF YOU COULD REMIND JAMES AS TO WHY HE'S HERE?

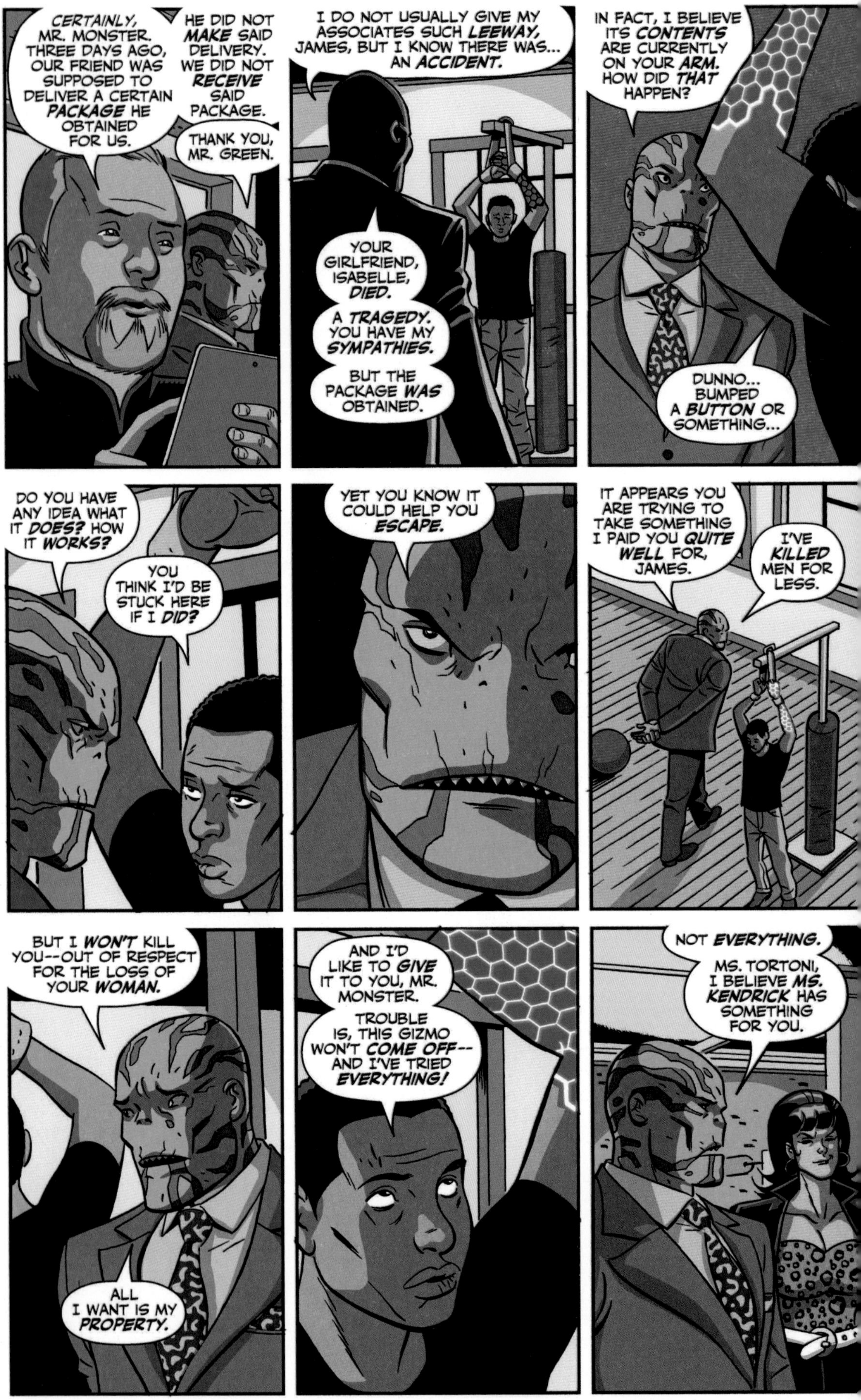
CERTAINLY, MR. MONSTER. THREE DAYS AGO, OUR FRIEND WAS SUPPOSED TO DELIVER A CERTAIN PACKAGE HE OBTAINED FOR US.
HE DID NOT MAKE SAID DELIVERY. WE DID NOT RECEIVE SAID PACKAGE.
THANK YOU, MR. GREEN.
I DO NOT USUALLY GIVE MY ASSOCIATES SUCH LEEWAY, JAMES, BUT I KNOW THERE WAS... AN ACCIDENT.
YOUR GIRLFRIEND, ISABELLE, DIED.
A TRAGEDY. YOU HAVE MY SYMPATHIES.
BUT THE PACKAGE WAS OBTAINED.
IN FACT, I BELIEVE ITS CONTENTS ARE CURRENTLY ON YOUR ARM. HOW DID THAT HAPPEN?
DUNNO... BUMPED A BUTTON OR SOMETHING...
DO YOU HAVE ANY IDEA WHAT IT DOES? HOW IT WORKS?
YOU THINK I'D BE STUCK HERE IF I DID?
YET YOU KNOW IT COULD HELP YOU ESCAPE.
IT APPEARS YOU ARE TRYING TO TAKE SOMETHING I PAID YOU QUITE WELL FOR, JAMES.
I'VE KILLED MEN FOR LESS.
BUT I WON'T KILL YOU--OUT OF RESPECT FOR THE LOSS OF YOUR WOMAN.
ALL I WANT IS MY PROPERTY.
AND I'D LIKE TO GIVE IT TO YOU, MR. MONSTER.
TROUBLE IS, THIS GIZMO WON'T COME OFF--AND I'VE TRIED EVERYTHING!
NOT EVERYTHING.
MS. TORTONI, I BELIEVE MS. KENDRICK HAS SOMETHING FOR YOU.

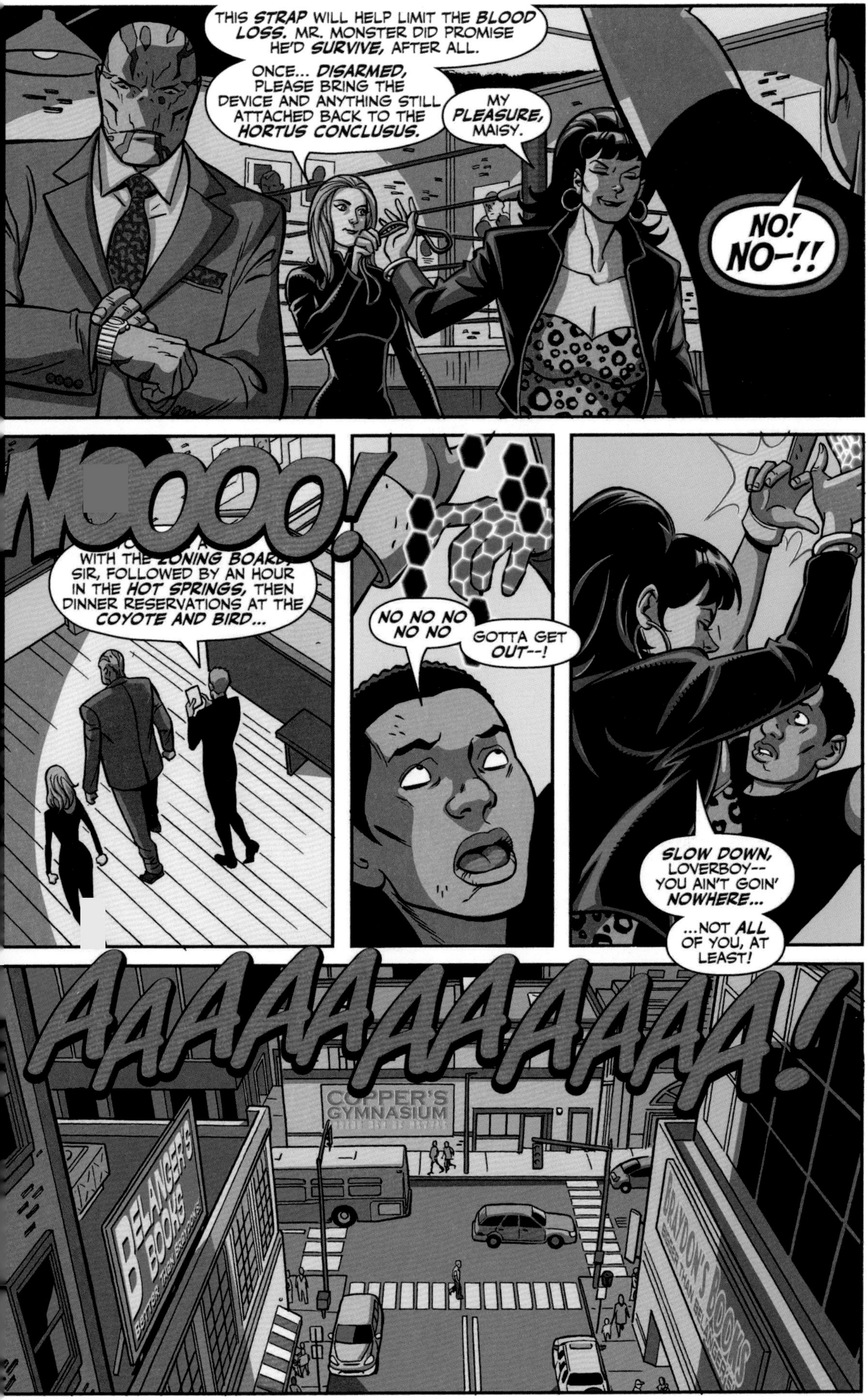

THIS STRAP WILL HELP LIMIT THE BLOOD LOSS. MR. MONSTER DID PROMISE HE'D SURVIVE, AFTER ALL.
ONCE... DISARMED, PLEASE BRING THE DEVICE AND ANYTHING STILL ATTACHED BACK TO THE HORTUS CONCLUSUS.
MY PLEASURE, MAISY.
NO! NO--!!
OOOO!
WITH THE ZONING BOARD, SIR, FOLLOWED BY AN HOUR IN THE HOT SPRINGS, THEN DINNER RESERVATIONS AT THE COYOTE AND BIRD...
NO NO NO NO NO
GOTTA GET OUT--!
SLOW DOWN, LOVERBOY-- YOU AIN'T GOIN' NOWHERE...
...NOT ALL OF YOU, AT LEAST!
AAAAAAAAAAAA!
COPPER'S GYMNASIUM
BELANGER'S BOOKS
BETTER THAN BRAYDON'S
BRAYDON'S BOOKS
BIGGER THAN BELANGER'S

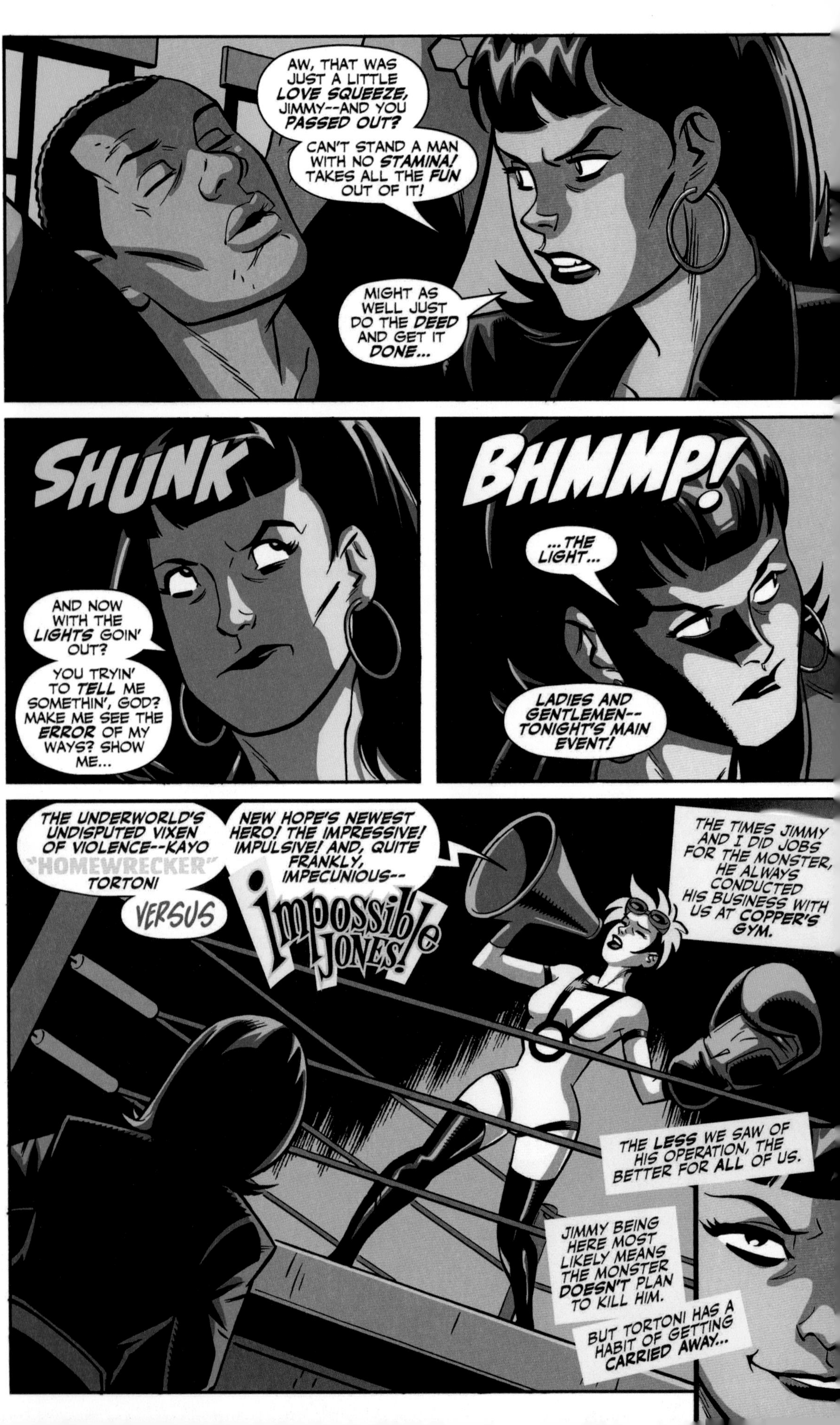

AW, THAT WAS JUST A LITTLE LOVE SQUEEZE, JIMMY--AND YOU PASSED OUT?
CAN'T STAND A MAN WITH NO STAMINA! TAKES ALL THE FUN OUT OF IT!
MIGHT AS WELL JUST DO THE DEED AND GET IT DONE...
SHUNK
AND NOW WITH THE LIGHTS GOIN' OUT?
YOU TRYIN' TO TELL ME SOMETHIN', GOD? MAKE ME SEE THE ERROR OF MY WAYS? SHOW ME...
BHMMP!
...THE LIGHT...
LADIES AND GENTLEMEN-- TONIGHT'S MAIN EVENT!
THE UNDERWORLD'S UNDISPUTED VIXEN OF VIOLENCE--KAYO "HOMEWRECKER" TORTONI
VERSUS
NEW HOPE'S NEWEST HERO! THE IMPRESSIVE! IMPULSIVE! AND, QUITE FRANKLY, IMPECUNIOUS--
impossible JONES!
THE TIMES JIMMY AND I DID JOBS FOR THE MONSTER, HE ALWAYS CONDUCTED HIS BUSINESS WITH US AT COPPER'S GYM.
THE LESS WE SAW OF HIS OPERATION, THE BETTER FOR ALL OF US.
JIMMY BEING HERE MOST LIKELY MEANS THE MONSTER DOESN'T PLAN TO KILL HIM.
BUT TORTONI HAS A HABIT OF GETTING CARRIED AWAY...

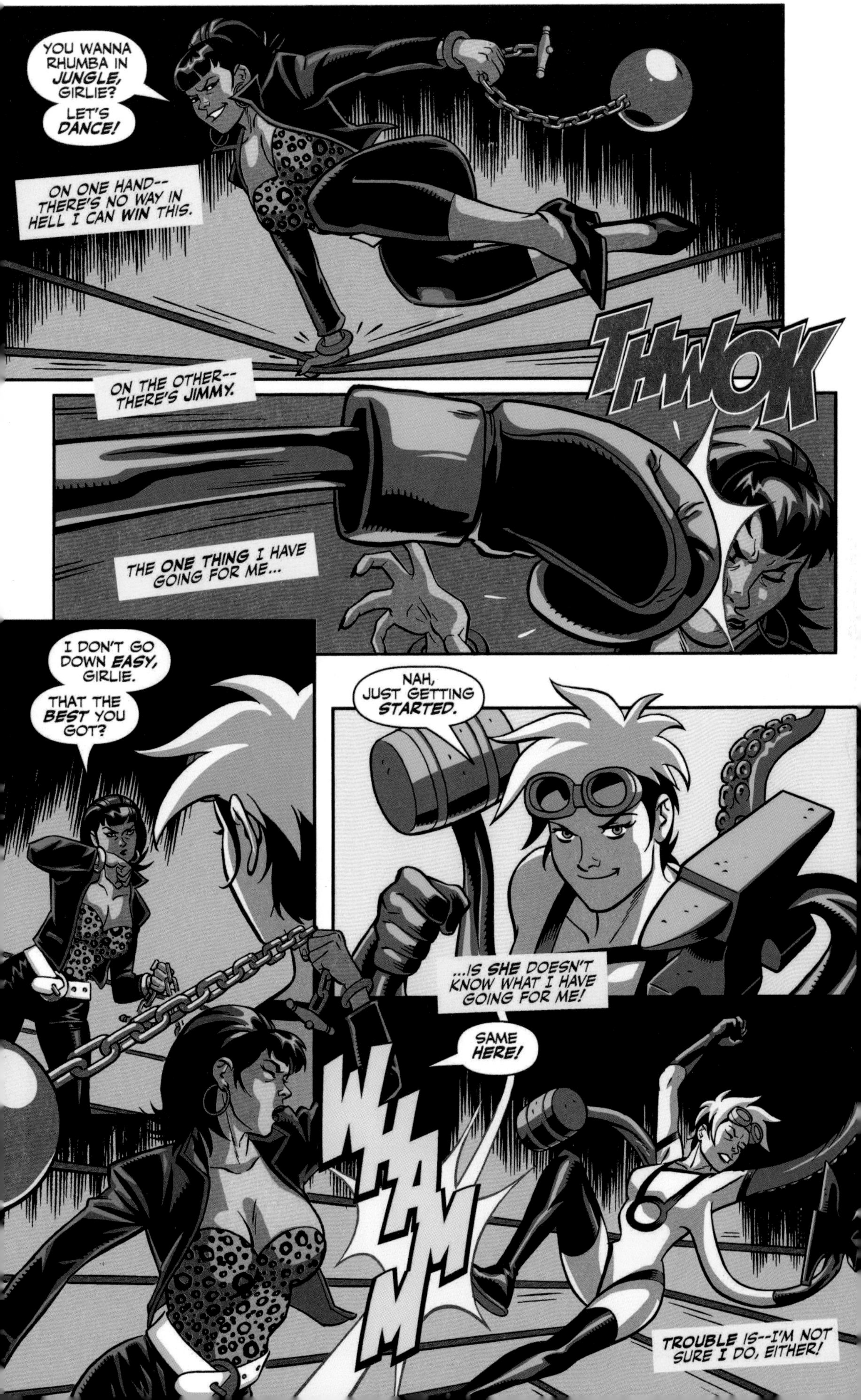

YOU WANNA RHUMBA IN JUNGLE, GIRLIE?
LET'S DANCE!
ON ONE HAND-- THERE'S NO WAY IN HELL I CAN WIN THIS.
THWOK
ON THE OTHER-- THERE'S JIMMY.
THE ONE THING I HAVE GOING FOR ME...
I DON'T GO DOWN EASY, GIRLIE.
THAT THE BEST YOU GOT?
NAH, JUST GETTING STARTED.
...IS SHE DOESN'T KNOW WHAT I HAVE GOING FOR ME!
SAME HERE!
WHAMM
TROUBLE IS--I'M NOT SURE I DO, EITHER!

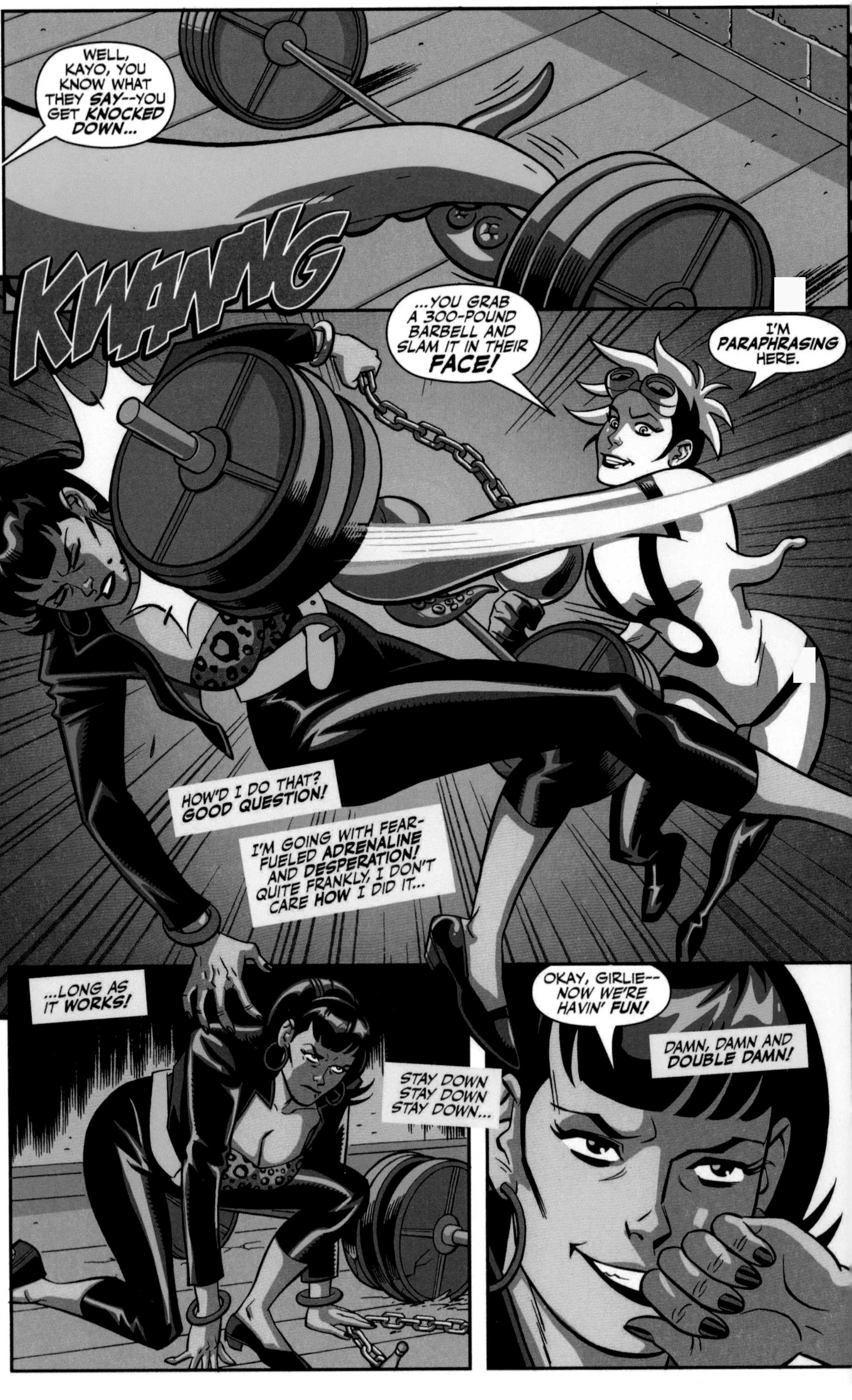

WELL, KAYO, YOU KNOW WHAT THEY SAY--YOU GET KNOCKED DOWN...
KWANNG
...YOU GRAB A 300-POUND BARBELL AND SLAM IT IN THEIR FACE!
I'M PARAPHRASING HERE.
HOW'D I DO THAT? GOOD QUESTION!
I'M GOING WITH FEAR-FUELED ADRENALINE AND DESPERATION! QUITE FRANKLY, I DON'T CARE HOW I DID IT...
...LONG AS IT WORKS!
STAY DOWN STAY DOWN STAY DOWN...
OKAY, GIRLIE-- NOW WE'RE HAVIN' FUN!
DAMN, DAMN AND DOUBLE DAMN!

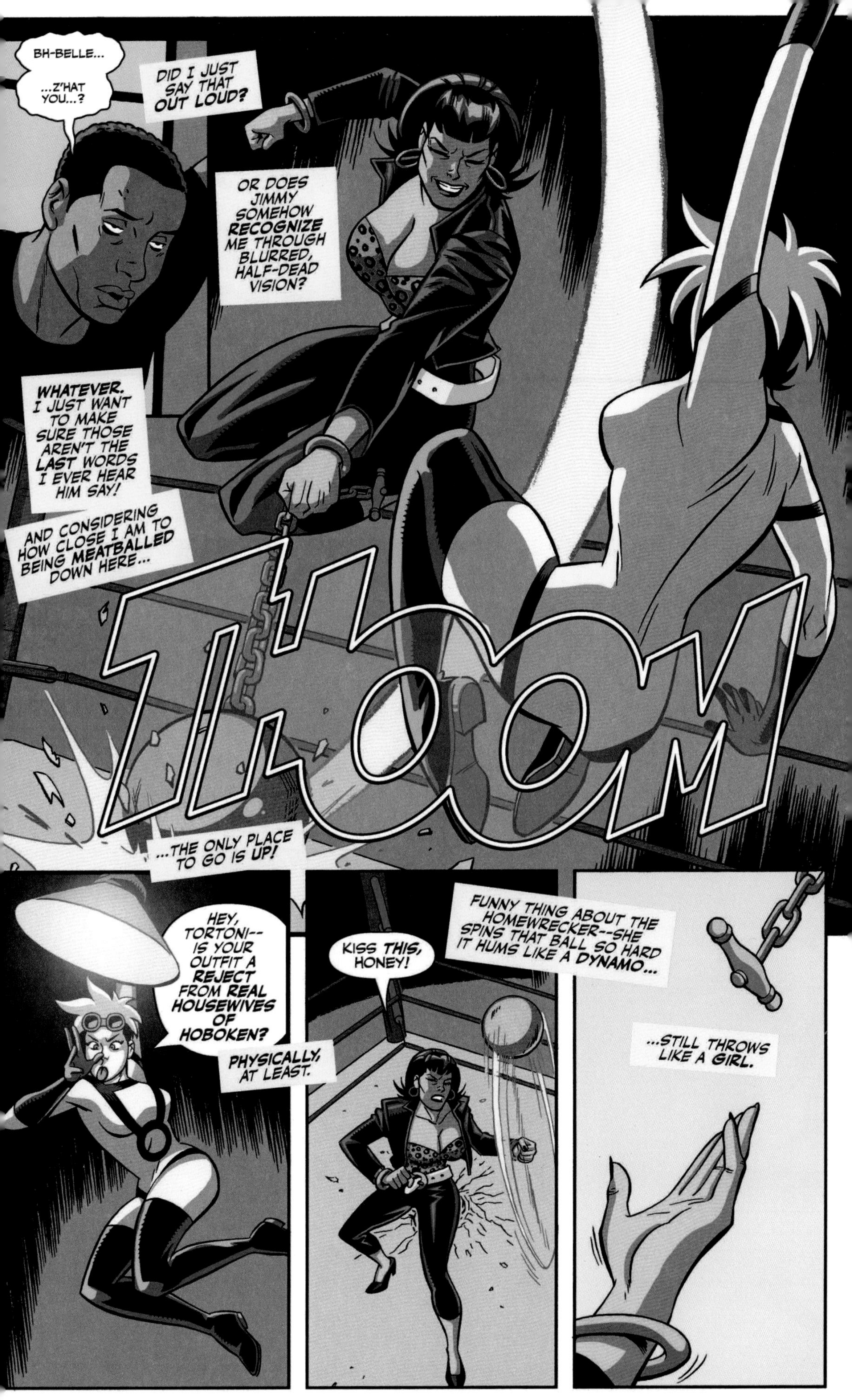

BH-BELLE...
...Z'HAT YOU...?
DID I JUST SAY THAT OUT LOUD?
OR DOES JIMMY SOMEHOW RECOGNIZE ME THROUGH BLURRED, HALF-DEAD VISION?
WHATEVER. I JUST WANT TO MAKE SURE THOSE AREN'T THE LAST WORDS I EVER HEAR HIM SAY!
AND CONSIDERING HOW CLOSE I AM TO BEING MEATBALLED DOWN HERE...
THOOM
...THE ONLY PLACE TO GO IS UP!
HEY, TORTONI--IS YOUR OUTFIT A REJECT FROM REAL HOUSEWIVES OF HOBOKEN?
PHYSICALLY, AT LEAST.
KISS THIS, HONEY!
FUNNY THING ABOUT THE HOMEWRECKER--SHE SPINS THAT BALL SO HARD IT HUMS LIKE A DYNAMO...
...STILL THROWS LIKE A GIRL.

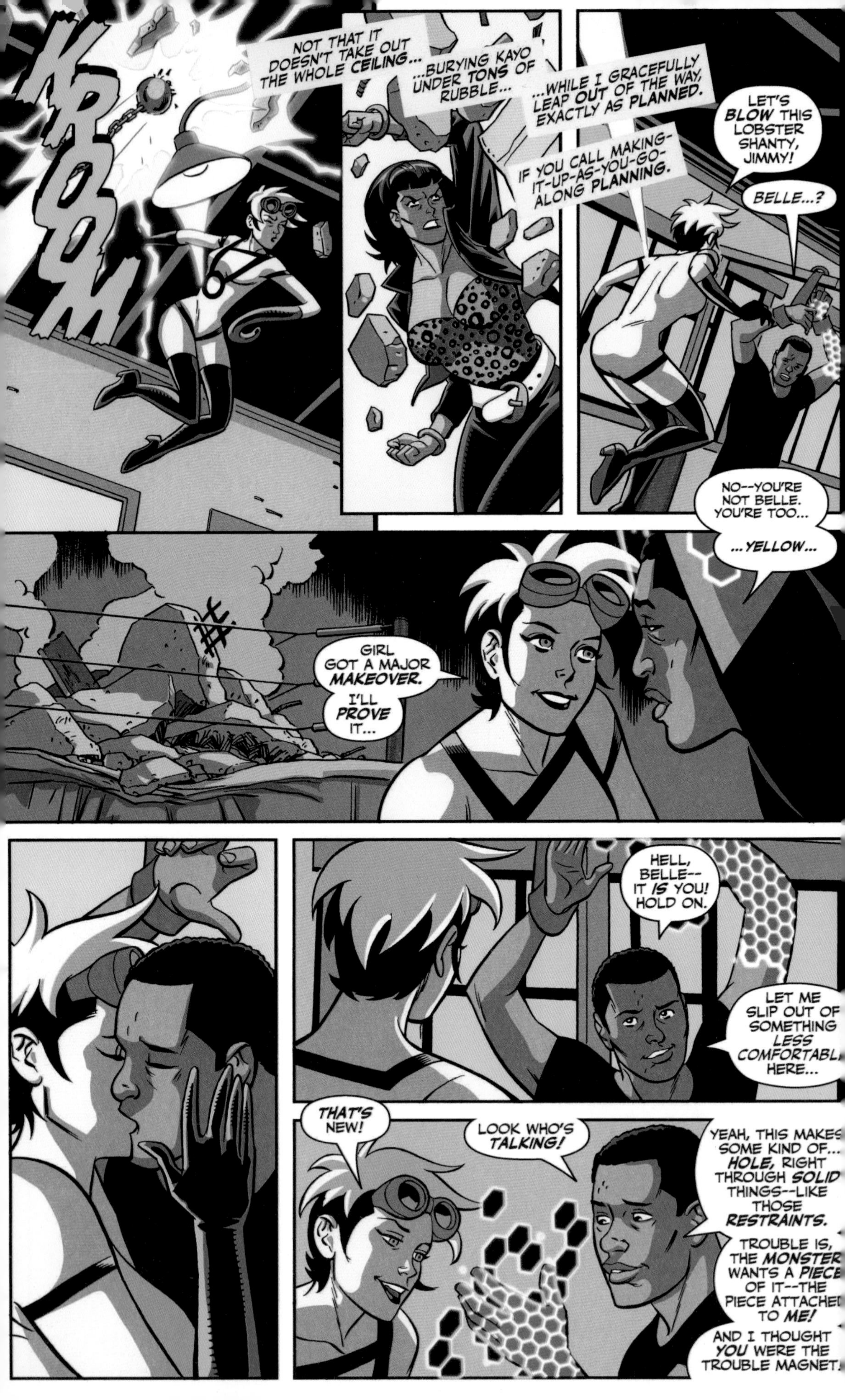
KROOM
NOT THAT IT DOESN'T TAKE OUT THE WHOLE CEILING...
...BURYING KAYO UNDER TONS OF RUBBLE...
...WHILE I GRACEFULLY LEAP OUT OF THE WAY, EXACTLY AS PLANNED.
IF YOU CALL MAKING-IT-UP-AS-YOU-GO-ALONG PLANNING.
LET'S BLOW THIS LOBSTER SHANTY, JIMMY!
BELLE...?
NO--YOU'RE NOT BELLE. YOU'RE TOO...
...YELLOW...
GIRL GOT A MAJOR MAKEOVER. I'LL PROVE IT...
HELL, BELLE-- IT IS YOU! HOLD ON.
LET ME SLIP OUT OF SOMETHING LESS COMFORTABL
HERE...
THAT'S NEW!
LOOK WHO'S TALKING!
YEAH, THIS MAKES SOME KIND OF... HOLE, RIGHT THROUGH SOLID THINGS--LIKE THOSE RESTRAINTS.
TROUBLE IS, THE MONSTER WANTS A PIECE OF IT--THE PIECE ATTACHED TO ME!
AND I THOUGHT YOU WERE THE TROUBLE MAGNET.

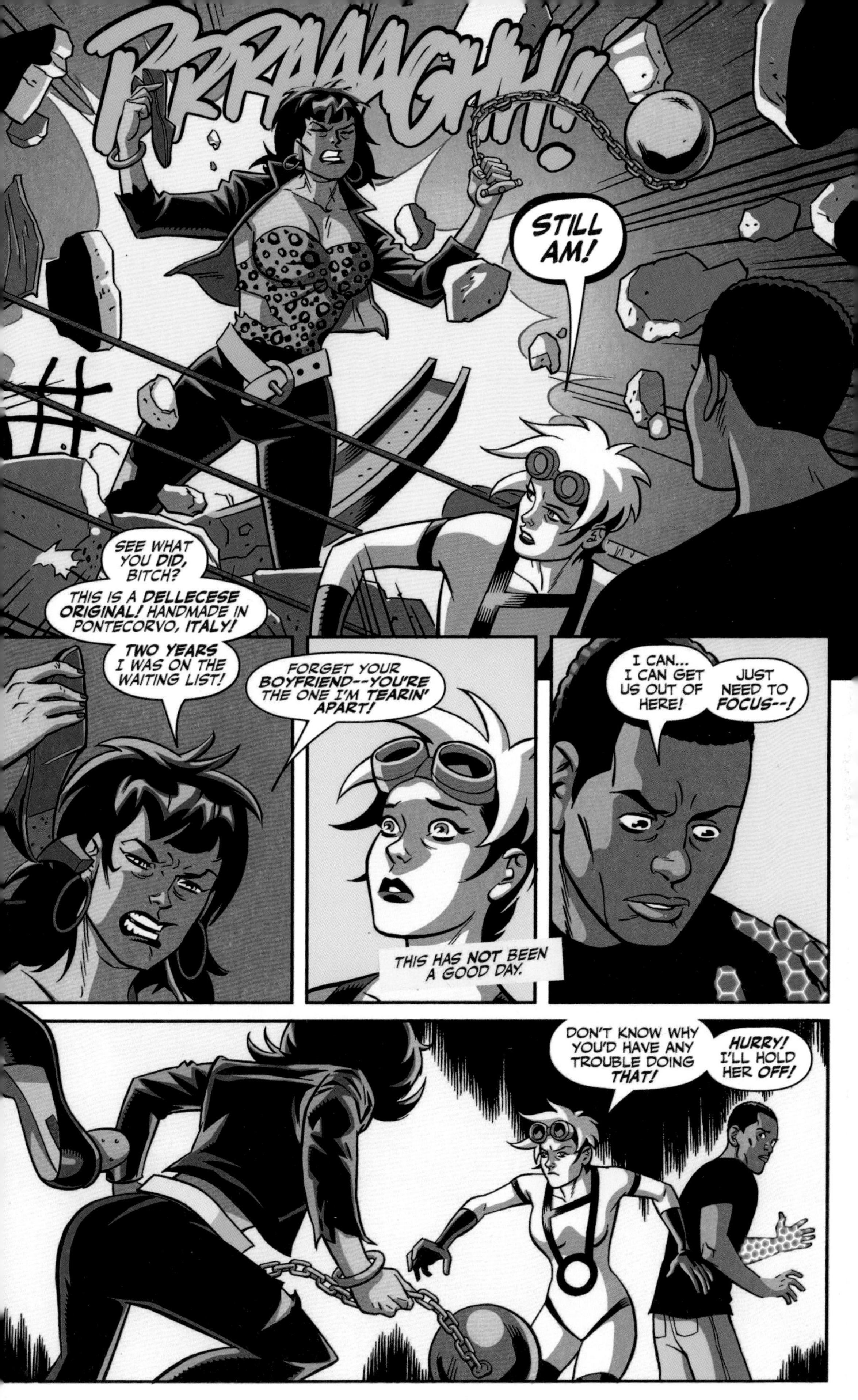
PRRAAAGHH!!
STILL AM!
SEE WHAT YOU DID, BITCH?
THIS IS A DELLECESE ORIGINAL! HANDMADE IN PONTECORVO, ITALY!
TWO YEARS I WAS ON THE WAITING LIST!
FORGET YOUR BOYFRIEND--YOU'RE THE ONE I'M TEARIN' APART!
THIS HAS NOT BEEN A GOOD DAY.
I CAN... I CAN GET US OUT OF HERE!
JUST NEED TO FOCUS--!
DON'T KNOW WHY YOU'D HAVE ANY TROUBLE DOING THAT!
HURRY! I'LL HOLD HER OFF!

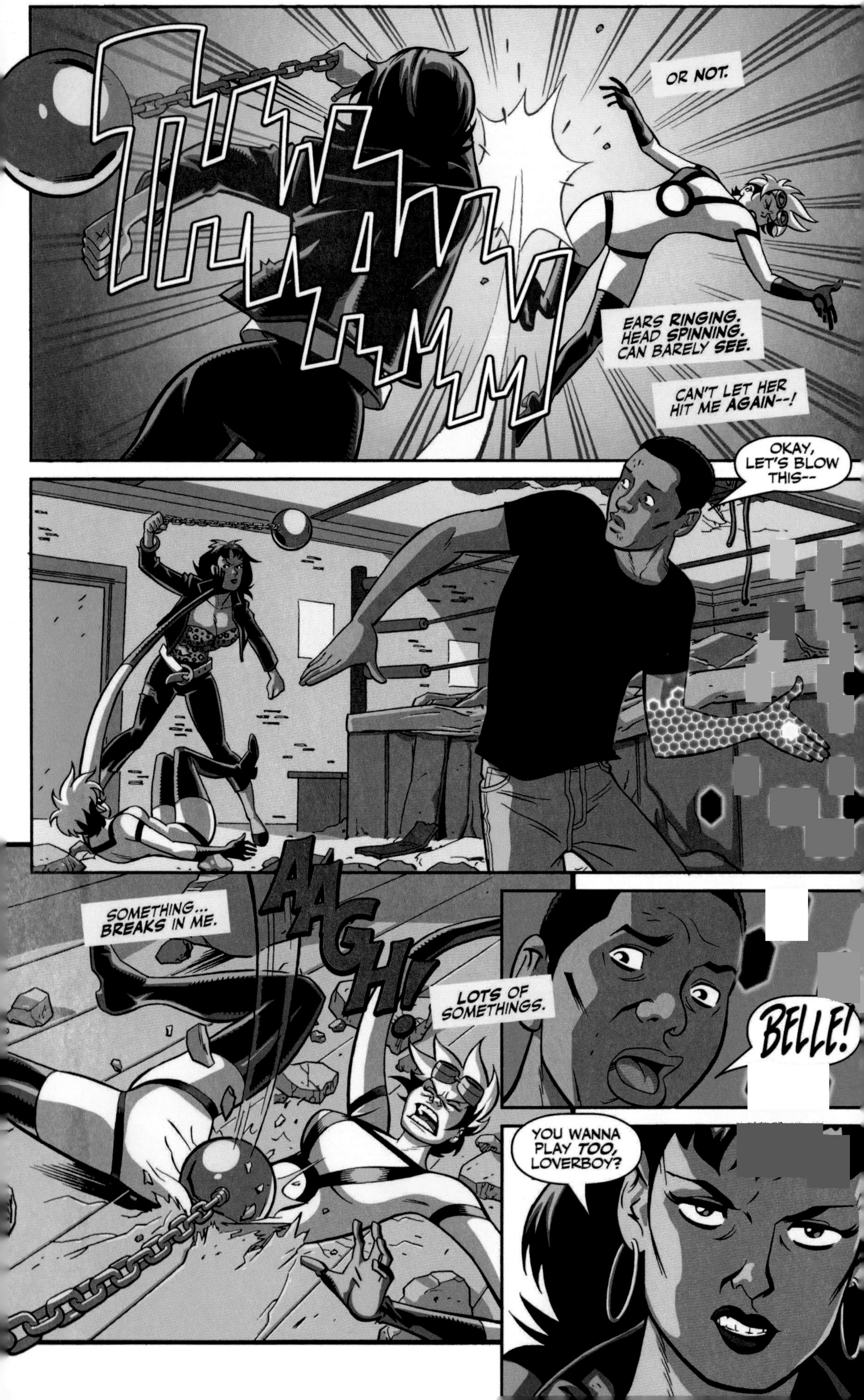
THWMMMM
OR NOT.
EARS RINGING. HEAD SPINNING. CAN BARELY SEE.
CAN'T LET HER HIT ME AGAIN--!
OKAY, LET'S BLOW THIS--
SOMETHING... BREAKS IN ME.
AAGH!
LOTS OF SOMETHINGS.
BELLE!
YOU WANNA PLAY TOO, LOVERBOY?

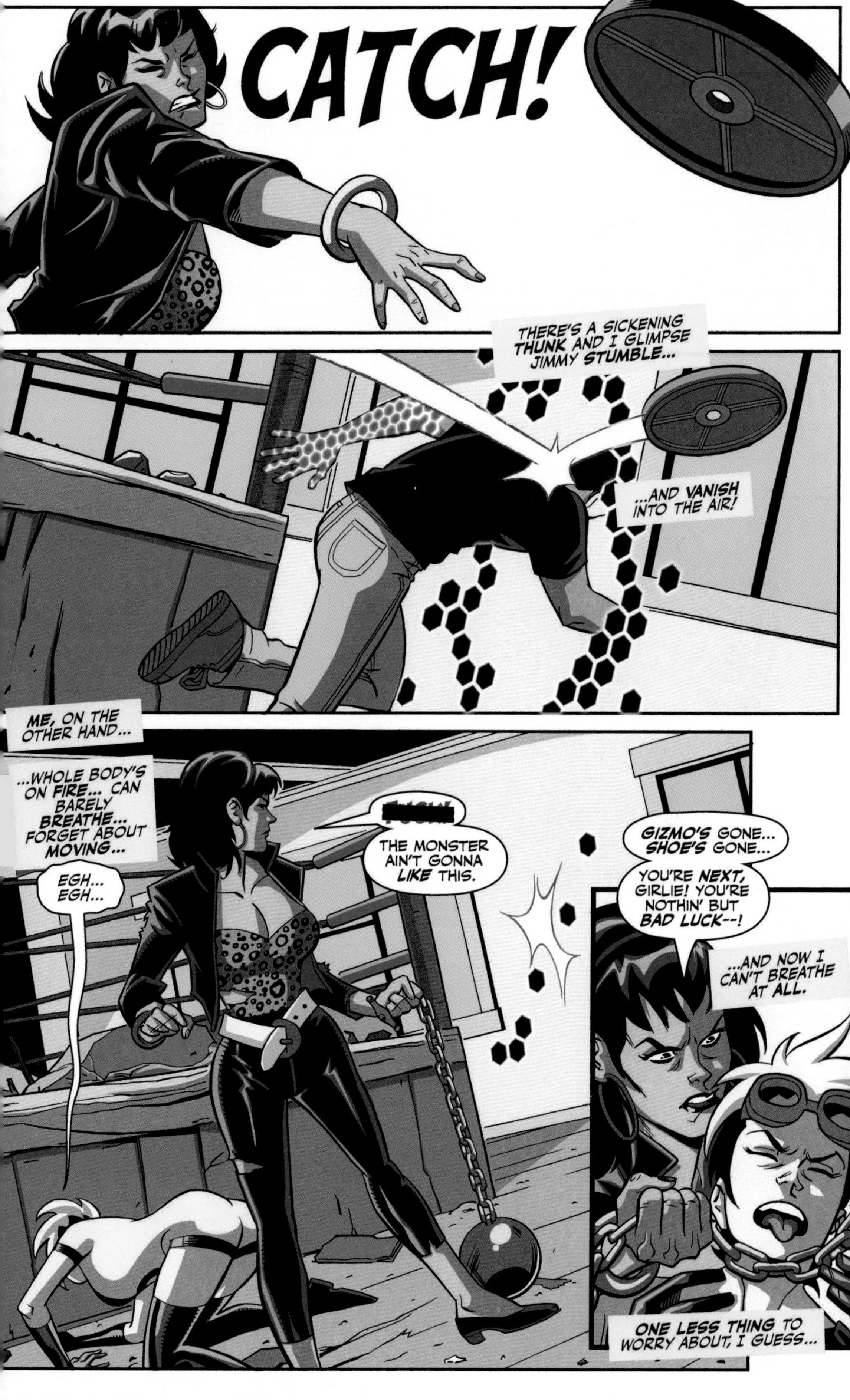
CATCH!
THERE'S A SICKENING THUNK AND I GLIMPSE JIMMY STUMBLE...
...AND VANISH INTO THE AIR!
ME, ON THE OTHER HAND...
...WHOLE BODY'S ON FIRE... CAN BARELY BREATHE... FORGET ABOUT MOVING...
EGH... EGH...
[redacted]
THE MONSTER AIN'T GONNA LIKE THIS.
GIZMO'S GONE... SHOE'S GONE...
YOU'RE NEXT, GIRLIE! YOU'RE NOTHIN' BUT BAD LUCK--!
...AND NOW I CAN'T BREATHE AT ALL.
ONE LESS THING TO WORRY ABOUT, I GUESS...

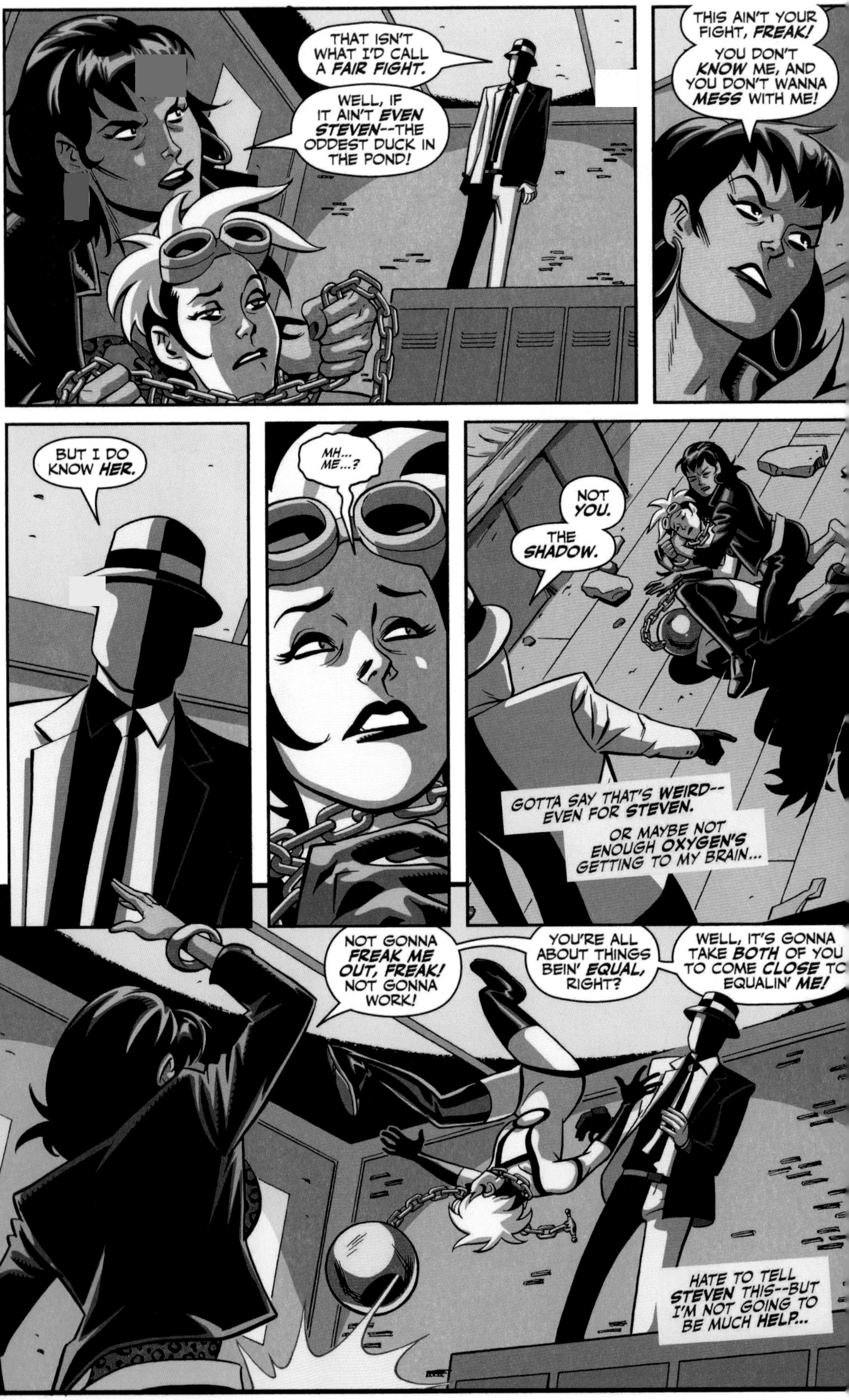
THAT ISN'T WHAT I'D CALL A FAIR FIGHT.
WELL, IF IT AIN'T EVEN STEVEN--THE ODDEST DUCK IN THE POND!
THIS AIN'T YOUR FIGHT, FREAK!
YOU DON'T KNOW ME, AND YOU DON'T WANNA MESS WITH ME!
BUT I DO KNOW HER.
MH... ME...?
NOT YOU.
THE SHADOW.
GOTTA SAY THAT'S WEIRD-- EVEN FOR STEVEN.
OR MAYBE NOT ENOUGH OXYGEN'S GETTING TO MY BRAIN...
NOT GONNA FREAK ME OUT, FREAK! NOT GONNA WORK!
YOU'RE ALL ABOUT THINGS BEIN' EQUAL, RIGHT?
WELL, IT'S GONNA TAKE BOTH OF YOU TO COME CLOSE TO EQUALIN' ME!
HATE TO TELL STEVEN THIS--BUT I'M NOT GOING TO BE MUCH HELP...

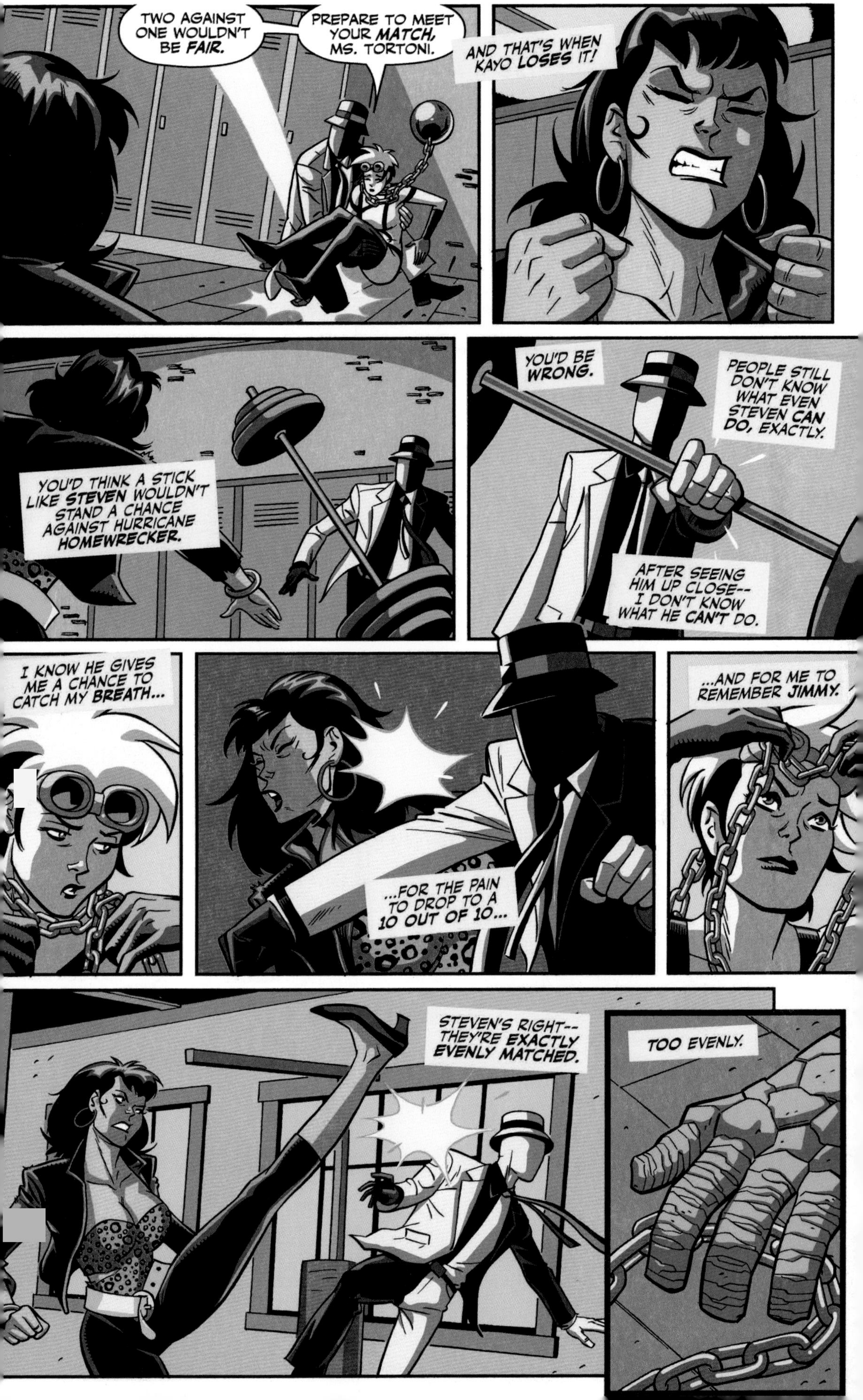

TWO AGAINST ONE WOULDN'T BE FAIR.
PREPARE TO MEET YOUR MATCH, MS. TORTONI.
AND THAT'S WHEN KAYO LOSES IT!
YOU'D THINK A STICK LIKE STEVEN WOULDN'T STAND A CHANCE AGAINST HURRICANE HOMEWRECKER.
YOU'D BE WRONG.
PEOPLE STILL DON'T KNOW WHAT EVEN STEVEN CAN DO, EXACTLY.
AFTER SEEING HIM UP CLOSE-- I DON'T KNOW WHAT HE CAN'T DO.
I KNOW HE GIVES ME A CHANCE TO CATCH MY BREATH...
...FOR THE PAIN TO DROP TO A 10 OUT OF 10...
...AND FOR ME TO REMEMBER JIMMY.
STEVEN'S RIGHT-- THEY'RE EXACTLY EVENLY MATCHED.
TOO EVENLY.

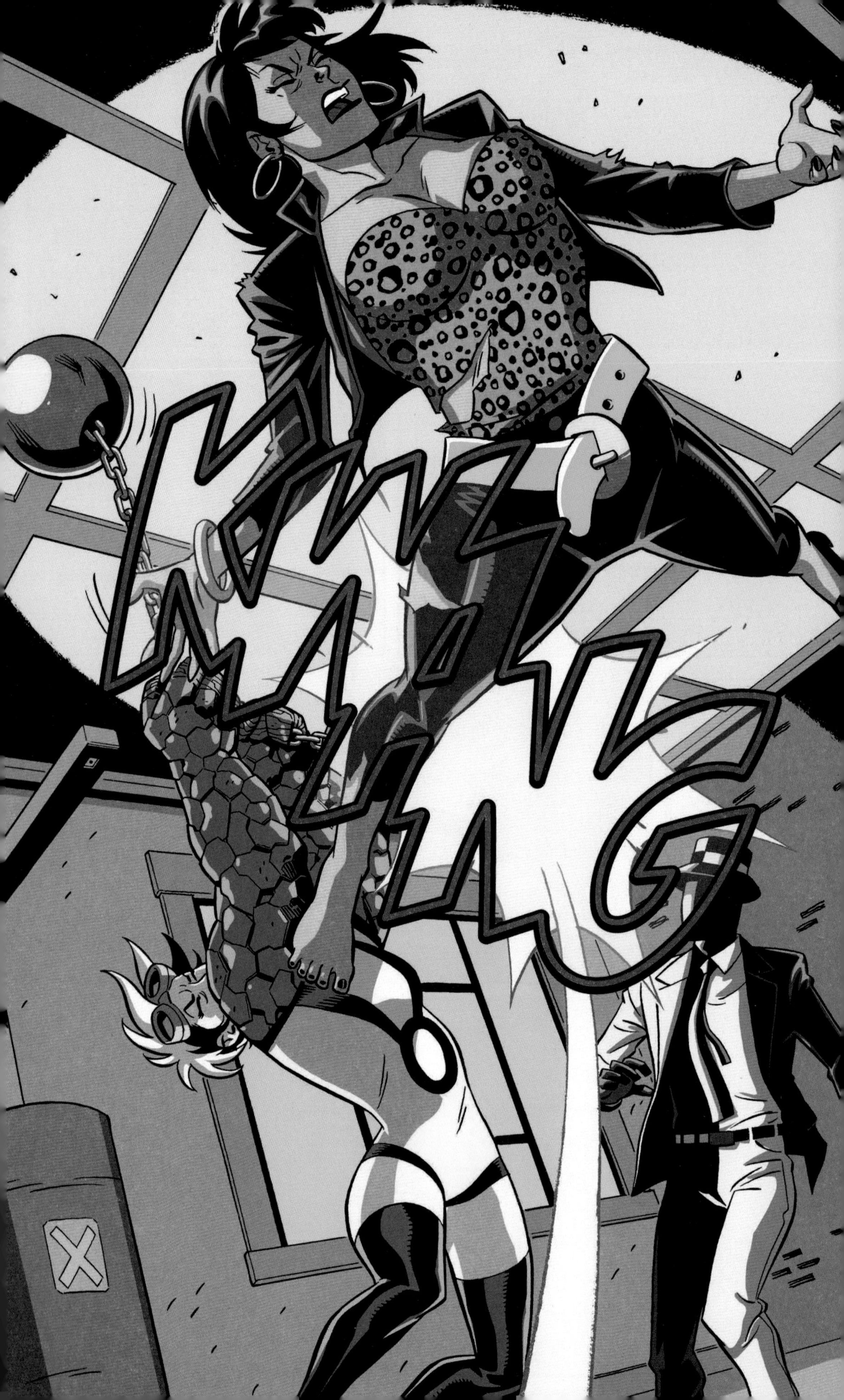

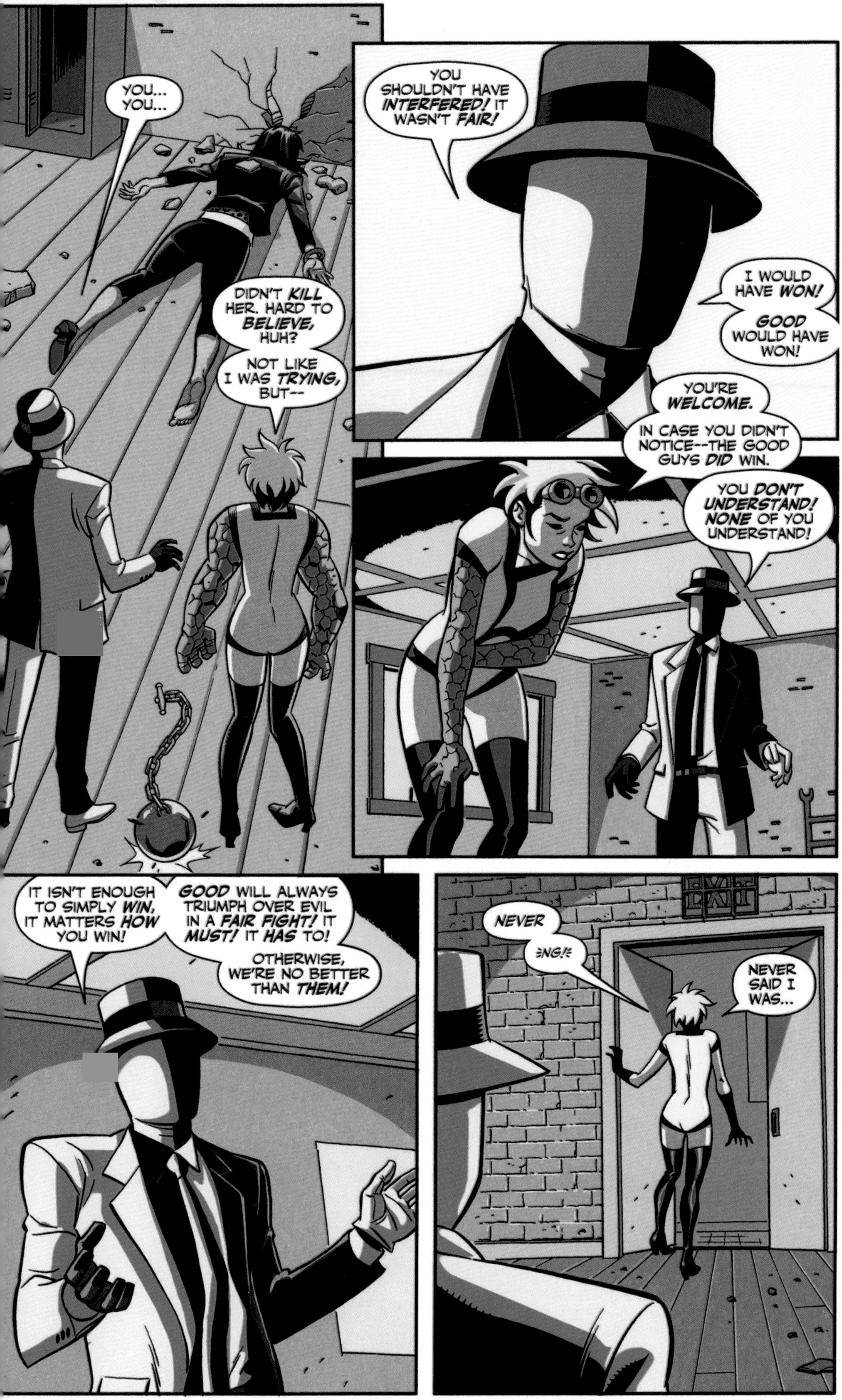
YOU... YOU...
DIDN'T KILL HER. HARD TO BELIEVE, HUH?
NOT LIKE I WAS TRYING, BUT--
YOU SHOULDN'T HAVE INTERFERED! IT WASN'T FAIR!
I WOULD HAVE WON!
GOOD WOULD HAVE WON!
YOU'RE WELCOME.
IN CASE YOU DIDN'T NOTICE--THE GOOD GUYS DID WIN.
YOU DON'T UNDERSTAND! NONE OF YOU UNDERSTAND!
IT ISN'T ENOUGH TO SIMPLY WIN, IT MATTERS HOW YOU WIN!
GOOD WILL ALWAYS TRIUMPH OVER EVIL IN A FAIR FIGHT! IT MUST! IT HAS TO!
OTHERWISE, WE'RE NO BETTER THAN THEM!
NEVER
NG!
NEVER SAID I WAS...

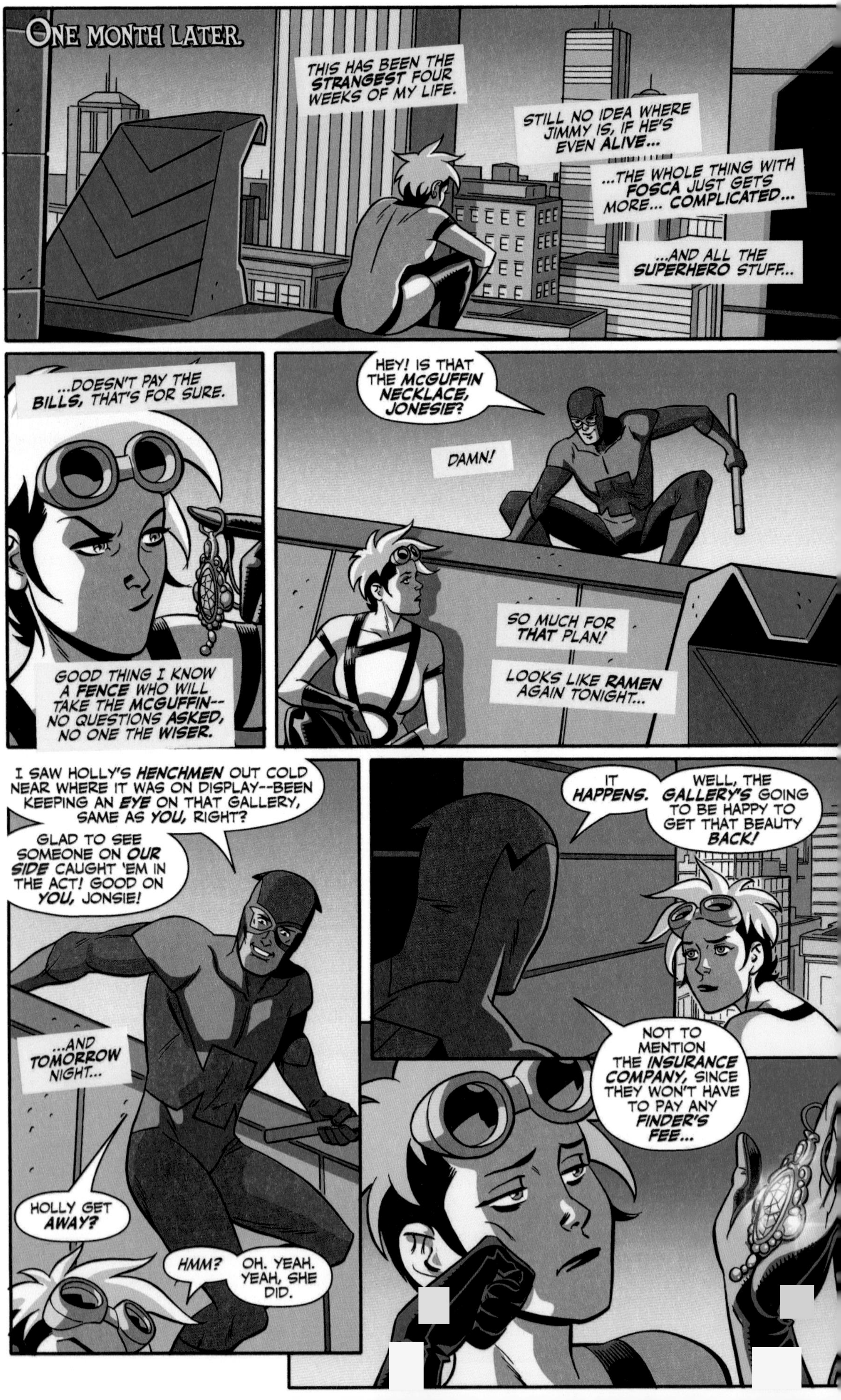

ONE MONTH LATER.
THIS HAS BEEN THE STRANGEST FOUR WEEKS OF MY LIFE.
STILL NO IDEA WHERE JIMMY IS, IF HE'S EVEN ALIVE...
...THE WHOLE THING WITH FOSCA JUST GETS MORE... COMPLICATED...
...AND ALL THE SUPERHERO STUFF...
...DOESN'T PAY THE BILLS, THAT'S FOR SURE.
GOOD THING I KNOW A FENCE WHO WILL TAKE THE MCGUFFIN-- NO QUESTIONS ASKED, NO ONE THE WISER.
HEY! IS THAT THE McGUFFIN NECKLACE, JONESIE?
DAMN!
SO MUCH FOR THAT PLAN!
LOOKS LIKE RAMEN AGAIN TONIGHT...
I SAW HOLLY'S HENCHMEN OUT COLD NEAR WHERE IT WAS ON DISPLAY--BEEN KEEPING AN EYE ON THAT GALLERY, SAME AS YOU, RIGHT?
GLAD TO SEE SOMEONE ON OUR SIDE CAUGHT 'EM IN THE ACT! GOOD ON YOU, JONSIE!
...AND TOMORROW NIGHT...
HOLLY GET AWAY?
HMM?
OH. YEAH. YEAH, SHE DID.
IT HAPPENS.
WELL, THE GALLERY'S GOING TO BE HAPPY TO GET THAT BEAUTY BACK!
NOT TO MENTION THE INSURANCE COMPANY, SINCE THEY WON'T HAVE TO PAY ANY FINDER'S FEE...

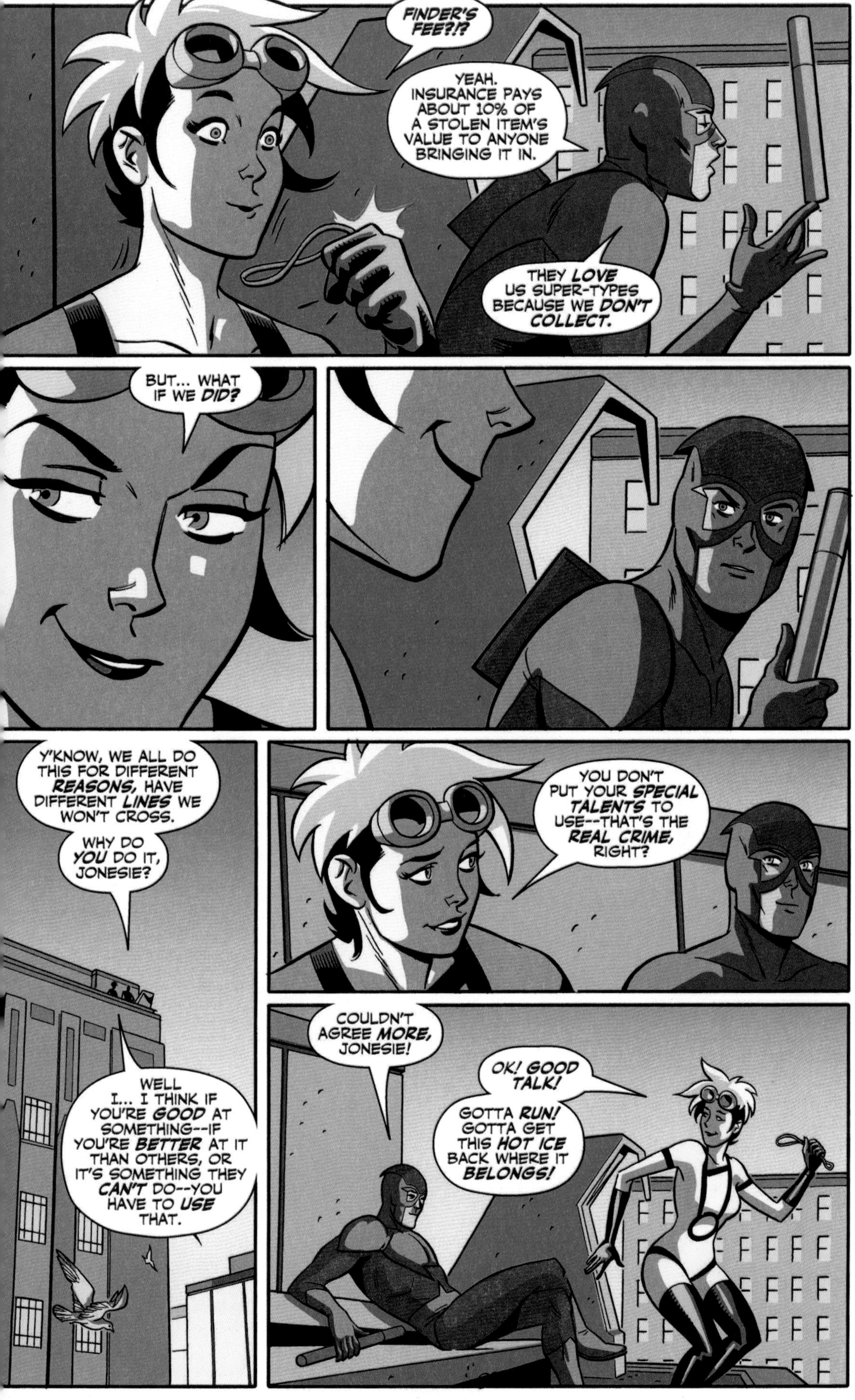
FINDER'S FEE?!?
YEAH. INSURANCE PAYS ABOUT 10% OF A STOLEN ITEM'S VALUE TO ANYONE BRINGING IT IN.
THEY LOVE US SUPER-TYPES BECAUSE WE DON'T COLLECT.
BUT... WHAT IF WE DID?
Y'KNOW, WE ALL DO THIS FOR DIFFERENT REASONS, HAVE DIFFERENT LINES WE WON'T CROSS.
WHY DO YOU DO IT, JONESIE?
WELL I... I THINK IF YOU'RE GOOD AT SOMETHING--IF YOU'RE BETTER AT IT THAN OTHERS, OR IT'S SOMETHING THEY CAN'T DO--YOU HAVE TO USE THAT.
YOU DON'T PUT YOUR SPECIAL TALENTS TO USE--THAT'S THE REAL CRIME, RIGHT?
COULDN'T AGREE MORE, JONESIE!
OK! GOOD TALK!
GOTTA RUN! GOTTA GET THIS HOT ICE BACK WHERE IT BELONGS!

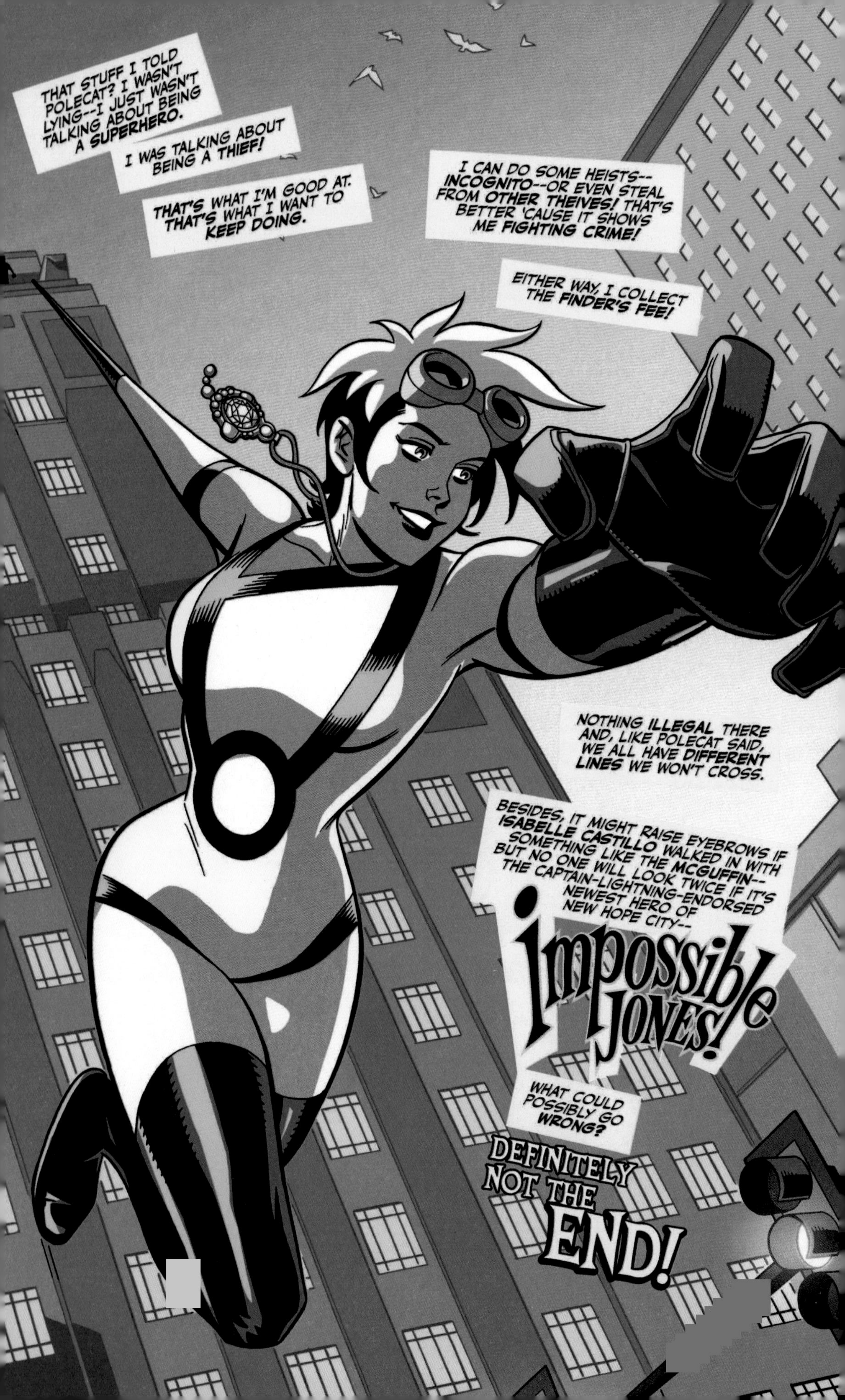
THAT STUFF I TOLD POLECAT? I WASN'T LYING--I JUST WASN'T TALKING ABOUT BEING A SUPERHERO.
I WAS TALKING ABOUT BEING A THIEF!
THAT'S WHAT I'M GOOD AT. THAT'S WHAT I WANT TO KEEP DOING.
I CAN DO SOME HEISTS--INCOGNITO--OR EVEN STEAL FROM OTHER THEIVES! THAT'S BETTER 'CAUSE IT SHOWS ME FIGHTING CRIME!
EITHER WAY, I COLLECT THE FINDER'S FEE!
NOTHING ILLEGAL THERE AND, LIKE POLECAT SAID, WE ALL HAVE DIFFERENT LINES WE WON'T CROSS.
BESIDES, IT MIGHT RAISE EYEBROWS IF ISABELLE CASTILLO WALKED IN WITH SOMETHING LIKE THE MCGUFFIN--BUT NO ONE WILL LOOK TWICE IF IT'S THE CAPTAIN-LIGHTNING-ENDORSED NEWEST HERO OF NEW HOPE CITY--
impossible JONES!
WHAT COULD POSSIBLY GO WRONG?
DEFINITELY NOT THE END!

Alternate Cover Gallery

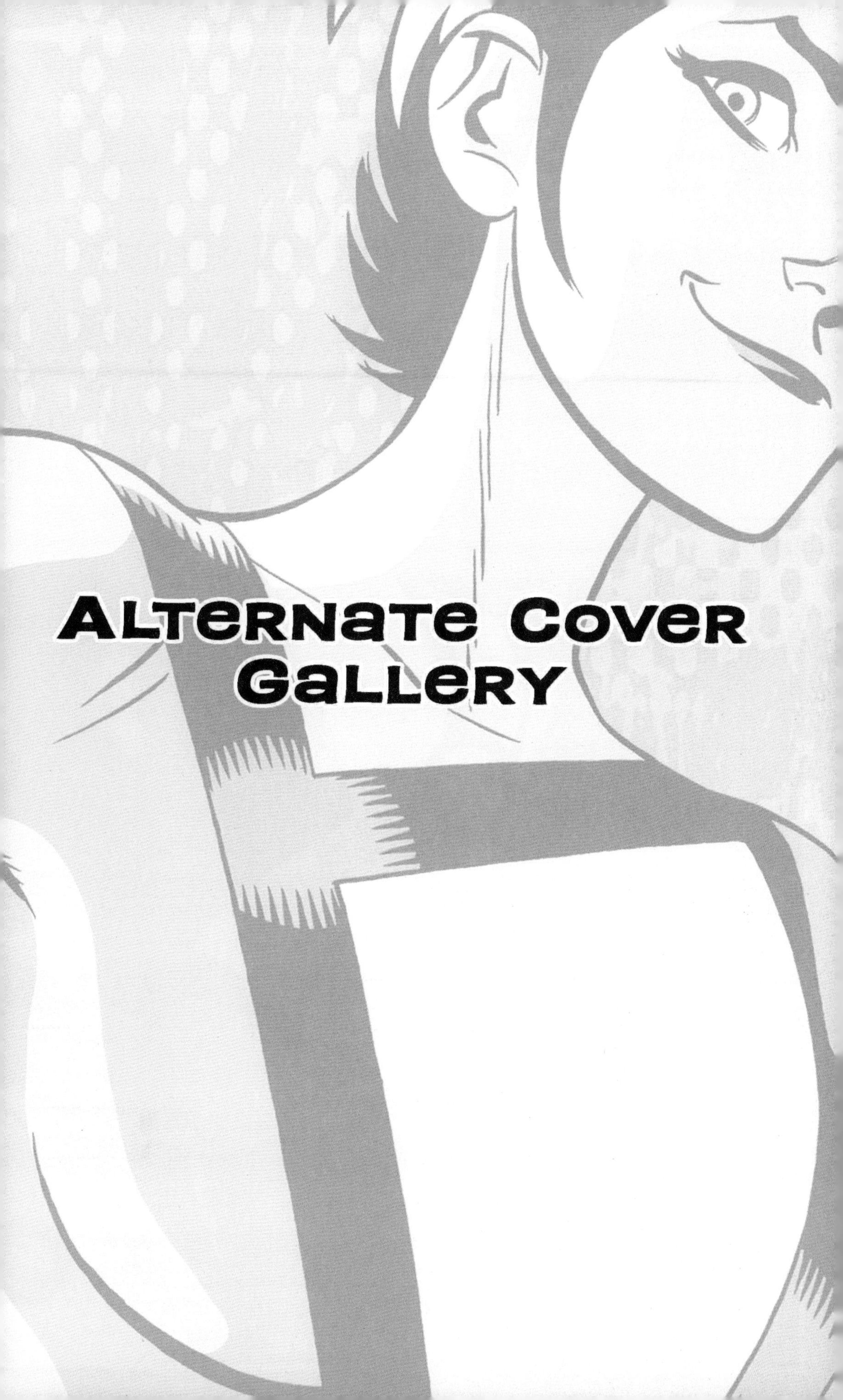

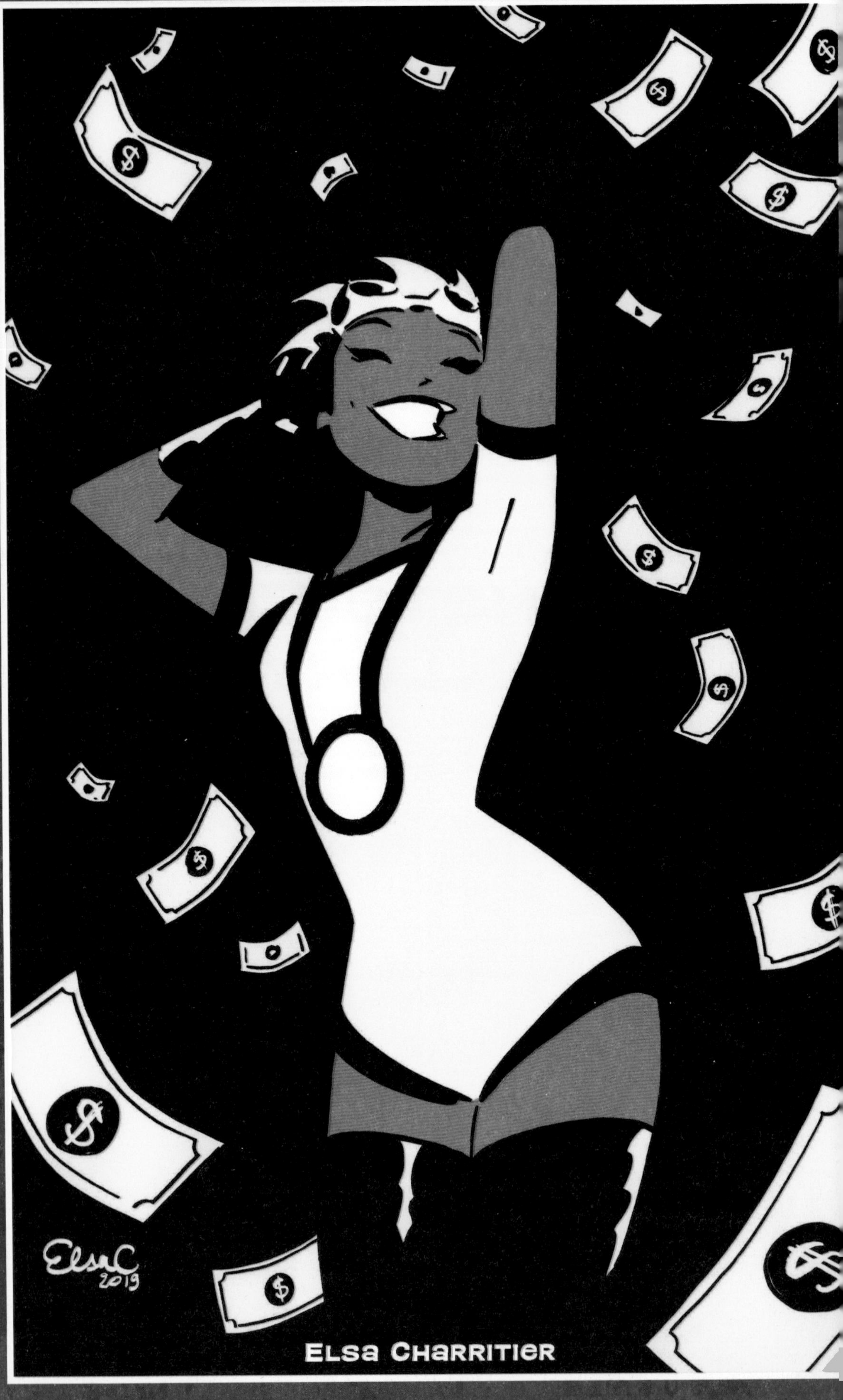
ElsaC
2019

Elsa Charritier

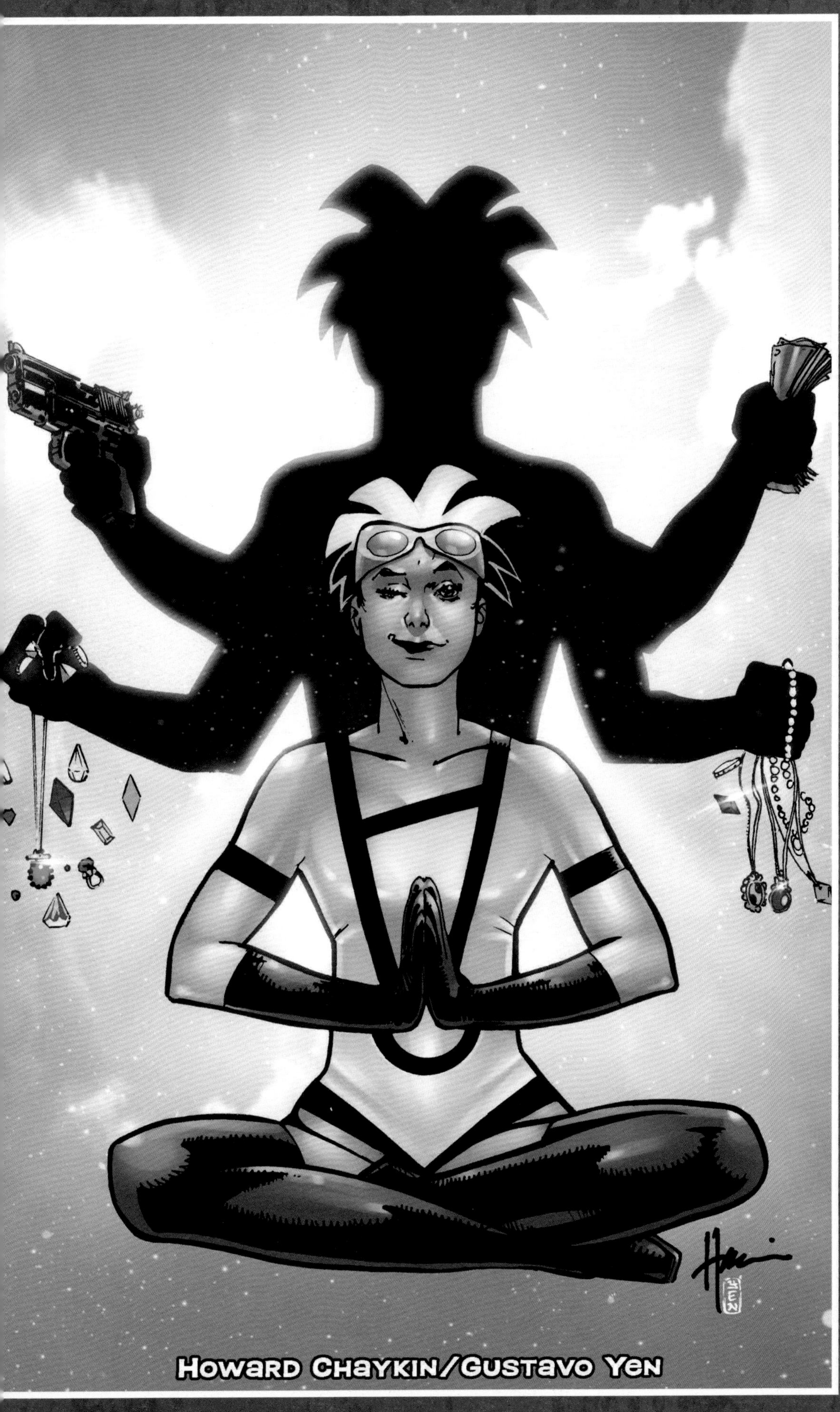

Howard Chaykin/Gustavo Yen

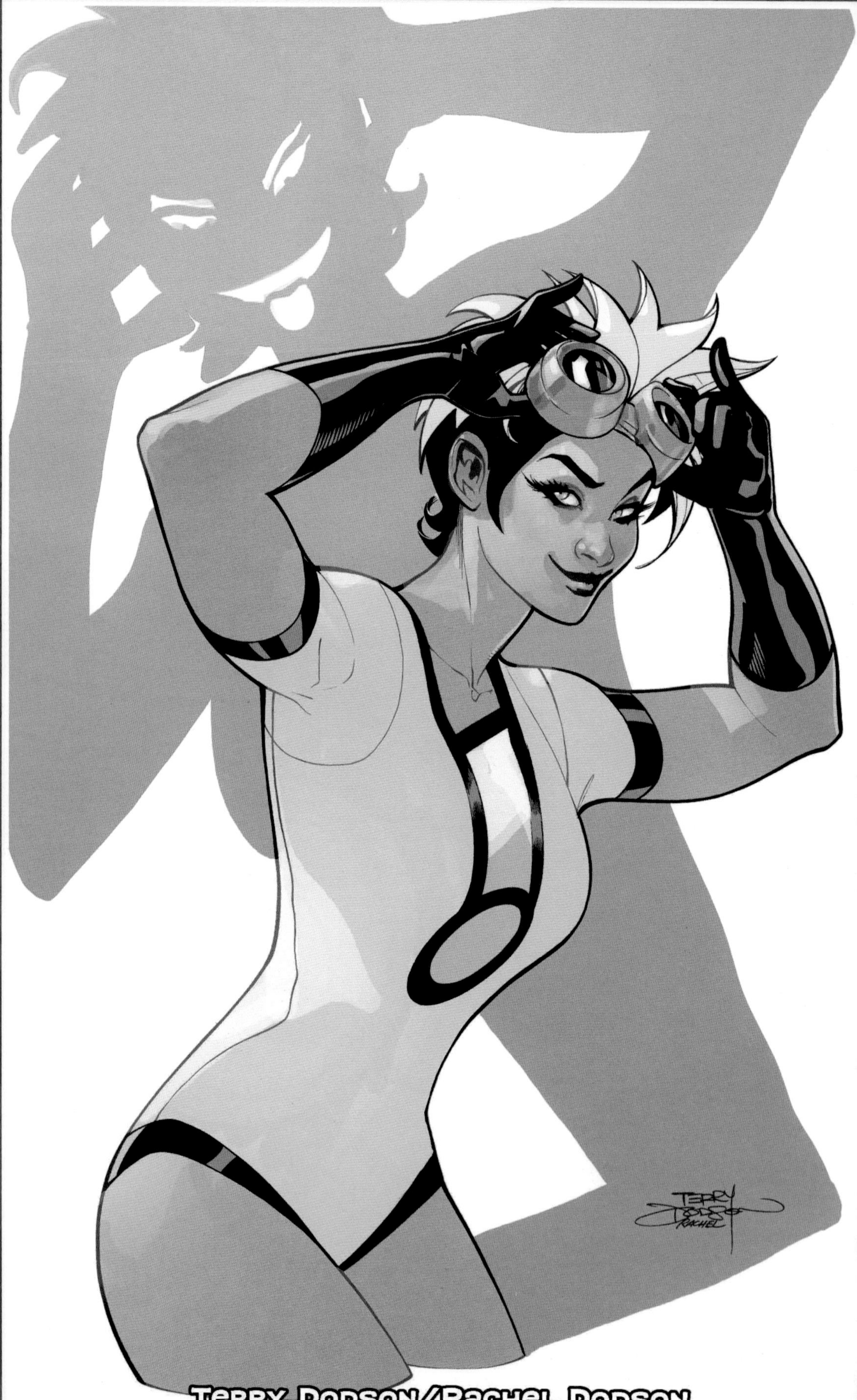
TERRY DODSON RACHEL

TERRY DODSON/RACHEL DODSON

SCOUT
GET READY
WRECKED!
4
$3.99
AVINA
THE BAYONNE
HOMEWRECKER!
TG KK 2020
TOM GRUMMETT/KARL KESEL/BILL CRABTREE

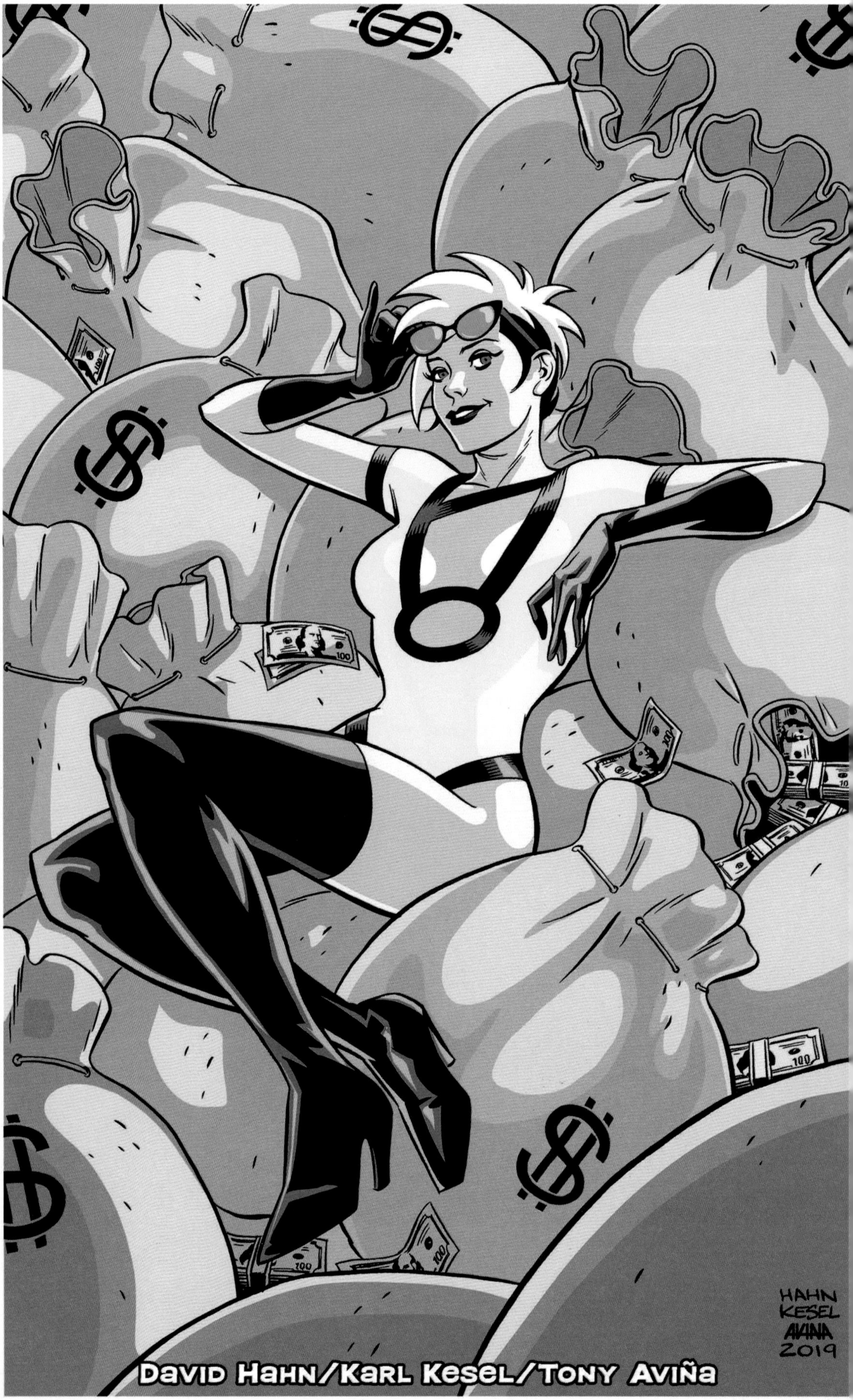

HAHN
KESEL
AVIÑA
2019
DAVID HAHN/KARL KESEL/TONY AVIÑA

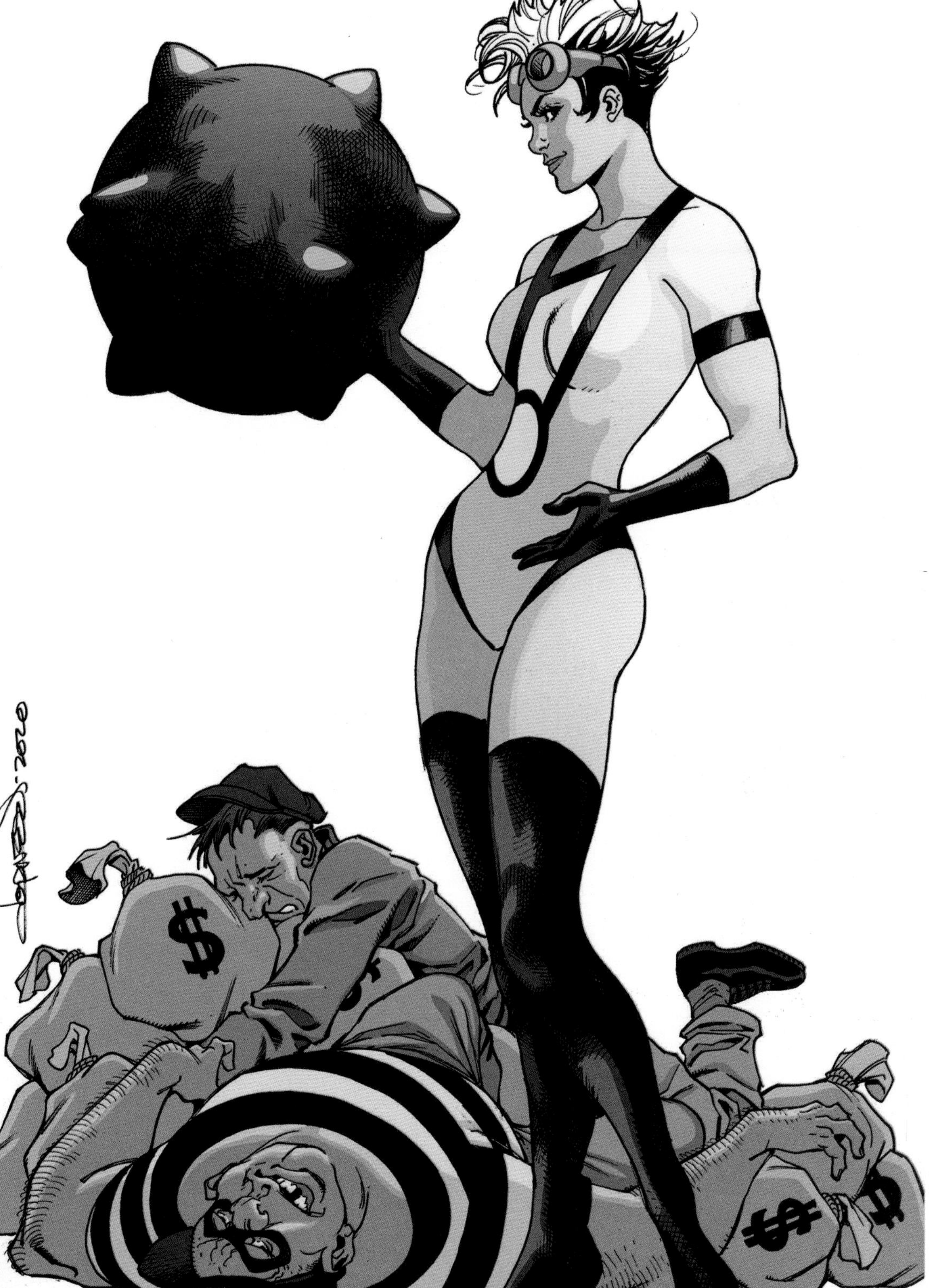

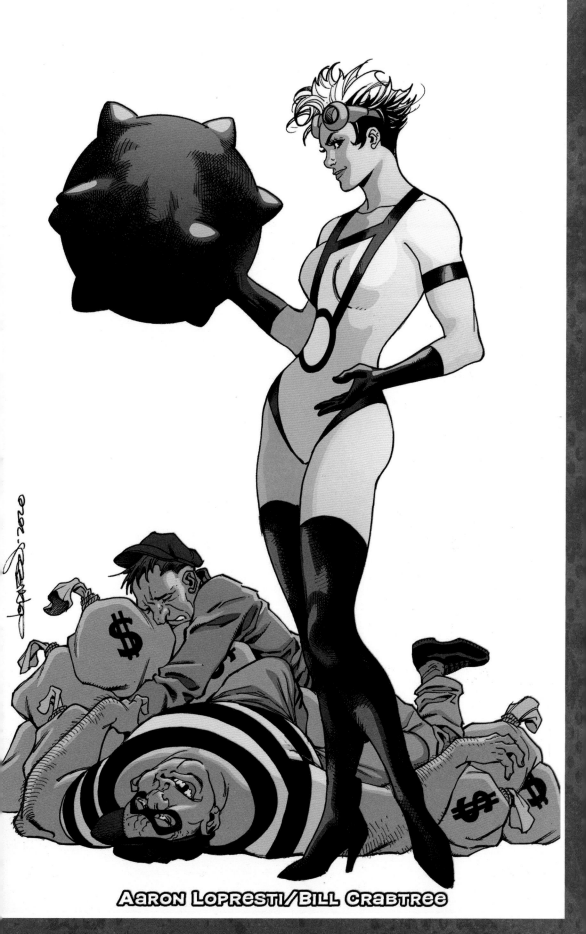

Aaron Lopresti/Bill Crabtree

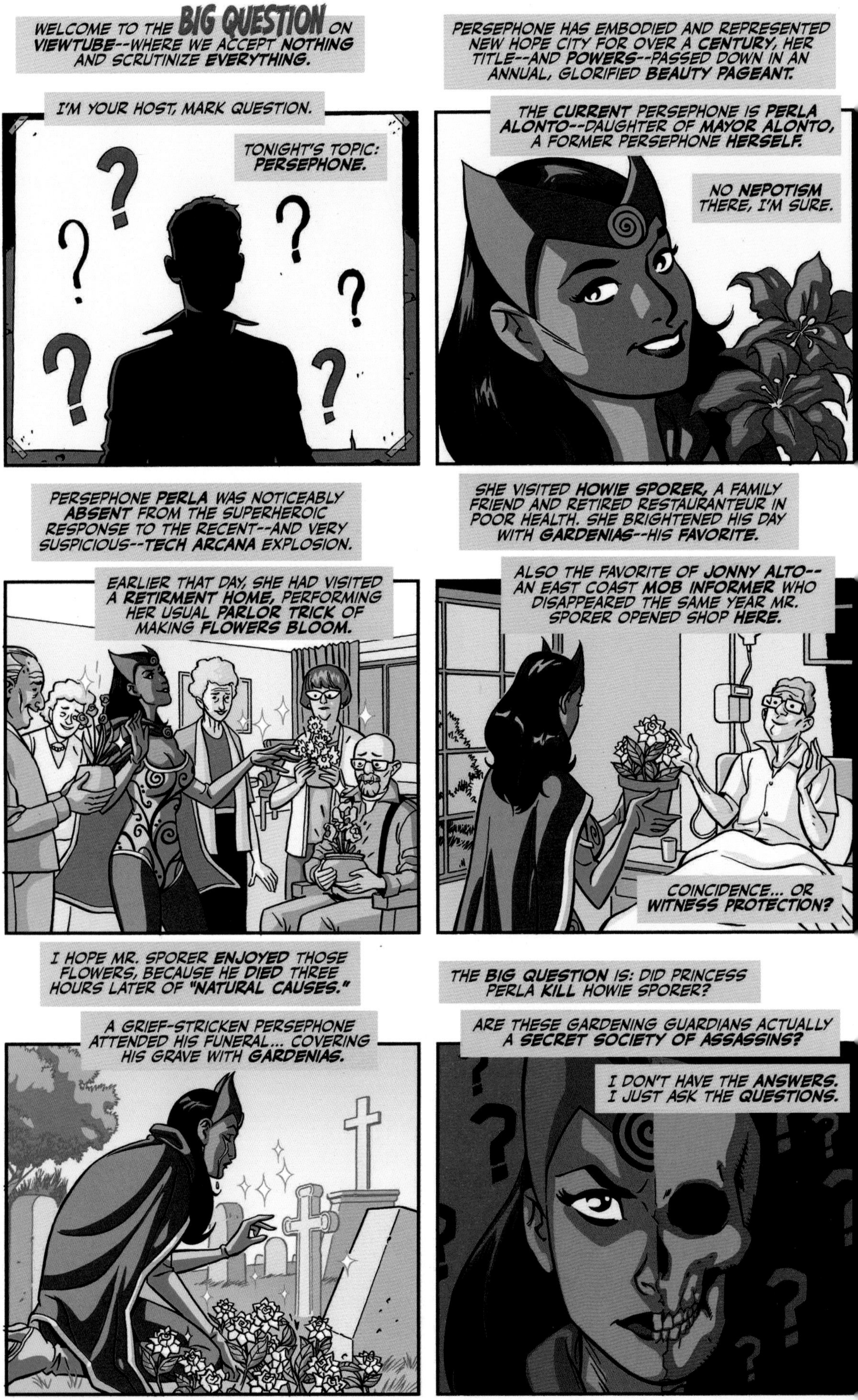
WELCOME TO THE BIG QUESTION ON VIEWTUBE--WHERE WE ACCEPT NOTHING AND SCRUTINIZE EVERYTHING.
I'M YOUR HOST, MARK QUESTION.
TONIGHT'S TOPIC: PERSEPHONE.
PERSEPHONE HAS EMBODIED AND REPRESENTED NEW HOPE CITY FOR OVER A CENTURY, HER TITLE--AND POWERS--PASSED DOWN IN AN ANNUAL, GLORIFIED BEAUTY PAGEANT.
THE CURRENT PERSEPHONE IS PERLA ALONTO--DAUGHTER OF MAYOR ALONTO, A FORMER PERSEPHONE HERSELF.
NO NEPOTISM THERE, I'M SURE.
PERSEPHONE PERLA WAS NOTICEABLY ABSENT FROM THE SUPERHEROIC RESPONSE TO THE RECENT--AND VERY SUSPICIOUS--TECH ARCANA EXPLOSION.
EARLIER THAT DAY, SHE HAD VISITED A RETIRMENT HOME, PERFORMING HER USUAL PARLOR TRICK OF MAKING FLOWERS BLOOM.
SHE VISITED HOWIE SPORER, A FAMILY FRIEND AND RETIRED RESTAURANTEUR IN POOR HEALTH. SHE BRIGHTENED HIS DAY WITH GARDENIAS--HIS FAVORITE.
ALSO THE FAVORITE OF JONNY ALTO--AN EAST COAST MOB INFORMER WHO DISAPPEARED THE SAME YEAR MR. SPORER OPENED SHOP HERE.
COINCIDENCE... OR WITNESS PROTECTION?
I HOPE MR. SPORER ENJOYED THOSE FLOWERS, BECAUSE HE DIED THREE HOURS LATER OF "NATURAL CAUSES."
A GRIEF-STRICKEN PERSEPHONE ATTENDED HIS FUNERAL... COVERING HIS GRAVE WITH GARDENIAS.
THE BIG QUESTION IS: DID PRINCESS PERLA KILL HOWIE SPORER?
ARE THESE GARDENING GUARDIANS ACTUALLY A SECRET SOCIETY OF ASSASSINS?
I DON'T HAVE THE ANSWERS. I JUST ASK THE QUESTIONS.

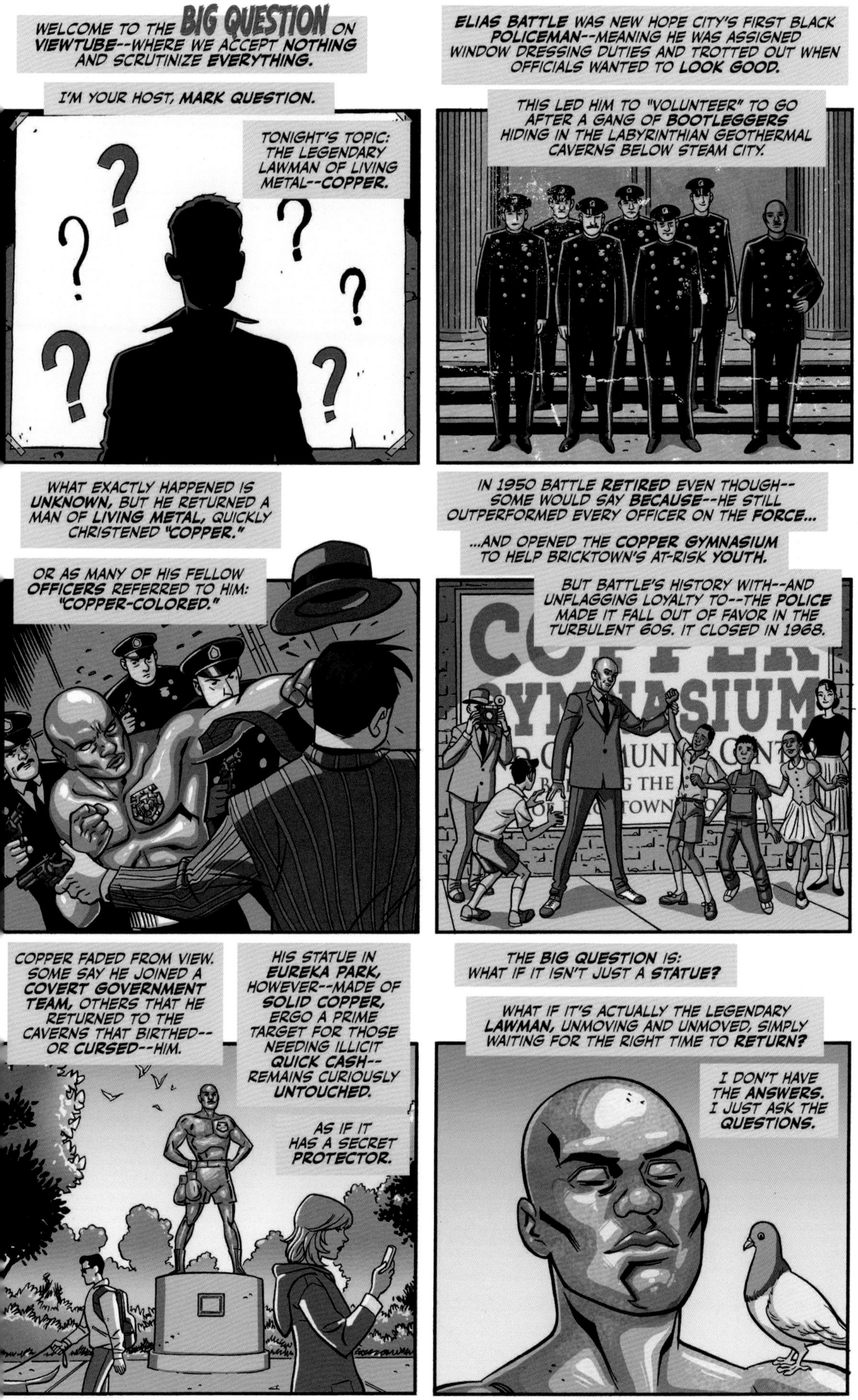

WELCOME TO THE BIG QUESTION ON VIEWTUBE--WHERE WE ACCEPT NOTHING AND SCRUTINIZE EVERYTHING.
I'M YOUR HOST, MARK QUESTION.
TONIGHT'S TOPIC: THE LEGENDARY LAWMAN OF LIVING METAL--COPPER.
ELIAS BATTLE WAS NEW HOPE CITY'S FIRST BLACK POLICEMAN--MEANING HE WAS ASSIGNED WINDOW DRESSING DUTIES AND TROTTED OUT WHEN OFFICIALS WANTED TO LOOK GOOD.
THIS LED HIM TO "VOLUNTEER" TO GO AFTER A GANG OF BOOTLEGGERS HIDING IN THE LABYRINTHIAN GEOTHERMAL CAVERNS BELOW STEAM CITY.
WHAT EXACTLY HAPPENED IS UNKNOWN, BUT HE RETURNED A MAN OF LIVING METAL, QUICKLY CHRISTENED "COPPER."
OR AS MANY OF HIS FELLOW OFFICERS REFERRED TO HIM: "COPPER-COLORED."
IN 1950 BATTLE RETIRED EVEN THOUGH--SOME WOULD SAY BECAUSE--HE STILL OUTPERFORMED EVERY OFFICER ON THE FORCE...
...AND OPENED THE COPPER GYMNASIUM TO HELP BRICKTOWN'S AT-RISK YOUTH.
BUT BATTLE'S HISTORY WITH--AND UNFLAGGING LOYALTY TO--THE POLICE MADE IT FALL OUT OF FAVOR IN THE TURBULENT 60S. IT CLOSED IN 1968.
COPPER FADED FROM VIEW. SOME SAY HE JOINED A COVERT GOVERNMENT TEAM, OTHERS THAT HE RETURNED TO THE CAVERNS THAT BIRTHED--OR CURSED--HIM.
HIS STATUE IN EUREKA PARK, HOWEVER--MADE OF SOLID COPPER, ERGO A PRIME TARGET FOR THOSE NEEDING ILLICIT QUICK CASH--REMAINS CURIOUSLY UNTOUCHED.
AS IF IT HAS A SECRET PROTECTOR.
THE BIG QUESTION IS: WHAT IF IT ISN'T JUST A STATUE?
WHAT IF IT'S ACTUALLY THE LEGENDARY LAWMAN, UNMOVING AND UNMOVED, SIMPLY WAITING FOR THE RIGHT TIME TO RETURN?
I DON'T HAVE THE ANSWERS. I JUST ASK THE QUESTIONS.